THE FOOD AND FEASTS OF THE APOSTLE PAUL

THE FOOD AND FEASTS OF THE APOSTLE PAUL

Inside the Early Church— with Menus and Recipes

DOUGLAS E. NEEL

ROWMAN & LITTLEFIELD
Lanham • Boulder • New York • London

Published by Rowman & Littlefield
An imprint of The Rowman & Littlefield Publishing Group, Inc.
4501 Forbes Boulevard, Suite 200, Lanham, Maryland 20706
www.rowman.com

86-90 Paul Street, London EC2A 4NE

British Library Cataloguing in Publication Information Available

Library of Congress Cataloging-in-Publication Data Available

ISBN 978-1-5381-0477-4 (cloth : alk. paper)
ISBN 978-1-5381-0478-1 (ebook)

∞™ The paper used in this publication meets the minimum requirements of
American National Standard for Information Sciences—Permanence of Paper for
Printed Library Materials, ANSI/NISO Z39.48-1992.

The Food and Feasts of the Apostle Paul is dedicated to Sally L. Neel. She was a professional musician, a good proofreader and writer, my food reviewer, and my loving wife. Her fingerprints are on every page of this book. She died as I was making edits to the final manuscript. May her soul and the souls of all the departed rest in peace.

CONTENTS

viii   *Contents*

ACKNOWLEDGMENTS

There are many people to thank for their support and assistance. An original set of drawings for the book were created by artist Heather Rose. She is very talented, with a background of illustrating books of all types. This was her first opportunity to draw a sarcophagus. Larry Walton and Wendy McAllistar both donated recipes for me to use. They are wonderful cooks, and their contributions are much appreciated. My son, Robert (Row) also deserves special mention. He created his own sourdough starter a number of years ago and has become an excellent baker. He assisted me when writing the chapter 6 recipe for a sourdough starter.

A number of people read and edited chapters for me. Several deserve mention. Nancy Greene, a retired librarian; Nicki Rippee, a retired university professor who guided many students with their theses and dissertations; and Katy Corbett, a teacher and proofreader with a fine eye—all took time out of their busy lives to assist me with this book. I especially want to draw attention to Nancy. She died in 2020 and was well loved by many people. She thoroughly enjoyed the task of reading chapters from this book. Her smile and inquisitive nature are missed.

The good people of St. Patrick's Episcopal Church in Pagosa Springs, Colorado, were invaluable. For three weeks in a row, I passed out copies of recipes for volunteers to prepare. We then gathered for either a Corinthian Lord's Supper or a Syrian Eucharist and sampled the dishes. It was a good method for testing recipes and using the ancient prayers of thanksgiving.

Sotiris Plemmenos, CFO of ESTI, a division of Lelia Foods in Greece, took a day out of his busy schedule to drive from Athens to Kalamata and give us a tour of two oil presses, one of which has been in operation since 1750 CE. We also toured an olive grove of old trees. The day was truly one of the highlights of our trip to Greece. While driving, he answered my many questions about olives and olive oil. His company's oil is made from Koroneiki olives. He also gifted us with a gallon of their gold medal oil for our use while in Greece and to bring back home.

The staff of Bridwell Library at SMU in Dallas must be thanked. Once again, they opened the stacks and computers to me for over a year, allowing me access to an outstanding theological collection. I am deeply grateful to Bart and Jackie Cox for allowing me to use their Dallas condominium while I was researching and writing.

Finally, I must acknowledge the team at Rowman & Littlefield. Their patience while I coped with serious illness, retirement, and the death of my wife was commendable. Their guidance has been invaluable. This is my second book to be published by Rowman & Littlefield, and both experiences have been quite positive.

MENUS AND RECIPES

1

THE APOSTLE PAUL AND FOOD

An Introduction

The master should have the selling habit, not the buying habit . . .
he should think a long time about building, but planting is a thing
not to be thought about but done.

—Cato, *On Agriculture*[1]

So, whether you eat or drink, or whatever you do, do everything for
the glory of God.

—Paul (1 Cor 10:31)[2]

It may surprise you to know that worship in many of the earliest Christian communities included a full meal. What was that meal like? What
did they eat? How did they eat? We suspect that worship meals in most
churches included both bread and wine just as services do today for many
Christian denominations. But did first-century Christians also share lentils,
cheese, sausages, and olive oil for dipping their bread? Did worshipers drink
flavored wine and snack on almonds and dried fruit during a sermon? And
where was the idea birthed for those young Christian communities that
they should eat a full dinner when they gathered? Jews and Gentiles originating from different areas of the Roman Empire were often members of
the same Christian community. Were the Jewish Christians offended when
their Greek friends wanted to eat pork or serve meat cooked with a cream
sauce? Were Roman Christians upset if their Jewish counterparts insisted
that the community keep a kosher diet?

As we look back on the first generation of Christians, it now seems
inevitable that the young movement would spread from Jerusalem and

Palestine to the rest of the Roman Empire. But to do so, the Christian message had to adapt to different cultures as it spread. In the process, the new communities often encountered conflict, sometimes because of the food they ate or did not eat. The conflicts were even more critical because they happened within the context of worship, which also was a common feast. Some of these conflicts were addressed in Paul's letters. Others were not. On occasion, instead of providing solutions, Paul's correspondence exacerbated cultural disagreements.

This book is designed to give you the opportunity to explore the New Testament Christianity of the many communities Paul started and visited through study and experience, by reading about the food and feasts of the Roman Empire, and by actually eating the kinds of food that were part of first-century life and worship.

FOOD, FEASTS, AND COMMUNITY

We know that meals and feasts build community. Most of us have experienced this aspect of a special feast, whether over a Thanksgiving turkey, at a church potluck, or during a wedding rehearsal dinner. The situation becomes more complex when different groups and cultures attempt to merge at a meal. Food and feasting can also define a family or group and differentiate them from one another, sometimes causing misunderstandings or even conflicts. For example, the expanding range of restaurant choices in the United States is symbolic of the growing diversity of peoples. I personally enjoy the arrival of a Guatemalan or an Ethiopian restaurant to my town, while others might be concerned with the influx of different peoples and their unusual food culture.

Paul confronted issues of community building among a diverse population in many of his young churches. The gospel message itself was birthed in Palestine among Jews. It relied on Hebrew Scriptures and a Jewish understanding of both "Messiah" and "resurrection." It came out of a culture where animal and other sacrifices were only offered at the temple in Jerusalem and where food and meals, both in homes and at celebrations within the vicinity of the temple precincts, were important to both religious and national identity.

But then the Christian movement extended from Palestine and was introduced into Greco-Roman colonies and cities around the Mediterranean Sea and beyond. Greeks, Romans, Egyptians, Eurasians, and diaspora Jews became part of the small communities called *churches*, and each brought its own food cultures. Some of the Gentile members of Paul's churches might have been familiar with Judaism, attracted by the ethics of the monotheistic religion. Others knew very little about Jews and were familiar only with a few basic tenets, such as the directive not to eat pork and the preoccupation with keeping the Sabbath rest. Paul saw his task as taking what was often considered a Jewish sect and presenting it in such a way that its message became relevant to everyone. In the process, his communities struggled with numerous issues, including food and feasting.

This book will explore the food and feasts of these young church communities and the cultural situations where they existed. It will look at the ways meals were prepared and eaten and how the form and format of the surrounding secular celebrations might have influenced early Christian worship.

THE CULTURES OF JESUS AND PAUL

Could any two people be more different than Jesus of Nazareth and Paul of Tarsus? And yet Paul's life and ministry were inexorably connected to Jesus. Both the dissimilarities and, at the same time, Paul's belief in the death and resurrection of Jesus profoundly impacted how he understood his life, his mission, and the communities he started and with whom he was connected. His background influenced his approach and priorities when facing the issues of his nascent churches, including the matters of food and feasting.

Jesus was a person of the *chora*, the countryside. He grew up in the small Jewish Galilean town of Nazareth that was situated near the large Roman city of Sepphoris. Perhaps he and his father worked as carpenters in Sepphoris, helping with the construction of public buildings and mansions for the wealthy. Sepphoris experienced a building boom during Jesus's early adulthood. At some point he moved to Capernaum and began his public ministry there. But the heart of his mission was among the small hill communities and the towns along the Sea of Galilee. It was here that he appeared to spend most of his time among farmers and fishermen. There is no record of Jesus ever taking his ministry into Sepphoris.

Jesus used stories to teach his followers and the crowds who came to see him. His parables and tales were filled with images of food production, feasts, and other pictures of rural life: a treasure buried in a field; laborers paid the same at the end of the day regardless of how long they worked; the silliness of hiding a lighted lamp under a bushel basket; a Godly Kingdom that was like a wedding feast, leaven, or salt; an evil neighbor sowing weeds that looked similar to the wheat that grew in the field; and a farmer sowing seeds that fell on rocks, thistles, but also on fertile ground, producing an abundant hundredfold harvest. We assume that none of the stories were transcribed during Jesus's lifetime. We know they were not recorded by Jesus. Yet because of their vivid, colorful nature, those who heard them remembered them for decades and shared them with family and friends.

Feasts and meals were an important element of Jesus's ministry. He ate with rabbis and Pharisees, enjoyed meals with his disciples, and celebrated at weddings and religious festivals. He even gave advice on proper banquet behavior. Some of his parables about the Kingdom were set at a banquet. One of these is the beloved parable of the prodigal son, which includes a feast in honor of the return of a wayward son.

Paul was a person of the *polis*, the city. He was born in Tarsus, an important municipality in the region of Cilicia, located in what is now southern Turkey, where he lived and breathed the Greek language and culture. He was both a Jew and a Roman citizen. The Greek version of the Hebrew Scriptures, the Old Testament, known as the Septuagint, were the texts Paul read and quoted. Paul preferred to write using the style of Greek rhetoric instead of parables and storytelling, and his letters evoke images of the gymnasium and stadium rather than the flock and field. Wealthy Greco-Roman men in their mid-teens were taught to use a rhetorical style of persuasive speech making and written compositions for the purpose of influencing and motivating others. It involved elements such as narration, refuting the arguments of others, and comparison for the purpose of praise or criticism.[3] The study of rhetoric prepared young men for careers in politics and law.

Paul made tents, a very lucrative trade that he possibly learned from his father. Tents were used by the wealthy and by the Roman army when they traveled. These tents were large, the size of small houses, and provided an attractive alternative to the dirty, bug-infested inns where common people usually stayed. Both the Book of Acts and Paul's own letters confirm that he continued to make tents after beginning his ministry as a means of financial support.

The Apostle Paul was extremely controversial during his lifetime. He still is. The New Testament is honest about Paul's nature, describing conflicts with civil authorities, pagan merchants, members of synagogues, temple leaders in Jerusalem, and even fellow Christians. In a very famous passage (Galatians 2:11–14), Paul describes his vehement disagreement with Peter, also called Cephas, about food. Paul remains a controversial figure for many people. His requirements that women remain silent at gatherings, keep coverings over their heads, and submit to their husbands result in claims that he was a misogynist. Even though several of his letters were the very first written of the collection of literature we call the New Testament, the absence of any quoted teachings or descriptions of the life of Jesus leads some modern scholars to discount his work. His gospel message of justification by faith sometimes results in the claim that he created a new and distinct theology, different from Jesus's teachings about the Kingdom of God and discipleship.

And yet Paul's missionary efforts resulted in promising Christian communities located in some of the most important cities of the Roman Empire. His letters paint pictures of the communal life of at least some of those communities and demonstrate some of the questions and issues raised by the first generation of Christ followers. There is no doubt that Paul had a religious experience and that it resulted in a profound change in the orientation of his life. This experience resulted in an evangelical zeal that lasted until his death.

FOOD AND RELIGION

There is an intimate connection between food and religion, and especially between food and worship. For thousands of years, most worship involved animal sacrifice followed by some type of celebratory meal. Not only did Greeks and Romans practice sacrifice, but the people they conquered did as well, including the people of ancient Palestine. This model of sacrifice and feasting continued into the first century CE and beyond for most ancient religions.[4] Early Christians, including Jewish Christians who lived away from the temple, dropped animal sacrifice from their worship but continued to share a celebratory meal. We can assume, at least for several decades after the death of Jesus, that Jewish Christians in Jerusalem continued to offer animal sacrifices in the temple especially on occasions such as Passover.

Paul's letters and other ancient Christian documents describe worship that included some type of cuisine. It is reasonable to ask, "What kind of meal?" For centuries, researchers assumed that Jewish meals, especially the Passover feast, were the primary models for Christian worship, but scholars over the last several decades have studied other meals, such as ancient Greco-Roman banquets, and found similarities between the forms of those feasts and first-century worship. We will explore and even enjoy some of those banquets and feasts.

ABOUT THE FOOD AND FEASTS OF THE APOSTLE PAUL

My wife and I spent time in Greece several years ago. We visited some of the outstanding archaeological sites and museums, but one of our primary goals was to immerse ourselves in the culture of southern Greece. To do that, we ate like the natives in restaurants enjoyed by locals. We altered the way we shopped, becoming at least short-term friends with shop owners and storekeepers. We rented a car and learned to drive like Greeks. We frequently became lost and quickly learned that speed limit signs and lane markings were only recommendations. We also visited olive orchards and oil mills, markets, and bakeries. We watched a skilled baker make phyllo dough and then use it to create a sweet pastry called *bougatsa*.

The trip helped me refocus my love of cooking. In Greece, my wife and I ate fresh food that was very well prepared. It was both wholesome and unpretentious and yet incredibly delicious. We ate wonderful meals, and I found myself wanting to cook. I wanted delicious, tart olive oil with crusty country bread. I wanted flavorful tomatoes served with strong thyme and hunks of briny feta cheese. I wanted grilled pork and lightly breaded calamari. I wanted to be able to walk through a market like the large one in old-town Athens and see insanely fresh red snapper, bell peppers, and pears.

For us, food became one of the important ways that we experienced the culture. In our case, it was the hospitality of the people that most impressed us. We were treated as long-expected guests that had finally arrived. Those very same shop owners I just mentioned drank coffee and ate pastries with us. Restaurant owners brought food to our table for us to sample. The people we met at the olive mills accepted us as friends, bringing us coffee and sweets or providing delicious lunches. Taxi drivers discussed church and politics with us. Our landlords filled our refrigerators with produce from their gardens, olive oil from their own orchards, and locally made feta cheese. Our small Greek vocabulary evoked smiles, if not corrections.

Did Paul enjoy the same degree of hospitality? What was his experience of the cities, the regions, and their cultures? I had to become intimate with Paul to write this book. Not only did I frequently read his letters, but I also studied what others think about him and attempted to immerse myself in the different cultures he experienced during his travels. To do so, I spent time along the Mediterranean, at a large seminary library, and in my kitchen. I tasted food and studied recipes. Friends and I made sausage, bread, vinegar, wine, and beer. I began cooking in clay pots, many designed to look like and function the same as ancient cookware. I brined olives and tried my hand at creating feta cheese. Ancient recipes became the main courses at dinner parties for families and friends.

THE BOOK AND THE RECIPES

Much to our delight, our first book, *The Food and Feasts of Jesus* ended up on the shelves of many college and seminary libraries and on reading lists for introductory classes on the New Testament. My coauthor and I were flattered and even surprised. But that was not our primary purpose in writing the book. We wanted readers with only a cursory knowledge of the Bible and a love of cooking to study and to experience the connections between foods, feasts, culture, and the life and teachings of Jesus.

Likewise, this current book is primarily intended for the common reader who wants to explore the association between food, culture, and the impact on first-century Christians. Individuals can read and enjoy this book, but I hope groups, such as book clubs and Bible studies, will use it together. My desire is that you will study the chapters and then use the recipes to experience and taste the ancient food culture with family and friends.

I have endeavored to thoroughly research the subject matter even though the primary audience is not academic. Endnotes are included when I believe they are appropriate and necessary. There is a bibliography for those who want more information about the subject of food and feasting in the Greco-Roman world and especially in Paul's Christian communities.

Most of the chapters are divided into three parts. The first section describes a meal or feast and provides cultural information about the location of a specific Christian community. The second section focuses on a specific type of food. The foodstuffs studied in these sections emphasize ingredients and cooking styles essential to Greco-Roman cuisine. Third, a menu and recipes for the chosen meal or feast complete almost every chapter.

When writing *The Food and Feasts of Jesus*, my coauthor and I found very few ancient Palestinian Jewish recipes. We first had to develop a list of food and flavorings available to the first-century cook and then research the cooking techniques most commonly used. We then created recipes that we still believe were quite authentic to that place and time. Once the focus moved north out of Palestine, I discovered, if not quite a wealth of material, certainly a larger collection of ancient food literature. Cooks for the wealthy Roman gourmet Apicius recorded a number of the recipes, enough to fill a book, though some of the collection may have been added after the first century. It should be noted that the name Apicius refers to the Roman gourmand who lived in the first century, and the collection of recipes from his cooks is called *Apicius*.

Several ancient writers on agriculture, including Columella, Cato, and Varro, not only described how to plant and care for various trees, vines, and crops but also recorded recipes for favorite foods and gave tips for food preparation. Pliny the Elder's multivolume *Natural History* was most helpful with large sections on all manner of farming and gardening. Even philosophers and playwrights provided descriptions of banquets and the types of foods that were served.

Ancient recipes can be problematic for the modern cook. They primarily are just lists of ingredients, only occasionally suggesting what cooking techniques were used in preparing the dish. Even though standardized measuring cups and spoons existed in the first century, measurements typically were not recorded by those writing and copying recipes. So as with other writers who have experimented with ancient food literature, I have used "trial and error" and educated guesses when developing the recipes in the book, beginning with the ingredients, experimenting with cooking techniques that were characteristic of the time, and then using ingredient amounts that produced a tasty product. Do realize that ancient cooks felt free to adapt recipes and change ingredients according to personal taste and availability. As such, all the recipes in this book are primarily guidelines. If a recipe includes an ingredient that is difficult to find or a flavor you do not like, then leave it out or substitute something else. For example, some call for coriander, or cilantro. I have found that coriander is an herb that people either love or hate. If you do not like coriander, then use an herb that was available in the first century, such as parsley or thyme, that you do like. To further complicate our effort to produce authentic flavors, there are a number of Greek and Roman recipes that use ingredients that are no longer available or not used for cooking. I have either substituted those ingredients or left them out.

I have used three approaches with the recipes in this book. Some of them are attempts to reproduce exactly the ancient version; some are my variations of ancient recipes; and some are my creations, where I use cooking techniques and ingredients available in the first century to produce a recipe in a certain style.

Why I Chose the Communities and Feasts in This Book

Early followers of Jesus formed communities throughout the northern and eastern Mediterranean Basin. A number of these communities were visited or started by Paul. As the author, I had the difficult task of determining which communities to describe and which to leave behind. Paul visited and started churches in many places that were important producers of food or wine. But we know little about his ministry in many of those locations. I focused on the communities where he seemed to stay longest and had the most influence. I have also included both Rome and Athens, where Paul spent time but did not, to our knowledge, start churches. Both of these cities became significant for Christians and were important cultural and culinary centers for the Roman Empire.

I have focused on many different feasts: Syrian, Turkish, Greek, Roman, Jewish, and Christian. I want us to experience a wide variety of meals, some of which may have directly or indirectly influenced the shape of primitive Christian worship. Almost all the chapters in this book focus on one city or region and one type of meal or feast. I have tried to choose a food or drink that is characteristic of the meal. In the process, I intend for us to learn about the culture that Paul encountered in each chosen community.

Wealthy and Poor

It is impossible with a book like this to ignore the culinary disparity between the wealthy and the poor in the Roman Empire. Archaeologists have found many signs of protein and vitamin deficiencies among the remains of the poor, especially among women and children. Their diets consisted almost entirely of grains with some legumes. Meat, poultry, and many vegetables and fruits were mostly absent from the meals of the poorest members of society. They certainly did not have access to the great variety of foodstuffs that successful artisans and the rich did. Wealthy Romans and Greeks used a wide assortment of herbs and spices, fruits, and vegetables in their food and at their meals. We will explore the impact of food shortages and famine on all strata of Greek and Roman society.

My Philosophy of Cooking and Entertaining

I have traveled on a food journey for decades. It began when I picked up a copy of *Gourmet* magazine in 1991, the fiftieth anniversary issue. I walked by the magazine stand in a Dallas market, and the photograph of chocolate mousse and raspberry cream dacquoise on the cover caught my attention. I thumbed through the issue, which contained five decades of recipes and beautiful photographs of delicious-looking fare. I had never seen food like that and certainly had never tasted anything like the cuisine described. I bought the magazine and soon prepared roasted fillet of beef with cornichon tarragon sauce, lemon bulgur timbales, and winter vegetables with horseradish dill butter. Serving the food that I found in this and other magazines brought me great joy, and my family and friends appreciated it, too.

I quickly moved beyond reproducing the recipes I found in print. I studied techniques and flavor combinations. I wanted to know how basic sauces were prepared and how they could be altered to incorporate regional ingredients and food styles. I took classes from a local cooking academy and honed my skills.

My *Food and Feasts of Jesus* coauthor and I often invited friends for dinner, whether it was a leg of lamb and salad or roasted chicken and sautéed asparagus. Whatever we served, it was usually good, the wine tasty, and the fellowship wonderful. Our almost weekly dinners lasted for hours. It was in this context that I began to understand the connection between food and hospitality. Offer your best no matter how simple or complex. Delight in your guests. Allow them to enjoy the food, the drink, and one another.

Now it is an exceptional day when I prepare roast fillet of beef with a cornichon tarragon sauce. I never did make a chocolate mousse and raspberry cream dacquoise. But food became even more important, and when tied to hospitality, it revealed itself to me as one of the great pleasures in life. With the help of yet another friend, I discovered the pleasures of Middle Eastern cuisine. She lived in Lebanon for ten years and became quite proficient at cooking what are to me very delicious and fascinating recipes. Cooking with her resulted in my early interest in biblical-period food. It also confirmed my belief in the connection between food and culture. Her Lebanese dishes allowed me to meet and taste a different culture while reinforcing my understanding of cuisine and hospitality, which are intimately connected.

My food journey continues. I know what it is like to make cheese, bread, sausage, and meat and vegetable stocks; to brine olives and to pickle vegetables; to grow one's herbs. I forage for mushrooms, and I know that there is nothing like the chanterelles and porcinis (boletus) that are found in the mountains where I live.

What have I learned over these many years? Loving, caring food preparation for family and friends is not so much about cookbooks and recipes. It certainly is not about the cooking competitions we can watch on television. It is a way of life.

I believe that food, community, culture, hospitality, and even religion are intertwined. To learn about a culture, begin with food. To build relationships, share a meal. Use food to extend hospitality. All these virtues—community, study, and hospitality—are characteristics of healthy religious communities as well.

I invite you to cook. Experience the cultures and cuisines that Paul experienced. Learn firsthand why Paul's communities disagreed about the food they ate. See how cuisine played such an important role in the life and worship of first-century Christian communities. You need not make your own sausage or cheese, but you should certainly cook to share and to extend welcome and hospitality to family and friends. Above all, experience firsthand how the meals you prepare can be used to build relationships and community.

2

THE GRECO-ROMAN LARDER

When I admitted to my family and friends numerous years ago that I was researching first-century food, especially the food and feasts connected to the life and teachings of Jesus, the most common response was, "How many possible ways can there be to cook and eat gruel?" Over several years, my investigations resulted in dinner parties where I tested recipes. Then churches and other organizations asked me to prepare first-century banquets for their members. Soon ancient foods and techniques evolved into favorites, and I coauthored and published a book of these findings. Not bad for a bowl of gruel, though I have discovered that gruel, also called porridge or *puls*, can be quite tasty when prepared properly.

The reality is that the people in the first-century Mediterranean region and Middle East had access to a wide variety of foods and ingredients. Foodstuffs available throughout the Roman Empire, and especially from northern and western Europe, the Middle East, and northern Africa, streamed into Rome and other large cities. The empire actively engaged in trade with India, allowing access to a variety of spices. Romans became especially interested in developing new strains of vegetables and fruits. Fish, pork, cheese, wine, olives, and crops from the countryside filled the markets of the empire. Even ice imported from the Alps at an extremely steep price was available to chill wine and water for the wealthy.

Many foods and ingredients that we identify with a Mediterranean diet were not yet available. It would be fifteen hundred years before tomatoes, corn, pinto beans, and potatoes became part of the diet. A very small amount of sugar cane was imported but only used for medicinal purposes. Italian diners waited centuries for tomato sauce, cornmeal polenta, pasta, risotto, and pastries sweetened with sugar.

With this chapter we will explore the foods and ingredients that Greeks, Romans, and others in the Mediterranean Basin had available, realizing that there was great variety. The poor in the large cities could not afford much more than very basic fare. Rome was an exception, giving grain for bread and porridge to its poorest citizens. They did not have access to spices and exotic flavorings except for salt and perhaps a small amount of pepper from time to time, which they may have received as a gift from a patron. Though also considered poor, a subsistence farmer with five to ten acres of land had grain, fruit trees, and a sizable kitchen garden with a wide variety of vegetables. Still, only the rich could afford a large assortment of herbs, spices, sauces, and other flavorings, all of which were available at the city markets.

GRAINS AND LEGUMES

Because of their importance to the diet, three food types are often considered the Mediterranean culinary triad or "trinity." They are grains, olive oil, and wine. Grains were by far the most important of the three. In fact, grains and legumes were the foundation of the ancient diet and provided most of the calories consumed by all people, rich and poor alike. Wheat and barley were grown around the Mediterranean, with much of the harvest exported to the large cities of the empire, especially to Rome with its one million people. Places like North Africa became "bread baskets" for the empire. Because grains could be stockpiled for a long period of time, they were a hedge against food shortage and famine.

Grains were prepared in many ways. They were parched, or dried and partially cooked, and then added to soups and stews. Parched wheat and barley easily became a pilaf. Flavorings such as onions, garlic, and any number of herbs and spices were added along with the water or stock. Grains were also used in a variety of soups to add flavor, thicken a broth, or make food more filling. Ground wheat and barley became gruel or flavorful porridges when simmered in water, milk, or stock. A variety of flavorings, grated cheeses, vegetables, and even meats were added to *pulses* to give them flavor. However, additional flavorings were not usually available to the poorest members of society. *Puls* made with barley, water, and a little salt was a typical dinner for many in the empire.

Bread replaced *puls* in everyday life as the staple food once the use of leavening became ubiquitous in the ancient Greco-Roman world. Bread was served at every meal. In the cities, and certainly in the countryside, many homes had bread ovens in their kitchens or in the courtyards. Community bakeries provided loaves for sale to those without ovens and often made their ovens available for the residents of neighborhoods to bring dough for baking. I suspect that on most mornings the neighborhood streets were filled with daughters and servants carrying dough to the ovens. The dough was marked with a unique brand to make the finished loaves easy to identify by its owners. Not only was it filling, but bread became the platform for sauces and relishes, and was even used as an eating utensil and as a napkin.

The wealthiest Romans imported rice from India, making it a very expensive grain. Most of what little rice that arrived in Rome was finely ground and used as a thickener for stews and soups. Occasionally it might be steamed and served as a side dish, but evidence demonstrates that rice as part of a meal was little more than a novelty at an expensive banquet.

The different types of beans, lentils, and peas are all considered legumes. Along with wheat and barley, legumes formed a major part of the ancient diet. They were eaten both fresh and dried. Fresh garden peas were a delicacy, cooked with herbs and other flavorings. Dried chickpeas or broad beans were soaked first and then kept at a boil most of the day in a special clay pot with inward-sloping sides and a small opening on top, preventing most of the moisture from evaporating while cooking. Seasonings ranged in complexity. Salt intensified the flavor of the beans just as it does today. So would a small piece of pork or beef. Cooking the beans in stock instead of water enhanced the taste.

In comparison, lentils were boiled only for a short time, thirty or forty minutes. Like other legumes, they were served as a complete meal, as part of a multi-dish dinner, or as a stew, sometimes with greens, sometimes with beans, meat, or poultry. Wine vinegar, onions, garlic, and herbs such as coriander leaf and lovage added flavor. So did *garum* (fish sauce) and drizzled olive oil that were included before serving.

Legumes were not respected or even liked by many people. They were considered food for the poor, though they were eaten by almost everyone. Like grains, once dried, legumes could be ground and used to make porridges and even bread-like patties as a replacement for bread. Ground legumes were a common substitute for wheat or barley bread during grain shortages.

Grains	Legumes
• Barley	• Chickpeas
• Einkorn	• Fava Beans
• Emmer	• Field Peas
• Millet	• Garden Peas
• Oats	• Lentils
• Rye	• Lupines
• Spelt	• Vetches
• Wheat	

VEGETABLES

Romans loved vegetables. Those who lived in the countryside, rich and poor alike, dedicated a significant piece of their land for their kitchen garden, most of which was used to grow vegetables. Some type of vegetable was almost always found on the table for meals. For those who could not regularly afford meat or fish, vegetables, along with bread and other grain dishes, provided the entire meal.

Vegetables were eaten raw, pickled, blanched, or as part of a salad. Vegetables were pureed and used as a dip or chopped and added to soups and stews. Celery and leeks were used for both purposes. Other vegetables such as asparagus, onions, and artichoke hearts were elements in baked egg dishes, called *patinas*, which tasted similar to crustless quiche. Vegetables like broccoli, Brussels sprouts, and cabbage were popular but did not have the well-formed heads or stalks as do the modern plants. Many of these vegetables were served with sauces, especially by the Romans. Lettuce and other greens were especially loved, and salads were dressed and eaten much as they are today.

Root vegetables were also very popular. Carrots, beets, turnips, onions, radishes, garlic, and even some flower bulbs were common. They were boiled and served with a sauce or pickled and dipped in olive oil or some other condiment. A mayonnaise-like aioli provided a popular dip for vegetables and was made with garlic in much the same way it is today. Root vegetables were also fried or chopped and added to soups and stews. They lent themselves to being pickled and then eaten throughout the year.

A word about eating flower bulbs: almost all are poisonous. There is speculation that perhaps the bulbs for narcissi or irises were used. Grape hyacinth bulbs are still eaten today in northern Italy and were most likely enjoyed in the ancient world. Flower bulbs taste quite bitter and must be boiled before they can be used. One ancient recipe suggested frying after boiling and then serving with a sauce of herbs, honey, and vinegar.[1] I recommend using young turnips instead.

Garlic, onions, and other members of the onion family such as shallots and leeks were essential elements of the Mediterranean diet. As with other root vegetables, they also were pickled and eaten as appetizers. Most soup and stew recipes began with onions, shallots, or leeks. Leeks and shallots were used when a more delicate onion flavor was required, just as they are today. In Egypt and the Middle East, garlic was an essential seasoning. In fact, most of the people of the Mediterranean loved the strong flavor of garlic in their foods. Romans were the exception. For some reason, they avoided the use of garlic, complaining, at least in literature, about the smell of their breath after eating. After the customary warning, Pliny advised that cooked garlic, baked or lightly cooked on a stove top, mellowed both the taste and the resulting smell.[2] Garlic was not entirely absent from Roman menus, just used with discretion.

Hops shoots were sought after in the spring. They grew wild in the countryside and looked and tasted similar to asparagus. When left to grow, the plant becomes a vine, and the buds, from the Middle Ages until the present, were used to flavor beer. Like asparagus, Romans steamed, boiled, or sautéed hops in oil. I have occasionally convinced the owner of a local microbrewery to give me some of his hops shoots in the spring. They are quite delicious when sautéed in olive oil with garlic and flavored with thyme, salt, and pepper. Some food historians believe that ancient writers, when referring to wild asparagus, were describing hops shoots.

Mushrooms and truffles were considered a delicacy just as they are today for many people. Mushrooms were not cultivated and had to be harvested from the countryside. But mushrooms were also feared. As today, those gathering mushrooms had to be very careful. Most varieties are poisonous and can cause a painful intestinal illness or even death. The Celts and Germanic peoples attributed "dark powers" to mushrooms. They were also used as a poison. It was rumored that the emperor Claudius died after eating poisonous mushrooms given to him by his wife Agrippina.[3]

Ancient frescoes show a variety of mushrooms, including chanterelles and porcinis as well as truffles. Though they could be used as a flavoring in soups, stews, and salads, mushrooms were typically the featured element in a dish with a sauce or a simple salad dressing. For the wealthy, large truffles likely were baked, roasted, or fried in the same way potatoes are prepared today.

Vegetables

- Artichokes
- Arugula (also called Rocket)
- Asparagus
- Beets
- Broccoli
- Brussels Sprouts
- Cabbage
- Cardoons
- Carrots
- Celery
- Courgettes
- Cucumbers
- Endive
- Garlic
- Grape Hyacinth Bulbs
- Hops
- Kale
- Leeks
- Lettuce
- Mushrooms
- Nettles
- Onions
- Parsnips
- Radishes
- Taro (Dasheen, imported from Africa and baked or fried like potatoes)
- Truffles
- Turnips

FRUITS AND NUTS

In his short lifetime, Alexander the Great (356–323 BCE), first the king of Macedonia and then all of Greece, conquered Asia Minor (western Turkey), Assyria, Palestine, Babylon, Persia, Egypt, and even a portion of India. His conquests had a profound impact on the culinary tastes of the Greeks and eventually the Romans and others around the Mediterranean Basin. Among other foods, he encountered fruits and varieties that were quite different from those previously known. His troops brought seeds, cuttings, and plants home to Greece where the plants and trees quickly adapted to the Mediterranean climate. He and his army also developed a taste for the spices and heavily flavored foods of India and Persia.

Apricots serve as an example. Originally from Tibet and Western China, apricot trees spread to India by the year 2000 BCE and continued traveling west until cultivation stopped in the area of Mesopotamia (modern Iraq). That is where Alexander the Great and his forces first encountered them.

By the time of the Apostle Paul, the fruit and nut trees brought home by Alexander the Great were well established. The Greeks and then the Romans built on this legacy by developing new varieties. These were added to the number of fruit-bearing trees and vines that either were native to the Mediterranean or migrated there long before Alexander. Figs, crab apples, cherries, dates, pomegranates, grapes, melons, and nuts such as walnuts, almonds, and pine nuts are a few examples. Markets in cities and towns, large and small, sold a wide variety of seasonal fruits and nuts. Even small subsistence farms grew an assortment of trees, giving their families access to fresh fruit and nuts and produce to sell at local markets.

The Greeks and Romans especially loved fresh raw fruit. Some fruits were dried for the winter. Because of their high sugar content, dates and figs were perfect candidates. Apples were sliced into rings and dried. Other fruits and berries were boiled, reduced to a syrup and then used as a sweetener or fermented. Fruits also were cooked, often in custards or egg pies, or covered with honey or a sauce and baked. Custards with blackberries, cherries, fresh figs, or currents were common. Dates were pitted and stuffed with a creamy cheese and any one of a wide variety of nuts, including pistachios, walnuts, almonds, and pine nuts. The cooks for the famous first-century gourmet Apicius had an unusual recipe, at least by modern standards, where peaches were cooked in olive oil and served with a cumin sauce.

Olives and the byproduct olive oil joined grains and wine as one of the three essential elements of Mediterranean food and cooking, part of the Mediterranean culinary trinity. Yes, olives are a fruit. It was necessary to brine and salt olives before eating them because they are extremely bitter when eaten raw. A bowl of olives was likely placed on the table in most homes for every meal. Minced olives were mixed with herbs and other ingredients to form a relish, a type of tapenade, and served with bread at both breakfast and dinner. The oil was even more valuable than the whole fruit. It was the primary oil for types of cooking and making hot and cold sauces. Flavored olive oil was a favorite side dish for dipping. Its uses were much more varied. Olive oil was the primary fuel for lamps. It was also used to make perfumes and medicines. Mediterranean life, both past and present, is hard to imagine without olives and olive oil.

A wide variety of nuts were grown. They were eaten raw, roasted, added to stews and other dishes as a garnish, and used in desserts. Nuts were ground and used in pastries and other dishes. Whether cooked or eaten raw, fruit and nuts typically were served after the main course as a type of dessert. At banquets, they were eaten during the second part of the meal, during what was called the *symposium*, while diners enjoyed wine, entertainment, and conversation.

Fruits

- Apples
- Apricots
- Blackberries
- Cherries
- Currents
- Damson Plums
- Dates
- Elderberries
- Figs

- Grapes
- Melons
- Olives
- Peaches
- Pears
- Plums
- Pomegranates
- Quinces

Nuts

- Almonds
- Chestnuts
- Hazelnuts

- Pine Nuts
- Pistachios
- Walnuts

MEAT, POULTRY, AND GAME

The people of the Mediterranean loved meat but did not eat it very often. Domesticated animals were too valuable. Almost all barnyard animals produced a commodity other than meat. Sheep were kept for their wool. Goats were prized for milk. Oxen were first and foremost beasts of burden, pulling plows and carts. Chickens and geese were valued for their eggs. Only pigs were raised solely for the table, which made pork the primary meat of the Roman Empire. When ancient food writers mentioned the word "meat," they almost always referred to pork. Jews were the one exception because of their religious abstinence from pork.

Second to the pig, sheep, which had been domesticated since 9000 BCE, remained a cherished meat. Because it was a common sacrificial animal, it was usually served at a feast. The size of a herd of sheep reflected the wealth of the owner. Before coins, sheep were used as currency. The meat of the lambs was preferred. Sometimes lambs were castrated and allowed to fatten quickly—the fatted calf referenced in the Bible (Luke 15:11–32, especially verse 23; 1 Samuel 28:24–25). Like pork, it was prepared in many ways. The Greeks preferred it roasted on a spit; Romans typically ate lamb boiled and served with a sauce and vegetables. It was also used to make meatballs and hash.

Goats had been raised in Greece for six thousand years by the time of Paul's mission trips. They were prepared for the table in much the same way as lamb. A suckling kid was considered a delicacy and was quite expensive because goats were not as prolific as sheep or pigs. That and their ability to provide milk for cheese made them a valuable asset.

And now the matter of the dormouse. Yes, Romans ate dormice. Note that a dormouse is not the same as a mouse or rat. They were considered a delicacy, and at least one ancient recipe calls for dormice glazed in honey and rolled in poppy seeds. Before they were eaten, dormice were brought inside and fattened. They were made to live in a homemade warren that was filled with its favorite foods: acorns, walnuts, and chestnuts. The dormice were then kept in the dark, causing them to eat constantly.

Several domesticated birds were raised by farmers for their own tables and to be sold at market. Chicken was by far the most popular. Native to India, chickens made their way to Europe around the year 6000 BCE. The Greeks called them "awakeners" or "Persian awakeners" because it was believed they originated in Persia. Long before the invention of time-keeping devices, cockcrows marked the approach of dawn. The chicken quickly supplanted both Guinea hens in Egypt and geese in Greece as the primary barnyard fowl.

Apicius and other ancient food writers often mention chicken, indicating its popularity. The Greeks preferred to cook poultry on a spit over a fire. Chickens were stewed, boiled and served with a sauce, or baked in a savory pie. Hens were typically eaten after three years when their egg production declined. Older birds were tough and so were stewed, boiled, or fricasseed to make them tender. Younger birds were naturally juicy and succulent, perfect for roasting. Male birds were sometimes castrated, making them grow larger and fatten at a young age. These were called *capons*.

Geese may have been usurped in the barnyard by the chicken, but they became the bird for a luxury meal. Goose liver was especially prized, even more so when the goose was force-fed grain or figs to produce a delicious and esteemed *foie gras*. Chickens were fattened in the same manner. Geese were treasured for their meat, fat, eggs, down, and feathers. They also had a reputation as effective "guard dogs." A popular story told how a gaggle of geese saved the Romans from being attacked by the Gauls during the siege of Rome in 390 BCE. Many of the citizens had fled the city, but the senators and soldiers stayed behind in the ancient fortress called the Capitol. The army of the Gauls attacked the fortress at night, but when they arrived, the geese began to honk, warning the Romans who were then able to win the battle.[4]

Smaller birds were raised in the barnyard for special meals and feasts. Pigeons and doves were the two most common. Many families, both in the countryside and in larger homes in the city, kept dovecotes and cages for raising pigeons. A family of more modest means used the smaller birds for stews and other recipes in which the meat was more of a flavoring. These birds were also roasted on a spit or baked in the oven.

The wealthy served and ate even more exotic birds. Peacock was usually one of the main dishes served at the special dinners and banquets of affluent Romans. Not that it tasted all that good, but it provided a spectacular presentation when carried into the banquet room on a silver platter with all its plumage fanned. The meat itself was often tough and stringy. Households hosting frequent banquets varnished the bird so it could be used multiple times. Other exotic birds found on the banquet table included crane, stork, parrot, flamingo, and ostrich.

The Greeks associated eating meat with sacrificing to the gods. Greek families usually did not eat meat apart from religious events. Because they were inexpensive, chickens were a common sacrificial animal among the poorer members of the population. Lambs, goats, and pigs all were commonly sacrificed. The Romans of the first century separated eating meat from ceremony and, because of the wealth of the empire, ate meat more frequently. The cities had thriving meat markets. Meat was made available to the Roman populace during large festivals.

Freshly killed game was not often found in the city markets and so did not factor in the daily diet, and it was quite expensive when it was available. Romans had a fondness for meat from animals that were killed violently with an arrow, spear, or sword, believing that the fierce death enhanced the flavor. Meat from animals sacrificed in the temple or killed in the coliseum was considered excellent for this reason and demanded a high price. For those who lived in the countryside, game supplemented the common meal of grains, vegetables, and fruit. Ironically, by the first century CE, much of the land in Italy, especially around Rome and the other major cities, had been sectioned, cultivated, and turned into farms and estates, leaving little land for wild animals.

A variety of game awaited the skilled hunter. Boar was very popular. It was roasted whole, often on a spit or in a large oven. It was also cut into smaller pieces and boiled in brine (salt water) and served with a sauce. Deer was also either roasted or boiled and sauced. Rabbits were originally brought to Europe by the Romans as domesticated animals. They preferred tame rabbits because they were fat and tender. As is often predictable, many escaped and quickly populated the entire continent. Hares especially were treasured by the Greeks who cooked them on a spit and simply served them hot with salt. They were not as well loved by the Romans, who preferred bigger game such as wild boar or their fat, domesticated rabbits. When they did eat them, Romans hunted hares raised on enclosed reserves to improve the flavor. Along with other cooking methods, such as stewing or fricasseeing, cooks stuffed hare and roasted or baked them in ovens and then served them with a sauce. Other more exotic game animals, such a bears, were served at banquets for the very wealthy.

Wild birds were also hunted and enjoyed. Grouse, partridge, woodcock, quail, thrush, cranes, and figpeckers commonly were sought by hunters. The Greeks cooked small birds whole on a spit with simple flavorings of olive oil and a spice such as silphium. They might be served with a sweet sauce. The meat from game birds was also baked in savory pies and used for stews.

Meat
- Dog (on rare occasions)
- Dormouse
- Goat
- Lamb and Mutton
- Pork
- Veal and Other Beef Products

Poultry
- Chicken
- Dove
- Duck
- Eggs from All Poultry
- Guinea Hens
- Goose
- Peacock
- Pigeon

Game
- Antelope (Persia)
- Bear
- Boar
- Crane
- Deer
- Figpecker
- Gazelle (Persia)
- Grouse
- Hare
- Lion
- Partridge
- Quail
- Rabbit
- Thrush
- Woodcock

FISH AND THE FRUITS OF THE SEA

Fish and seafood were an important part of the Mediterranean diet. Much of the Roman Empire, especially before it expanded into northern Europe, was located along or near the Mediterranean Sea. For example, Greece alone has over eight thousand miles of coastline. Many of the cities and towns not located directly on the coast were not far away. The Mediterranean Basin also had access to freshwater lakes and rivers that were teeming with fish and delicacies such as eels.

Aristotle divided Mediterranean fish into three classifications: deep-sea fish, in-shore fish, and rockfish. Shellfish such as shrimp, a type of lobster, squid, and octopus were in a separate class and were also enjoyed.

Fish were expensive, even along the coast. Fresh fish especially was costly. Salted fish was less pricey, but also less desirable. The process of salting fish leeched out the water, causing them to dry. Once dried, they lasted longer and were easier to transport. Dried fish then had to be soaked in fresh water to reconstitute them before cooking. Fish also were pickled or used to make *garum*, fish sauce. These alternative means of preparation resulted in less expensive (but still costly) products. *Garum* was the cheapest means for common people to consume the taste of fish.

There were numerous techniques for cooking fish and other seafood. It was baked, roasted, stuffed and steamed, boiled and served with a sauce, grilled, stewed, baked in an egg patina, and ground and made into "fish" balls and sausage. Small fish, such as anchovies, were fried in a skillet.

This is a very partial list of the fish and seafood available in the first century CE:

Fish

- Anchovies
- Bluefish
- Bonito
- Bream
- Carp
- Chub
- Crabs
- Cuttlefish
- Dolphin (only on very rare occasions)
- Eel (especially Conger)
- Grayling
- Little Rockfish
- Mullet
- Octopus
- Oysters
- Perch
- Pike
- Sardines
- Sea Bass
- Sea Urchin
- Shark
- Sole
- Squid
- Tuna

MILK AND MILK PRODUCTS

People had known for millennia that certain domesticated animals produced more milk than was needed to feed their young. A certain amount was set aside each day for the family to drink. Cows were sometimes milked, and the milk used for cheese. But cattle were seen almost exclusively as beasts of burden. The milk from goats, sheep, and occasionally mares, asses, and even camels was preferred.

Milk was a drink that was much loved but rarely available in the cities. Of course, farmers and shepherds had ready access to a very large amount. But milk spoils quickly without refrigeration, and only the wealthiest city dwellers paid to have fresh milk rushed to their homes.

Because of the speed of spoilage, almost all milk was made into cheese. Cheese making was in fact an ancient art. Archaeologists have found cheese strainers in the area of Thessalonica that date from 3000 BCE. With the addition of rennet, the milk curdles when heated and separates into curds (solids) and whey (liquid); the curds were placed into wicker baskets to allow excess whey to drain. To make a harder cheese, a basket or plate with weights was placed on top of the curds. Some cheeses were salted, that is, salt was added to the curds before they began to drain or rubbed on the outside of the finished product. Almost all cheese was stored in a saltwater brine resulting in a product very much like modern feta. The cheese was washed before serving.

Two types of rennet were used. Animal rennet, which forms naturally on the inside of the stomach lining of young animals, was used most often. The stomach of a young lamb or calf butchered for sacrifice was set aside just for the purpose of making cheese. The sap from a fig tree also contains rennet and was used:

> The fig sap was first squeezed out into wool. The wool is then washed and rinsed, and the rinsing put into a little milk, and if this be mixed with other milk it curdles it. (Aristotle)[5]

The Romans especially liked very fresh cheeses—products like cheese curds, ricotta, or cottage cheese—and usually served it with honey. Harder and brined cheeses like feta were sometimes washed to remove the salt and eaten with honey as well. Also prized was cheese that had been molded into small shapes, such as cones, cylinders, or pyramids.

Just as today, smoked cheeses were popular. The common method was to place a hard cheese or a cheese that was still aging near a smoky fire.

The challenge was to keep the fire and the cheese cool enough to not cook and ruin the product. Applewood was most often used. The opinion of at least one ancient food scholar is that the cheese used for smoking might have had a taste and texture similar to cheddar.[6] The best smoked cheeses reportedly were made in the city of Rome itself.

A recent archaeological find reveals even more about the texture and taste of ancient cheese. A number of newspapers reported an announcement by Egypt's Ministry of Tourism and Antiquities that two thousand 600-year-old bricks of cheese were found at the Saqqaru archaeological site. The announcement was made on September 10, 2022. Experts believe the cheese had the taste and texture of modern Halloumi cheese. This cheese is made in Crete and is available in many grocery stores and Mediterranean markets.[7]

Making yogurt was another method for converting milk before it spoiled. Yogurt has a tangy flavor and creamy texture. Honey was added, and it was eaten with fruit or combined with other foods and sauces. Yogurt was also drained to make a soft cheese-like product. It was placed in a porous cloth and hung for ten to twelve hours, allowing the liquid whey to slowly be removed.

Butter was little known and rarely made or used by the people living in the Mediterranean Basin. For the Romans, butter was a food product that represented the northern European barbarians and thus avoided.

Milk products

- Butter (away from the Mediterranean Basin)
- Cheese
- Yogurt

HERBS, SPICES, AND CONDIMENTS

The regions of the north and east Mediterranean each seasoned their food with slightly different flavorings, using the leaves and seeds from local plants. For example, the Greeks used coriander (also called cilantro), oregano, thyme, and pennyroyal, a type of mint. They had two different words for herbs, the first, *khloe* or *hedysmata khlora*, meaning the green herbs that were chopped or pounded into a paste with a mortar and pestle. According to the time of year, these herbs were either fresh or dried. They were used to flavor meat, stews, vegetables, or other dishes. The other word for herbs, *phyllas*, likely meant "bitter herbs" or salad leaves.[8] The Greeks typically finished their dinner with a salad and dressing in order to cleanse their palate.

By the first century, those living in Rome and the other large cities in the empire had access to a wide variety of spices and flavorings imported from around what is now Europe and from India and beyond. Still, Romans loved using local herbs as part of their food preparation. They favored a large variety of herbs in their food and were especially partial to coriander, oregano, lovage, rue, parsley, celery leaf and seed, and mint.

Lovage and rue often were added in tandem. Lovage has a peppery bitterness that made it quite popular, so much so that *Apicius* used it in almost every savory recipe. The leaves, roots, and seeds were utilized, but most ancient recipes fail to specify which. It was sometimes used in place of pepper, which could be quite expensive in the first century. Parsley and celery leaves have a similar flavor but are not as bitter; over the course of centuries, these two herbs gradually replaced lovage in the kitchen. Today lovage is almost never used in North America and only infrequently in Europe. Sometimes lovage is added to potato or other soups in northern Italy.

Rue was used both for medicinal and culinary purposes. It grew wild in the northern and eastern areas of the Mediterranean, though it was also included in almost all kitchen gardens. Pliny the Elder recorded the interesting folk story that rue tasted better if stolen from someone else's garden. Ancient writers admitted that rue could be dangerous and, when eaten in large amounts, might cause miscarriages. It was used only in small amounts because of its reputation. Since both lovage and rue were bitter, they were often balanced with sweet flavorings, such as honey, sweet wine, mint, or perhaps a fruit syrup.

Many other herbs were available but not often used. As today, first-century cooks had favorites and used those most often. You should as well. Use parsley if you do not like cilantro. Replace basil, which was infrequently added to a dish anyway, with mint or with a very different herb such as oregano. A partial list of the culinary herbs of the first-century Mediterranean region follows:

Herbs

- Basil
- Bay Leaves
- Celery Leaves
- Coriander
- Dill
- Fennel Leaves

- Lemongrass
- Lovage
- Marjoram
- Mint
- Mustard Plant
- Myrtle Leaves
- Oregano
- Parsley

- Pennyroyal
- Rosemary
- Rue
- Sage
- Savory
- Sorrel
- Spikenard
- Thyme

SPICES

Whereas most herbs were grown locally, spices often came from lands some distance from Rome, including Egypt, Arabia, Judaea, Syria, Armenia, Mesopotamia, and India. Seeds, bark, roots, and the saps of plants were and still are considered spices. Aromatic spices were available for a variety of uses, including for perfumes, incense, cosmetics, and medicine. Our interests are the culinary uses of many of these same flavorings.

The Greeks, with their simple, straightforward cuisine, used locally grown herbs and seasoned foods with spices far less frequently than their Roman neighbors. Mastic, poppy seeds, saffron, sumac, and silphium were the ones used most frequently. Greek writer Theophrastus said of the heavy-handed use of spices that most such aromas would ruin food, though they might be acceptable in wine. Greek cooks also used locally grown seeds for seasonings, especially anise, coriander, and cumin seed. The ability to procure spices increased after the conquests of Alexander the Great opened both land and sea routes to spice-producing countries.

The Romans had access to spices from around the known world. Because of their great costs, exotic spices represented both wealth and generosity, especially when shared with friends and clients. Rome sent on average 100 million sestertii, or 25 million denarii to India, China, and the Arab Peninsula, which was considered the cost of luxury. Romans used pepper primarily, but were also fond of ginger, spikenard (nard), myrrh, and other spices such as cardamom, cinnamon, and cloves.

The spice silphium was second perhaps only to pepper in popularity. Silphium was called *laser* by the Romans and was the resin of a plant grown near Cyrene in Libya. The stem and roots were also used as flavorings. Saffron may have been the gold banner of ancient spices. It is the stigma of a flower in the crocus family. Harvesting was and is extremely difficult and labor-intensive because the three stigmas each flower has must be harvested by hand. Between seventy and eighty thousand of them are needed to produce one pound of saffron. It had many uses, including flavoring food and wine and producing a red or yellow dye for clothing. Medicine and a popular aphrodisiac were both made with saffron. Very wealthy Romans scattered it around their beds on their wedding nights and in banqueting rooms. It is believed that saffron was dropped before the feet of the emperor on special occasions as a sign of extravagance.

Spices

- Anise Seed
- Asafetida
- Bay Berries
- Caraway
- Cardamom Seed
- Celery Seed
- Cinnamon
- Cloves
- Costmary
- Cumin Seed
- Fennel Seed
- Fenugreek

- Ginger Root
- Juniper Berries
- Mastic
- Mustard Seed
- Myrtle Berries
- Pepper
- Poppy Seed
- Saffron
- Sesame Seed
- Silphium (Laser)
- Spikenard (Nard)
- Sumac

SPECIAL SAUCES AND LIQUID FLAVORINGS

Liquid flavorings were used as marinades, in sauces, and to enhance the taste of many types of foods. Vinegar, wine, honey, and the omnipresent *garum* or fish sauce are just several examples. Wine vinegar was most common, but vinegars made with different fruits or infused with different types of herbs and spices were common as well.

A variety of sauces were essential to the kitchen. Modern cooks often reduce or boil wine as the base for a sauce, usually in the same pan in which meat is cooked. For first-century cooks, *must* was reduced and kept as a flavoring to be used for future cooking. Must is the freshly pressed juice from fruit, usually grapes, when making wine, often still containing the skins and seeds. For making sauce, the must was cooked and strained. Ancient cooks kept several thicknesses of the juice. If cooked to a syrup, it was called *defrutum* or *saba* (*sapa*). *Saba* is still made in Italy and other Mediterranean countries. Cooks also used raisin wine, called *passum*, to flavor foods and sauces. Reduced wine that was fully fermented was referred to as *caroenum*. *Passum*, *defrutum*, and *caroenum* will be used in some recipes in this book.

Honey was extremely important as a sweetener because sugar was not yet part of the pantry. It was used to make pastries, was poured over cakes, and became the primary ingredient in custards and other desserts. Not only was honey used for the sweet endings of special meals, but it also found its way into numerous savory dishes and sauces. First-century diners were especially fond of sweet-and-sour flavors, and the sweetness was provided by honey, fresh or dried fruit, and syrups such as *defrutum* and *passum*.

Garum, also called *liquamen*, was a fish sauce that was likely not that different than East Asian sauces such as *nuoc mam* or *nam pla*. The sauce was used for a wide variety of foods, including egg pies and custards. Small dried fish and fish parts such as heads and tails were covered with a salt brine and the mixture fermented in the sun for months. The resulting sauce was dipped off the top and strained into containers for storage and sale. *Garum* meets two culinary needs, one for salt, and the other for *umami*, the meaty, brothy flavor that is considered as basic as sweet, sour, bitter, and salty. *Umami* is found especially in fermented sauces and foods, such as sauerkraut, mushrooms, and soy sauce, and in many fresh vegetables, such as tomatoes, spinach, and celery. When used sparingly, the fishy taste of *garum* is not noticed, and it adds a luscious base to broths, sauces, and savory recipes, balancing the overall flavor.

A partial list of liquid flavorings:

- *Defrutum*, *Saba* (must, boiled until a syrup)
- *Caroenum* (reduced, fermented wine)
- *Garum*, also *Liquamen* (fish sauce)
- Grape Must (sweet, unfermented grape juice)
- Honey
- *Passum* (raisin wine)
- Syrups Made from Fruit Juices
- Vinegar, Flavored Vinegars

EXTRAVAGANT AND FORBIDDEN FOODS

Some foods were surprisingly extravagant and eaten only by those who were incredibly rich. One such dessert reportedly was eaten by Cleopatra in order to impress Mark Antony during his visit to Egypt. The story is told by Pliny the Elder in his *Natural History*. He prefaces the story by telling the reader that Cleopatra owned the two largest pearls at the time. The story continues that Mark Antony enjoyed a number of meals of the best and most exotic foods Egypt offered. He queried if anything could possibly surpass such extravagance. Cleopatra was not impressed with his boorishness and said the value of 10 million sesterces (approximately $16.7 million) could easily be added in one meal. Mark Antony and Cleopatra then wagered whether she could really provide a banquet worth that much additional money.

The next day, after yet another amazing feast, she had a servant bring a dish of very acidic vinegar to the table. She removed one of her pearls from one of her ears and dropped it into the vinegar. Those at the feast watched it dissolve into a slush. She drank it. Cleopatra then reached for the second pearl, and Lucius Plancus, the referee for the wager, stopped the meal and declared that Cleopatra clearly was the winner.[9] Scholars have debated the historicity of the event, but the story serves our purpose. It was only the great wealth and power of two people such as Mark Antony and Cleopatra that would make such a story believable two thousand years ago and still interesting for us today.

Apicius constantly searched for new and fascinating flavors. One story relates that he sailed from Rome to the coast of Africa in search of larger and sweeter prawns. As he approached shore, fishermen rowed out to his boat holding samples of their famous shellfish. After observing them, he determined the prawns were no better than those available in the Roman seafood market. He immediately instructed the captain of his boat to turn and head home before even reaching the coast.

Apicius eventually discovered from his bookkeepers that he had feasted through most of the fortune he had inherited. He responded by committing suicide after a particularly opulent banquet rather than settle for a more common diet and lifestyle.

There are stories of other extravagant meals: food wrapped in gold leaf for a lavish banquet or an emperor who had dishes seasoned with pearls and precious stones. But instead of eating the gold, onyx, and pearls, banqueters were free to remove the treasures from their food and take them home. Edible delicacies might include camels' feet, moray intestines, partridge eggs, brains, tongues from birds such as flamingos and thrushes, or colorful parrot heads. The emperor Elagabalus reportedly served six hundred ostrich brains at one banquet. Even as wealth poured into Rome and the extravagance of banquets increased, very few of its citizens, even wealthy ones, could afford this degree of opulence. Yet they competed to offer meals that were more excessive and impressive to their friends.

Some foods were forbidden. It is well-known that Jews did not eat pork. They also avoided fish without scales, such as catfish and eels, and all shellfish, including shrimp, oysters, and lobster. All the blood in meat that was part of the Jewish diet had to be drained before it was eaten. Egyptians also avoided pork, though archaeologists have discovered enough bones from hogs to convince them that this rule was rarely followed.

Most Mediterranean people avoided reptiles of all types and seemed to have stayed away from turtles and tortoises. Greek authors mocked Egyptians for supposedly eating grubs and snakes, but the Greeks were known to eat cicadas, though some considered the bug to be sacred and refrained from placing them on the menu. Dog, puppy, and horse meat were generally avoided, and certain birds were not eaten. Animal brains were considered a delicacy by all but the followers of Pythagoras. Pythagoreans also refused to eat fava beans.

Herons, owls, and vultures were forbidden, and the ibis was considered sacred by the Egyptians. The Greeks and Romans believed certain fish were sacred and to be avoided, including dolphins and pilot fish. Both fish swam with ships and were believed to be guides by sailors. Anyone who broke this rule was believed to have polluted their household.[10] Yet others thought the prohibitions against eating these fish were unnecessary and enjoyed them as a delicacy.

Even with these restrictions, the Mediterranean Basin and the lands beyond provided the Roman Empire with a wealth of foodstuffs. Great variety was available to those who could afford it. Still others struggled to guarantee that a bowl of porridge, beans, a bit of cabbage, a few slices of onion, and bread were on the table for the evening meal.

SOME THOUGHTS ON THE ANCIENT PANTRY

There was no shortage of ingredients and flavorings. Many modern cooks should be inspired after looking at the first-century pantry. Like the modern Mediterranean diet, this chapter describes a food lifestyle that is healthy and rich with variety. Whole grains and vegetables dominated the table. Fish and poultry were added sparingly, and meat was reserved for special occasions, though wealthy first-century Romans consumed it regularly. This was and still is a healthy diet. If only modern cooks used this kind of flavor diversity for their food preparation. But we must remember that this abundance of foods and flavorings was not universally available. A large part of society ate almost nothing but grain- and legume-based foods: *puls*, beans, lentils, and bread. The work of modern archaeologists demonstrates that many people in the first century, especially in the cities, suffered from protein and vitamin deficiencies.

The people in our society crave three flavorings more than all others: salt, sugar, and fat. Because of our relative wealth we can afford to have constant access to foods that satiate these cravings. The choices are abundant. Restaurant meals, including fast-food eateries, prepackaged and frozen foods, and snack foods commonly contain large amounts of salt, fat, and sugar and also include copious amounts of preservatives and artificial flavorings. Foods advertised as "low fat" use sugar, salt, or chemicals to compensate for the absence of the flavor provided by fat. The results of a diet high in sugar, salt, and fat, especially polyunsaturated fat, often include obesity, heart disease, and diabetes. And yet the healthy foods and flavorings described in this chapter are within the reach of most of the people in our country. We realize the need for a radical dietary change, but breaking the addictive cycle of eating foods loaded with sugar, salt, and fat is difficult. "Who has time to cook?" is the wrong question. "Who cannot afford to prepare healthy, tasty meals for their families and loved ones?" is what we should be asking.

Now for my confession. I personally try to avoid all prepared and frozen meals. I gave up most fast foods years ago. Snack foods, perhaps the greatest offenders, are difficult to avoid, and I do occasionally indulge. But what about a snack composed of a handful of olives, almonds, and a slice of feta cheese? It will quench our desire for salt but help us to avoid excess fat and sugar. Sodas are loaded with sugars and salt and are difficult for many of us to stop drinking. Eventually I was able to replace diet sodas with water, coffee, tea, and an occasional glass of nice wine. Of course, neither coffee nor tea were available in the first century, but I drink them nonetheless. I am busy and do frequent restaurants, but I attempt to make healthy food choices, realizing that restaurant food is higher in salt and fat than the same dishes prepared at home. Our cravings for salt, sugar, and fat make a good food lifestyle difficult, but the effort is worth it.

I believe that food and the ways it is eaten are excellent means to learn about the people in different nationalities and cultures. Our country has a fast-food culture. We use fast food as a quick fix for hunger in the midst of our busy lives. And because of that, we sacrifice quality and health. Isn't that sad?

The chapters that follow explore some of the different Mediterranean food cultures that the Apostle Paul most definitely encountered. Lands where figs, some olives, a slice of cheese, or a handful of pistachios were the fast foods of the day. Enjoy the journey.

3

FOOD, FARMING, AND THE KITCHEN IN THE GRECO-ROMAN WORLD

Only about 4.2 percent of the people in developed nations work in agriculture. The number is even smaller in the United States. But the same is not true for much of the world, and is certainly not historically true. Forty percent of the global workforce is engaged in agriculture, 75 percent in the world's poorest countries. In the United States, in the year 1800 CE, 80 percent of our ancestors worked as farmers and ranchers. Much of what they grew was for family consumption; the rest was sold to help purchase the things that could not be made at home. This was the pattern for the ancient world. Approximately 80 to 90 percent of the population was involved in agriculture. Many were subsistence farmers with small tracts of land. Their goal was to live on their own harvests.

Do most of us even know a full-time farmer or rancher? While my father was finishing his doctoral studies at the University of Tennessee, my family lived in a small rental house on what was most likely a subsistence farm. Our house was separated from the main home by a field inhabited by the family cow. There was also a goat, a number of hens, a large kitchen garden, a few fruit trees, and a cornfield. It was a small child's dream. I helped collect the eggs and watched the farmer's wife milk the cow and goat and churn the

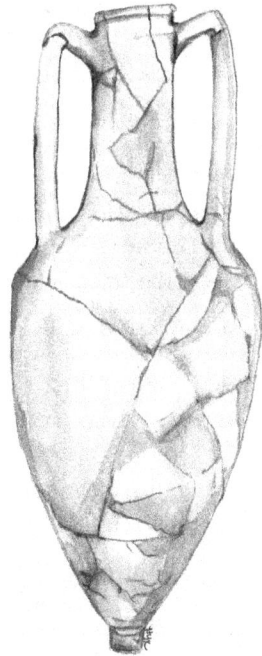

Amphora, used for storing wine. *Heather Rose*

cream for butter. The cornfield made a perfect setting for playing hide-and-seek with my sister. The couple that owned the farm worked most of the day weeding, harvesting, and canning. Even during the winter, there were eggs to gather and animals to milk.

Then there are the amateurs: gardeners who grow tomatoes and squash during the summer. I dabbled a bit and kept a nice herb garden until I moved to Colorado. I quickly realized after the move that the neighborhood deer and the black bear that occasionally meandered up and down the street enjoyed my basil and parsley before I did. Most of my harvest now takes place at the local grocery or the town's small farmer's market. For most of us, if we do grow food, it is only to supplement what we purchase at a store. I know only one person who grinds grain for the flour to bake bread. He buys the grain online!

THE ANCIENT FARM

For centuries, small subsistence farms were the norm throughout the Mediterranean Basin. Long before the first century, many of the citizens of Athens owned five to ten acres of arable land outside the city. It was farmed by the family, perhaps a slave or two, and seasonal workers, who were also landowners, assisting neighbors with plowing, planting, and harvesting. The same type of farming existed in Syria, Palestine, and the area we now know as Turkey, all of which were lands where the Apostle Paul traveled and started churches.

Seven or eight acres might be the norm, but farms fluctuated greatly in size. Some farms were only two or three acres. The average subsistence farm on the Italian Peninsula fell between three and six, but private farms owned by the wealthy were substantially larger. Cato, a Roman writer who lived from 234 to 139 BCE, suggested that farms should be approximately one hundred *iugera* or sixty-six acres in size: "If you ask me what is the best kind of farm, I should say a hundred *iugera* of land, comprising all sorts of soils, and in a good situation."[1] Note that Cato, along with his friends and acquaintances, were wealthy gentlemen farmers and influential Roman citizens and politicians who could afford much larger stretches of land.

Farmers also rented land from the owners of large estates. A family might own four acres of land and then rent an additional ten to twenty acres, leased in five- to ten-acre plots from a wealthy landowner. Leasing land provided several advantages. The rented land was not necessarily connected to the original farm. The farmer then had the advantage of different soil types often located in diverse microclimates. One stretch of land might be ideal for wheat or barley; another suited to olive trees and grapevines. One area might have sufficient rainfall, while only a few miles away the crops would struggle because of the lack of moisture. Land diversity and microclimates still provide agricultural advantages and challenges in the northern Mediterranean Basin to this day.

The primary crops of the northwest and northern Mediterranean were grains, legumes, vegetables, fruit, and livestock. Again, from Cato:

> A vineyard comes first if it produces bountifully of good quality; second, a watered garden; third an osier-bed [willows used to make baskets]; fourth, an olive yard; fifth, a meadow; sixth, grain land; seventh, a wood lot; eight, an arbustum (orchard); ninth, a mast grove [tall, straight trees of the type that can be used as a ship's mast].[2]

It is likely that Cato listed the crops in the order of importance for the ancient Roman farmer. Most farmers agreed with him. It is interesting that he does not specifically mention livestock, though he certainly does elsewhere in his treatise. The meadowland, item five, undoubtedly was used for grazing. But it is puzzling that grain and fruit orchards are placed toward the end of the list. Fruit trees were often part of the kitchen garden for most rural households. Fruit was grown for the family and then for the local market. The exception was the orchard where fruit was grown in large quantities strictly for commercial purposes.

Why were grains, especially wheat and barley, ranked so low? They continued to be the major element in everyone's diet, rich or poor. But as Rome continued to grow and its population reached one million, local farmers could no longer meet the city's grain needs. It might be that by the time Cato wrote *On Agriculture*, grain was already being imported from Africa and Sicily. Italian farmers concentrated on the more financially lucrative grape and olive crops.

This certainly was the case when the Apostle Paul was founding and visiting small Christian communities around the western and northern Mediterranean. So much grain was exported into the city that prices dropped, not that Roman farmers completely stopped growing wheat, barley, and other grains. But massive imports had an impact on the economy of many regions around the Mediterranean. Areas that once had grown a variety of crops for local and regional consumption instead grew wheat for Rome.

The average subsistence farmers continued to grow grains with the goal of having enough to last, not only throughout the year but also for the future, with a sufficient surplus stored in case of bad crops and shortages. Additional excess, especially in the form of olive oil, wine, wheat, and a variety of fruits, was taken to market or sold to brokers. Farm families also took homemade household wares to sell at regional markets.

Subsistence farming continued as the norm for many farmers in the first century CE. Some owners received their land for military service, others through inheritance. Cato wrote this about farmers: "It is from the farming class that the bravest men and the sturdiest soldiers come, their calling is most highly respected, their livelihood is most assured and is looked on with the least hostility, and those who are engaged in that pursuit are least inclined to be disaffected."[3]

THE THREAT TO THE FAMILY FARM

The idea of the self-sufficient farm family was attractive, but how frequently was it achieved? As today, small family farms often faced peril. The risks of bad weather, disease, and pests were always present. A farmer might lease land as a tenant farmer and purchase seed for the crop, but if the yield was small for any reason, then the tenant farmer was left with a large debt that he might not be able to afford.

The economy of Rome and much of the Italian Peninsula changed in significant ways several hundred years before the first century CE, shifting as Rome waged wars to conquer new lands. Most of the soldiers were the men who worked the small farms. They were required to supply their own weapons, equipment, and even food. Both the cost of outfitting husbands and sons and their absence placed great economic stress on families. The stress was exacerbated if the men were absent for an extended length of time or if they were killed in battle.

The families of soldiers lived on reserves, both monetary if there was any, and on food stores. The booty soldiers collected from victories helped families and farms survive. But in many cases, these assets were eventually depleted. Farms were forfeited to the state, usually for nonpayment of taxes, and these were purchased by wealthy neighbors. Many small farms were lost. Soldiers returning home discovered that their land and livelihood had disappeared. Some remained in the army. Some became tenant farmers, even on the very land they lost to bankruptcy. Others moved to cities where they attempted to find work as laborers. However, those who distinguished themselves might be awarded land by their commanding officer.

Rome's military successes provided an ongoing, large influx of slaves. Instead of tenant farmers, a number of the bigger farms gradually began using slaves as laborers. Displaced tenant farmers discovered that the best option for survival was to move to larger cities, especially to Rome. This trend continued for centuries: "Rome continued to evolve from a society of peasant citizen farmers into an empire of massive, slave-run plantations and cities overflowing with impoverished citizens."[4]

The loss of family farms also resulted in violence. Rome in the second century BCE experienced several revolutions and riots among soldiers. Reforms were made but often inadvertently pitted the aristocracy against landless citizens. However, by the time of the Apostle Paul, Rome had settled its citizen revolutions and controlled not only the Mediterranean Basin but also much of western Europe, the area that is eastern Turkey, much of the Middle East, and northern Africa. Despite the large number of slave-run plantations on the Italian Peninsula, subsistence farms still played a large role in food production and the Roman economy.

GRECO-ROMAN ATTITUDES TOWARD FOOD

"The Greeks did not just eat to live; on the contrary, from the earliest times, dining had enormous social importance."[5] The Greeks were known for their simple fare, that is, until Alexander the Great and his armies began sending new herbs, spices, fruits, and vegetables home for cultivation. Recipes then became more complex and reflected those encountered in Persia and India. Likewise, Romans ate simple meals until they conquered the Greeks, Mesopotamians, Egyptians, and peoples of Asia Minor centuries after Alexander the Great. It was within the context of conquest that Roman soldiers were introduced to much more international and sophisticated cuisines.

For Greeks, eating at home meant eating together as a family rather than a grand banquet every night as we might suppose. The same was true for Roman families—in fact, for families all around the Roman Empire. Some men occasionally spent an evening at an elaborate banquet as an occasional treat, but certainly not the average farmer. These families especially looked forward to the evening meal. Most members of the family spent long days in the fields, in the kitchen garden, at the loom spinning wool and making clothing, or at the oven baking bread and preparing the evening meal. After a long day of work, the evening meal was an important respite, perhaps the only time when everyone in the household gathered together. It provided the opportunity to discuss planting, harvests, or surplus produce to be sold at market.

Roman families were not close. Arranged marriages were normative, and their purpose was for giving birth and raising children. Husbands typically were much older than their wives, and couples did not cherish each other. Other than their children, they did not have much in common. Parents rarely showed outward signs of love for their progeny. In wealthy families with large homes, the husband and wife lived in separate bedroom suites. Dinnertime truly was family time.

In many ways the importance of the evening meal has the same potential for the twenty-first century. With most families, school and work schedules make it difficult for the entire household to gather as a whole at any time during the day. And modern households are significantly smaller. The ancient household included extended family and might number as many as fifteen or more adults and children. The evening meal can and should be an important social occasion where conversation and mutual support are as important as the food that provides the setting. In essence, meals have the ability to build community, even small communities such as a family.

EATING IN THE FIRST-CENTURY WORLD

The Greek custom was to eat two meals; Romans ate three. The early meals were small and light. A typical Roman breakfast consisted of bread, cheese, and fruit. A noonday meal for both the Romans and Greeks might include a hard-boiled egg, easily packed vegetables, or perhaps a leftover piece of fish, and a cup of wine. Especially for the farmer and the laborer, the food for lunch had to be portable because it was carried to the fields or the workplace likely in some type of a bag or satchel. It is possible that many people ate these light meals while standing or sitting in the field or at a workbench. This pattern of light meals, either one or two, was repeated around the Mediterranean Basin.

Dinner was different. It was the best and largest meal of the day. Except for the poorest members of society and for slaves, dinner could be a multicourse meal. It might be plain and simple, sometimes even monotonous, but it was the best that the family and perhaps the servants and slaves had to offer. The meal certainly focused around the Mediterranean trinity of food: grains, olive oil, and wine. The first course of appetizers might include bread and vegetables. Lettuce was especially popular because it was believed to aid in digestion. Bulbs, such as turnips and radishes, found their way to the table as an appetizer. The Greeks typically ate bread with honey, cheese, and olive oil. The main course followed, usually a thick soup or porridge made of wheat or barley with additional flavorings added. On special occasions, sausages, a meat stew of some sort, most likely with chicken or another type of poultry were served. Fish was boiled or grilled and served on very special occasions, though it was rare when a common person could afford fresh fish. Bread was served at this course as well. The food for both courses was cut into small pieces to make it easier to eat with the thumb and two fingers. This course was followed with some sweet or salty food as a dessert at the end of the meal. Wine was the drink of choice; most of it was consumed with the dessert.

The very wealthy ate reclining on couches, leaning on an elbow and using their free hand to take food from the small table in front of them. The poorest families might have crouched on the floor around a large bowl of lentil stew and a loaf of bread or perhaps they sat on cushions around a table with three short legs for stability. When not in use, the legs were removed so the table could be taken from the room, allowing space for other activities. Families of average means most likely sat on benches and chairs, though even so, especially on special occasions, the men of the family reclined for their dinner.

Wealthy first-century diners from the Mediterranean region occasionally used spoons when eating soup, but for everything else they used their fingertips to eat. The right hand was utilized for food and the left for washing. Grabbing food with the entire hand was considered barbaric. There were never forks at the table. Knives were also utensils only a barbarian would use at the table, though there is archaeological evidence that, even in the cultured community of Athens, they were available for diners at cheap, low-class taverns.

Eating from common bowls or platters was the normative experience. Several smaller tables might serve for an extended family of ten to fifteen people. Deep bowls held the porridge, soup, or legumes. By the first century, plates of cheap pottery sometimes were used. These plates were not glazed, so they quickly absorbed food smells and became stained and were thrown away after several uses. The wealthiest Romans could afford porcelain plates and fine drinking vessels of the sort that are now in museums. Bread was used both as a plate and as an eating utensil.

Drinking vessels were made from an assortment of materials in a variety of shapes. Subsistence farmers might use wooden cups, but most vessels were pottery. Terra-cotta wine cups might have exquisite paintings on both the exterior and the interior. Artists painted the bottom of cups so pictures were revealed as the wine was consumed. Bronze casting and glassblowing were both advanced crafts and used to make drinking vessels.

Napkins were not commonly used. Greasy fingers were wiped on tablecloths, sleeves, bread, and even on the hair of slaves. Wealthy Romans occasionally used napkins, and gentlemen sometimes were known to keep the cloth in their toga throughout the day. This way their napkins were available for luncheons at the gymnasium, at a tavern, or if they were invited to an evening banquet with a friend or sponsor.[6]

THE KITCHEN, WHERE MEALS WERE PREPARED

As one might imagine, the scope and type of kitchen varied greatly according to the size of the house and the wealth of the household. Helpful information about houses and kitchens has especially been gleaned from archaeological digs at Pompeii and Herculaneum. The poorest families typically had one large room, called the *atrium*, which was used for all daily activities, such as weaving and grinding flour. Small bedrooms were attached to the atrium. A hearth was built into a corner or wall where meals were prepared. Storage for pots and cooking utensils was built into the hearth. The house might have a storeroom for foodstuffs. The houses belonging to the poor typically had no windows, so there was no escape from smoke. Fires were common.

In many homes, the kitchen was either in a room especially set apart for food preparation or in a lean-to built in the courtyard. The lean-to kitchen was the most common for ordinary households. It was built with attention given to the prevailing wind direction, so the breeze removed much of the smoke. These kitchens usually included a small oven for baking bread and cakes, a water basin, and burners that were little more than holes built into a brick base that housed a wood or charcoal fire. The base was often constructed against the courtyard or kitchen wall. The bread oven was also ideal for baking fish, suckling pigs, poultry, and other small animals. Separate from the kitchen area, families often had a spit for roasting skewered meat, sausages, and very firm fish. Spit-roasted lamb, goat, and pigs were especially popular in Greece.

Archaeologists have found a number of portable hearths, or braziers, in Pompeii. They were used in small homes or in apartments built above street-side businesses. Portable hearths were made of metal with metal legs.

They had fireboxes and several large round holes above the fire for holding clay pots and pans. Portable hearths doubled as ovens for cooking meats. They were ideal for cooking or reheating stews or sauces. Brazier-baked bread was also prepared on these portable hearths. Because they could easily be transported, they were used by catering businesses, which took them for guild banquets and funeral meals.

The kitchens for the wealthy had large spits and ovens. A cook for a wealthy household often prepared big animals, such as an entire lamb, goat, or hog, with the spit or oven for banquets. They might have several ovens, one for bread and pastries and another for meat and stews.

Both wood and charcoal were used for cooking. Wood smoke imparted a flavor that was desirable for some foods, such as meats and stews, but not so much for dishes with delicate flavors like egg patinas and sauces. Charcoal was likely used most often and was less smoky, but without sufficient ventilation, fumes accumulated and caused health problems for the cook and all who worked in the kitchen.

KITCHEN TOOLS

Many of the kitchen utensils that are found in the modern kitchen, especially the nonelectric-powered ones, were available to the ancient cook. Knives of all sizes and purposes, spatulas, whisks, sifters, skewers for grilling meat, and mortars with pestles were all used frequently to prepare even simple meals. The mortars and pestles were extremely helpful tools. In a time before blenders, electric grinders, and Cuisinart products, they were used to grind herbs and spices and to emulsify sauces. Mortars and pestles were made from a variety of materials, including clay, bronze, and wood. The Romans were especially fond of mortars made of lead because they added a "sweetness" to their food. We now know it also contributed to lead poisoning.

Spoons of various types and sizes were present. As in my kitchen, spoons were made of wood or metal, and even a few were made of bone. Cooks used spoons for stirring, tasting, and serving. Some were specialized; a spoon with a sharp point enabled diners to remove snails (escargot) from their shells. Even though first-century diners still used their fingers to eat most foods, spoons found their way to the tables of the wealthy for the purpose of sipping soup.

Different types of pots and pans were used for a variety of purposes. Clay cookware was the most common, though occasionally households owned bronze or copper pans and skillets. As today, metal pots and especially copper cookware cost significantly more than other types. Even kitchens for average families had mixing bowls, pots, kettles, and casseroles. Cookware was used for stewing, braising, deep-frying, and boiling. Frying pans and skillets were placed directly over the fire or on the coals and were often used to prepare small fish. Cooks kept tall clay pots that sloped inward and had small openings at the top. The sloping side enabled the steam to be captured and, once the moisture condensed, it ran back into the pot. Pots like these were especially helpful for cooking beans, keeping them from becoming too dry. But pots, pans, and casseroles also had lids.

Specialty pans were common. Round pots with wire handles were designed for cooking stew or *puls*. Baking crocks were dome-shaped and had lids. Charcoals or wood coals were then scattered on the sides and top. The baking crock could cook a single loaf of bread, a small chicken, or something like a bowl of stew. There was one specialty pan with indentions for baking mushrooms, including stuffed mushrooms, a well-loved appetizer. A pan called the *patina* looked very much like a tart pan and was used to prepare egg-based dishes, also called *patinas*, that were similar to crustless quiches. Patinas could be either savory or sweet; egg dishes with onions, herbs, asparagus, anchovies, peaches, or pears were all popular.

For a special occasion, the cook or a slave brought the patina to the table for service, though most food was transferred from the pot to a service platter. Platters could be both metal and terra-cotta. They could be round or oblong. Wealthy families could have platters made of bronze, silver, or gold and shaped like flowers, fish, or, most popular, shells.

Ancient cooks used all of these tools for two different cooking methods. The first was known by the Roman word *hepso*, cooking in liquid. This technique included boiling, stewing, braising, and frying. Cooking dry, or *opto*, included baking, roasting, and grilling. Just as today, cooks used a small amount of olive oil when dry cooking in a fry pan or skillet.

VEGETABLES AND THE KITCHEN GARDEN

Kitchen gardens were very highly prized. Even though herbs and vegetables were extremely important throughout the empire, they were especially loved by the Romans. A kitchen garden by law was not to be confused with a farm. Pliny the Elder explains in his *Natural History*, "From our Laws of the Twelve Tables, the word 'farm' never occurs—the word 'garden' is always used in that sense."[7] Pliny goes on to explain that the kings of Rome cultivated their own kitchen gardens with their own hands, expressing a certain sense of importance and sanctity connected to growing vegetables.

The Latin word for garden is *hortus*. It literally means an *enclosed* garden, often in a courtyard. Traditionally gardens included herbs, fruit trees, and perhaps some vegetables. Pools of water and fountains were available for watering plants and to provide a pleasing ambiance. The gardens usually also included a statue of the god of gardens, Priapus. He had a beard, a Phrygian cap, and often a painted red face.

In time, the concept of *hortus* expanded, as did the size of the gardens. Kitchen gardens in the countryside could be as large as an acre. Remember that a household was composed of multiple generations as well as servants and slaves. A large garden was needed to provide vegetables, not only during the growing season but throughout the year. The garden adjoined the farmhouse and was irrigated by a nearby river or well. Pliny recommended eight men prepare the land for the kitchen garden by turning the soil and then mixing in manure to a depth of three feet. The garden then was divided into plots with "borders and sloping, rounded banks."[8] Paths wound between the plots so family members and slaves could weed and harvest. The Romans understood irrigation, fertilizing, grafting, pruning, crop rotation, and even vegetable placement in order to avoid insects and disease.[9] Wild cucumber soaked in water and poured onto unwanted pests was a well-known insecticide, and insect-eating birds were promoted.

Townhouses in the large cities did not have an acre of land to set aside for this type of kitchen garden unless the owners were incredibly wealthy. Pliny described how some Romans followed the example of the Athenians by bringing the *chora* to the *polis*, the countryside to the city. More typical was the townhouse that surrounded an interior courtyard with vegetable plants in pots that were moved to receive optimal sun or shade.

Pliny demonstrated that even the *plebs* brought the countryside into the city by placing pots and boxes of herbs and vegetables in their windows. In this way, he wrote, the poor could look out onto the countryside and enjoy the fresh fruits of the earth.[10] It is worth noting that Pliny lamented that, by the first century, many of the vegetables grown by subsistence farmers and available to most people had become so specialized that only the upper classes could afford them. For example, asparagus grew wild in the Italian Peninsula and was harvested and eaten by many. But with cultivation and improvement, only the wealthy and the farmer with a kitchen garden had access to asparagus. As Pliny complained, "But I protest, how little does garden produce cost, how adequate it is for the pleasure and for plenty, did we not meet with the same scandal in this as in everything else?"[11]

Traditionally the kitchen garden was the responsibility of the women in the family. It might take eight men to prepare the garden for planting, but it was the daily responsibility of the women to weed the garden and harvest the vegetables as they ripened. Surplus vegetables and fruit were pickled or dried and stored for the winter. Vegetables were also taken to the market and sold so the farm family could buy other essentials such as salt or farm equipment.

Many of the wealthiest Romans took great care and pride in the cultivation of vegetables. They often retained direct oversight of the kitchen garden. They were delighted with their vegetables and served them at banquets and other meals with great pride. Roman aristocrats were also involved in cataloguing and developing new strains of vegetables. For example, not satisfied with wild asparagus, they continued to cultivate and improve asparagus until very large ones, three to a pound, were developed. Techniques were also developed to keep the color of asparagus white.

EATING AND ENJOYING VEGETABLES IN THE FIRST CENTURY

Pliny described the types of vegetables in a kitchen garden:

> Some plants growing in gardens are valued for their bulb, others for their head, others for their stalk, others for their leaf, others for both, others for their seed, others for their cartilage, others for their flesh, or for both, others for their husk or skin and cartilage, others for their fleshy outer coats.[12]

He considered cucumbers as an example of vegetables composed of cartilage and flesh, radishes and turnips as root vegetables, and fennel as one where the bulb, stalk, frond, and seeds were all used in food preparation.

Both culinary and medicinal herbs were also grown in the kitchen garden. As with vegetables, various parts of the herb were used. For example, both the leaf and the seeds of the coriander (cilantro) plant were used as flavorings in food preparation.

It was the practice of many Mediterranean people to eat vegetables with their evening meal and, from time to time, have raw or leftover vegetables with their light lunch. Until the first century, vegetables were eaten at the end of the main meal or banquet. This was certainly the way Greeks and Romans ate them. But customs change. For first-century banquets and other formal meals, vegetables were served first, as an appetizer. Cooked and raw, they were eaten with a sauce or a dip that might be as simple as olive oil, vinegar, and *garum*, or a more complex salad dressing. Vegetables also played a vital role at ordinary meals, served along with the main dish, as part of a stew or casserole, or featured in a patina.

THREE FAVORITE VEGETABLES IN
THE GRECO-ROMAN WORLD

In this section, I will examine three vegetables popular in the entire Mediterranean Basin. All three shared an important place on the ancient table.

Cucumbers

Cucumbers are a fruit that is prepared and eaten as a vegetable. Food archaeologists are not sure exactly where they originated. Some believe they first grew wild in northern India and were initially cultivated there. Some strains might have come from northern Africa. It appears that Egypt was the first place in the Mediterranean Basin to grow them, where they were eaten as a type of melon. Jews took seeds to Palestine, and cultivation gradually worked its way north into Asia Minor, and then to Greece and Italy. The exact origin of cucumbers is difficult because they were picked and eaten young while the seeds were still very soft. The seeds were consumed along with the rest of the skin and flesh, making them unavailable for archaeologists.

Cucumbers grow on vines. They can be trellised, but they were usually allowed to grow along the ground, with hay or straw placed under them to keep the fruit from becoming bruised. Supposedly Greek farmers soaked the seeds in milk and honey before planting them to make the flesh sweeter. Pliny discussed how the vegetable could be manipulated to change its shape and made impressive for friends and clients at a banquet or special meal.

Cucumbers were much loved around the Mediterranean and still are. They were a favorite of those who lived in Egypt and Palestine. The Greeks regularly served cucumbers, eating them raw, with a dip, or as part of salad. A salad might be as simple as peeled cucumber with a tablespoon or so of *garum* or *oenogarum* (*garum* with wine) splashed on before serving, or as complex as having a dressing made from pennyroyal, mint, honey, pepper, red wine vinegar, garlic, and a pinch of the exotic asafetida. *Apicius* used parboiled cucumber in a pâté. They were baked, boiled, added to stews, and prepared in the same way a modern cook might an eggplant. Peeled and shredded cucumber made a delicious sauce when added to yogurt. Small cucumbers and long, thin varieties were the most popular for eating because of their cool, watery sweetness. Just as today, small ones were also chosen for pickling and storage. When left to grow to full size, the fruit became quite large and apparently not very tasty. Ancient writers compared full-grown cucumbers to gourds, and like gourds, they were dried, hollowed, and used for storage.

The emperor Tiberius was very fond of cucumbers, reportedly eating them daily. To assure his uninterrupted supply, the emperor's kitchen gardeners had cucumber beds mounted on wheels so they could be moved to the shade during the heat of the summer day and placed under frames covered with transparent rock during wintery periods, protecting the plants from the cold while still allowing access to the sun.

Lettuce

Lettuce was perhaps the most popular vegetable in the Roman Empire. "Nothing is more typically Roman than lettuce and salad."[13] For Pliny the Elder, a lettuce salad must have been close to the perfect food. It was inexpensive to prepare and healthy to eat:

> These products of the garden were most in favour which needed no fire for cooking and saved fuel, and which were a resource in store and always ready; hence their name of salads, easy to digest and not calculated to overload the senses with food, and least adapted to stimulate the appetite. . . . There was no demand for Indian pepper and the luxuries that we import from overseas.[14]

Wild lettuces that were both spindly and bitter grew in the prehistoric world from Asia to the southern Mediterranean. Lettuce as we know it today was first cultivated by the Egyptians in the third millennium BCE. Egyptian tomb paintings show lettuces that look very much like a type of romaine lettuce. Persians enjoyed salads and served lettuce at their royal banquets. However, the Romans were the ones who popularized and especially prized serving and eating lettuce salads at meals.

Pliny the Elder wrote that the Greeks distinguished three different types of lettuce. He described even more varieties, some with crinkly leaves or flat leaves, or leaves of different colors. The stalks were different as well: broad, round, triangular. Popular lettuce plants were known by the region of origin. Cappadocian lettuce from central Turkey was a favorite, and its seeds were brought to both Greece and Rome long before the first century CE. In fact, I suspect that by the first century, most of the lettuces grown in the northern and northeast Mediterranean regions were variations of romaine. In time, gardeners improved the variety by cultivating only the plants that tasted and grew the best. That process was already underway by the first century CE.[15]

Ancient doctors claimed that lettuce had a variety of medicinal properties. Pliny relates how the doctor Musa cured the emperor Augustus by prescribing raw lettuce. He writes that this was a "good advertisement" for the vegetable.[16] Along with curative properties, ancient Egyptians claimed that lettuce was an aphrodisiac. Lettuce was considered sacred to Min, the god of love and fertility. The Greeks perceived it differently, as an anti-aphrodisiac. Despite that reputation, the Greeks enjoyed the taste of lettuce and considered it both nutritious and wholesome. At Greek banquets, it was often served in salads with rocket, also called arugula, which both Romans and Greeks considered to have amorous properties, thus counteracting the nonromantic feature of Cappadocian lettuce.

Perhaps the Greeks were at least somewhat medically accurate. The sap in lettuce has soothing properties that can help diners unwind and even sleep. High levels of magnesium in lettuce assist with relaxation. As one might suspect, most of the magnesium and the element of relaxation has been bred out of modern lettuces.

Lettuce was more than just a salad plant. It was also added to soup and patinas, and it was used as a food wrapper in much the same way as grape leaves. One Roman philosopher sprinkled his lettuce with wine and honey the day before harvesting, calling it "'green cakes' given to him by the earth."[17] Other greens and herbs, including arugula, kale, chicory, endive, parsley, watercress, cabbage, and beet greens, were sometimes added to the salad. Salads were dressed with vinegar, *garum*, oil, and salt, but for a banquet or special meal the dressing might be quite complex. Lettuce was best eaten fresh as it begins to wilt quickly after it is harvested.

Onions

Onions and other bulb vegetables from the onion family, such as garlic and leeks, were essential to Mediterranean cuisine. They still are. They were one of few root vegetables that were eaten raw, cooked as a separate dish, or used as a flavoring. *Apicius* used onions in many recipes, but only as a base seasoning.

There is some disagreement about the origin of onions. Some scholars believe they originated in central Asia: Afghanistan, Iran, and Pakistan. Others posit that they were indigenous to a larger territory, growing from Palestine to India, and that the Mediterranean Basin was a secondary center of origin. The Egyptians likely were the first to cultivate onions and garlic around 3200 BCE. They believed that the onion was a symbol that represented the universe. Pliny the Elder writes that "in Egypt people swear by garlic and onions as deities in taking an oath."[18] The Egyptian peasants found onions to be a spicy relief to the daily diet of dates and fish. Onions became part of the pay for those who labored on the Great Pyramid and were even supplied for the dead as sustenance as they journeyed into the afterlife.

Onions are very rich in mineral salts, sulfur, and vitamin C. Because of the vitamin C, they were used by both Greek and Phoenician sailors to ward off scurvy. Onions contain the chemical alkyl sulfide, which causes their distinctive smell. Another chemical, syn-propanethial-S-oxide, is released when onions are cut, prompting the release of tears. All ancient cooks knew that onions had a strong, pungent smell and made one cry while slicing. Xenophon wrote a humorous dialogue in which he and his friends discuss a passage from the *Iliad* where Homer promotes eating raw onions:

> "Gentlemen," said Charmides, "Niceratus wants to go home stinking of onions so that his wife will think absolutely no one would kiss him."
>
> "No doubt," said Socrates. "If we don't live up to our reputation, we will be ridiculed. The onion is the best side-dish, given that not only does food become more tasty, but drink does as well."[19]

It was believed that onions stimulated thirst. Romans served them all through the meal, and afterward during the symposium, the "drinking" portion of the evening, so guests would consume plenty of wine.

Pliny the Elder described a wide variety of available onions. The colors ranged from white to red, flavors from sweet to pungent. Many were raised to become large round bulbs. Some were small and were planted in clusters so they did not become large. As today, green onions, scallions, and spring onions had very little bulb and were raised for the culinary use of the green stem. Pliny proclaimed that the onions originating from Crete and the Ascalon region of Palestine were the most esteemed. He speculated that both of these varieties had a similar origin, but the Ascalon onions were sweeter. Some of the recipes in *Apicius* specifically call for Ascalon onions. It calls for the bulbs to be stored in a dry environment with good circulation of air. Pliny recommended that they be stored in chaff. Centuries before the time of Jesus and Paul, they were kept and sold in net bags.

Onions were prepared in a variety of ways. The cooks for wealthy Romans used them almost entirely as a seasoning. They were diced and then mashed with a mortar and pestle to become part of a sauce. Sliced onions or small pearl onions were added to meat stews and pots of beans or peas to give flavor. *Apicius* has a recipe for meat and onions. Columella's book on agriculture includes a technique for pickling onions. These were eaten as an appetizer or used as a replacement for fresh or dried onions when preparing a meal. They were also used as an ingredient in patinas, such as those with asparagus and onion. An onion patina was quite similar to a modern quiche Lorraine but with no crust.

DINNER WITH A FARM FAMILY

Our meal for this chapter focuses on bread and vegetables. It is a typical dinner and does not feature meat. Characteristically, the principal elements include a soup made with a grain and bread. Everything else is served as an appetizer or side dish.

I suggest that you serve the meal family style. All elements should be placed in common bowls and shared by the diners. Unless you have a soup tureen or an appropriate serving dish, you can bring the barley soup to the table already in bowls. Each diner may also want a small plate for the appetizers.

Try eating this meal without forks or spoons. Some first-century families had spoons solely to use for soup. Very small dishes of salt and pepper are also appropriate. I use small sushi dishes intended for soy sauce or the small bowls for simple dips such as flavored olive oil. Even a small plate will work.

Wine is certainly an authentic drink. Coffee and iced tea are not. But this is your meal; do what you want.

You can sit at a table, but it might be interesting to try sitting on cushions on the floor. Put the food on a coffee table or another table with short legs. If you use a table, sit on benches if you have any. Rustic-looking dishes are preferable.

You make the decision regarding napkins!

MENU: DINNER WITH A FARM FAMILY

Choose from the following recipes:

Barley Porridge (*Puls*)
Barley Soup for Plebeians
Lettuce, Green Onions, and Hard-Boiled Egg Salad
Rustic Bread
Mint Dipping Sauce
Cabbage Soup
Boiled Turnips and Raisin Sauce
Pickled Red Onions
Wine and Seasonal Fruit (from the market)
Cheese Curds or Cottage Cheese (from the market)

RECIPES

Barley Porridge (Puls)

Pomegranate seeds are available in many supermarkets. They are unnecessary, but they are delicious. This porridge with a slice of bread makes a filling meal.

- 4 cups of water
- ½ tsp. salt
- 1 cup barley flakes
- 1 tbs. honey

- 4 eggs
- ¼ cup pomegranate seeds, optional

Bring the water to a boil and add the salt. Add the barley flakes and return to a boil. Reduce to a simmer and cook for 20 minutes, stirring frequently. As barley porridge nears completion, stir in the honey and start cooking the eggs. You may use any method you choose. I prefer either eggs over easy or poached eggs. Spoon barley into each bowl. Top with an egg and garnish with a tablespoon of pomegranate seeds.

Barley Soup for Plebeians

It might be interesting to prepare both versions of this soup and have your family or guests do a taste test. You can add leftover meat or sausage to the second version to make it even more special.

- 1 cup pearl barley
- 1 cup red lentils

- 6 cups chicken stock
- 2 tsp. salt

Additional ingredients to make the dish special:

- 1 tbs. olive oil
- 1 leek, white and light green part, chopped fine
- 1 cup spinach

- 2 tsp. dried dill or 2 tbs. fresh dill
- 1 tsp. pepper

Soak the barley overnight. Drain the barley. Combine barley, lentils, and stock in a large pot. Bring to a boil. Be prepared to skim off whatever impurities rise to the top. Add salt and turn heat to a simmer. Cook until barley breaks down and becomes thick. Adjust seasoning before serving.

To make the soup special: Soak the barley overnight. When prepared to cook, drain the barley. Pour 1 tablespoon olive oil in a hot pot. Add the leek and sauté. Add the barley, lentils, and the chicken stock. When soup is beginning to thicken, after approximately 30 to 40 minutes, stir in the spinach, dill, and pepper. Continue to cook until spinach wilts. Adjust seasoning and serve. You may top either version of this soup with olive oil when it is finished.

Lettuce, Green Onions, and Hard-Boiled Egg Salad

I like using a ratio of 1:2, one part vinegar to two parts olive oil, for my salad dressings. Use a ratio of 1:3 if you prefer a less acidic dressing. You may add additional vegetables to your platter.

- Romaine and other lettuces
- 10 green onions, trimmed
- 6 hard-boiled eggs, cooled and cut in half

- 1 tsp. thyme, divided use
- Salt
- Red or white wine vinegar
- Extra-virgin olive oil

Tear romaine lettuce into large pieces. Add other lettuces, such as "spring mix." Place on plates with the green onions and eggs. Add half the thyme to the salad. Put a pinch of salt on each egg half. Mix the vinegar and oil, the rest of the thyme, and salt in a small bowl and use as a dip. Alternatively, pour the dressing over all the contents of the salad.

Rustic Bread

A delicious bread that is not hard to make. It will become a favorite.

- 1 tbs. quick-rising yeast
- 1 cup plus 1½–1¾ cups water
- 4 cups white unbleached flour

- 2½ cups whole wheat flour
- ½ cup cracked wheat
- 3 tbs. olive oil
- 1 tbs. honey
- 1 tbs. salt

If using a mixer with a dough hook: combine yeast with 1 cup of 110-degree water in the mixer bowl. Leave until yeast is activated. Add the flours and cracked wheat, the rest of the water, olive oil, honey, and finally the salt. Mix for 5 minutes; let rest for 15 minutes, then mix for another 5 minutes. The dough should be slightly wet. If the dough is too damp, add flour 1 tablespoon at a time. If too dry, add water 1 tablespoon at a time.

Use a plastic bench scraper or large spatula and scrape dough onto a floured board. Briefly knead and place in an oiled bowl. Cover with a kitchen towel (not terry cloth) or plastic wrap and let rise until doubled, approximately 60 to 90 minutes, depending on the temperature of your kitchen.

Punch down the risen dough and turn out onto the floured board. Knead briefly and divide into two loaves or keep as one large loaf.

Preheat oven to 500 degrees. Place the dough in the bottom of a well-seasoned Dutch oven. Alternatively, place the loaves on an oiled cooking sheet (half sheet).

Cover with a floured towel or plastic wrap and let rise for another hour. Place the dough in the Dutch oven and score with a razorblade knife and cover with the top. Turn down the oven to 450 degrees. Bake

30 minutes and remove the top. Bake another 15 minutes. Very carefully remove from the oven and empty the bread onto a cooling rack. Let cool for 2 hours before cutting.

Alternatively, after the oven has preheated and the loaves have risen, place the sheet with loaves in the oven. Throw several ounces of water against the side of the oven to produce steam. Quickly close the oven door and turn the temperature down to 450. Cook for 30–35 minutes or until nicely browned.

Mint Dipping Sauce

A farm family could not have afforded saffron, so its use here is optional. Use as a dip for bread.

- ½ cup fresh mint
- 1 tbs. pickled green peppercorns or 1 tsp. ground pepper

- 1 pinch of saffron, *optional*
- 1 tbs. honey
- ½ cup olive oil
- 3 tbs. white wine vinegar

Finely cut the mint leaves into ribbons and set aside. Combine the rest of the ingredients. Stir in the mint and set aside so flavors can combine.

Cabbage Soup

- 1 tbs. olive oil
- 1 lb. pork or pork sausage
- 1 onion, chopped fine
- 3 garlic cloves, minced
- 2 tsp. caraway seeds
- 1 tsp. each dried thyme, celery seed, and ground sumac
- ¼ cup white wine

- 1 head cabbage, cut into ¾-inch pieces
- 8 cups chicken stock
- 2 bay leaves
- 4–5 myrtle leaves
- 1½ tsp. salt
- 1 tsp. pepper
- ½ cup yogurt and dill to garnish

Sauté the pork in the olive oil. Add the onion and garlic and cook until opaque. Add the caraway seeds, thyme, celery seed, and ground sumac. Add the cabbage to the pot and then the wine. Let the wine reduce, and then add the chicken stock. Wrap the bay and myrtle leaves in cheese cloth and add to the pot. Season with salt and pepper. Cabbage will be wilted and pork cooked through when finished. Adjust seasoning and top each serving with yogurt and dill.

Boiled Turnips and Raisin Sauce

The sauce can be used for many dishes including as a dip for bread.

- ½ cup raisins
- 2 small turnips, washed, peeled, and cut into bite-sized pieces
- 2 tbs. plus ½ tsp. salt, divided use

- 1 tsp. mustard seed
- 6 peppercorns, *optional*
- ¼ cup red wine vinegar
- ½ cup olive oil

Place raisins in a small bowl and cover with boiling water. Soak for 30 minutes. Bring enough water to a boil that will cover the turnips. Add 2 tablespoons salt to the water and then boil turnips for 20 minutes or until soft.

For the raisin sauce: Crush 1 teaspoon mustard seed with a mortar and pestle. Then crush the peppercorns. Rough chop the raisins and then add the remaining salt and the raisins to the mortar and continue to crush. Then add the wine vinegar and olive oil and make into a paste.

Alternatively, use a blender and blend mustard seed, salt, peppercorns, wine vinegar, and olive oil all at once.

Adjust the seasoning and serve turnip pieces covered with the sauce.

Note: Most farmers would not have had access to pepper, so you may omit it.

Pickled Red Onions

These provide a nice garnish for most of the savory recipes in the book. You can also use rice vinegar instead of the last three ingredients, a "not-very-first-century" alternative.

- 1 cup of thinly sliced red onion
- ½ cup red wine vinegar
- 2 tbs. honey
- ¼ tsp. salt

Place the red onions in a jar or small bowl. Mix the vinegar, honey, and salt and pour over the onions. Allow to macerate for 12–24 hours.

ADDENDUM

Roman Class Structure

R oman class structure was well defined by the first century CE. Each of the various strata had its own relationship to food, farming, and food production, which this brief introduction will help to illustrate.

Landowners and farmers existed in almost all strata of the Greco-Roman social order. The *senatorial order* were the true aristocrats, engaged in running the empire as members of the senate. Senators owned land, sometimes very large holdings, and were incredibly wealthy, with fortunes worth as much as 100 million denarii (about $20 billion).[1]

They were not allowed to engage in business or trade, which was considered "basically dishonest since it involved buying products at one price and selling them for a higher price without doing anything to increase their value," so much of a senator's monetary worth was invested in farm- and pastureland.[2] A young man from a senatorial family began his career as *cursus honorum* ("course of honors" or colloquially "ladder of offices"), and had a variety of career opportunities. But first, as with many class opportunities, he had to claim a monetary and property threshold worth at least 250,000 denarii ($12.5 million). The young senator began his career with a job such as road management or legal work. He also spent time as a military officer, a tribune. After this "training period" the young senator might work as a judge or have oversight of some type of public welfare such as grain distribution. He also could remain in the military. Eventually non-Romans and those living outside the Italian Peninsula could become senators.

The *equestrian order*, beginning centuries before the period of the Apostle Paul, originated from Roman citizens who served the army on horseback. They had to furnish their own weapons, supplies, and horse, thus the name. Later the term expanded to define the order beneath that of senator. As with *cursus honorum*, those in the *equestrian order* had to meet minimal qualifications, including a monetary worth of 100,000 denarii (equivalent to $5 million), proof that the family was born free (not slaves) for two generations, and possession of an excellent moral character. A long-serving centurion stood a good chance of becoming an equestrian. He also had a good opportunity to become a senator.

Equestrians filled positions such as the military tribune for auxiliary legions, treasury official, and procurator and governor of a region. Pontius Pilate was an *equestrian*, as was Claudius Lysias, who examined Paul in Jerusalem, and Marcus Antonius Felix, who heard Paul in Caesarea. Because they were not senators, they were free to invest their financial resources in a wide range of commercial ventures. Many of them made fortunes participating in trade, tax collection, and a wide variety of businesses. Like senators, equestrians invested in agricultural land. The transition from business to farming helped *equestrians* gain respectability.

Aristocrats from the cities around the empire made up the *decurion order*, the bottom rung of the upper-class orders. Members of the local senates that ruled colonies and municipalities comprised the *decurion order*. In the eastern part of the Mediterranean, these were Greek or Hellenized Near Easterners, including sympathetic Jews, Herodians, and many in the temple priesthood.[3] They were often traders, merchants, and locally wealthy landowners. Qualifications to be accepted as part of the *decurion order* were set locally and included ownership of property, age, and involvement in reputable businesses. Service as a *decurion* could be costly. They were required to work their first year without compensation and make large financial contributions to their communities. In exchange, they received preferential treatment, including access to water supplies, food, and legal privileges.[4] Paul knew at least two *decurions* that became Christians: Dionysius the Areopagite in Athens (Acts 17:34) and Erastus, the treasurer of Corinth (Romans 16:23).

Everyone else, meaning most of the people in the Greco-Roman world, were considered either the *populus integer*, the respectable populace, or *plebs sordida*, the poor. The respectable populace included shopkeepers, craftsmen, and small landowners. They might have been Roman soldiers or even centurions. Many were financially able to employ laborers or own slaves. They represented a wide range of wealth, from very successful business owners to subsistence farmers. Some were Roman citizens, though those that lived in the Roman provinces likely were not. The wealthiest of the *populous integer* attempted to imitate the aristocracy in their lifestyle. Most found companionship by belonging to guilds and other associations. They were considered honest and respectable by the aristocratic orders, though those who were not Roman citizens were thought to have less status. Most of those named by the apostle Paul in his letters and who populated his churches belonged to the *populous integer.*[5]

The poor, or *plebes sordida*, tended to be tenant farmers and day laborers. Some of the poor families owned small farms at one time but lost them because of their inability to pay debts. By the first century, most had migrated to the large cities in order to look for work. In fact, the *plebes sordida* spent a significant amount of time looking for work. They were considered equal in status to the lowest slaves and often did the same kind of labor. The *plebes sordida* were considered "shabby people" by most Romans, liars and cheats who did not have the financial resources to live a virtuous life.[6] Interestingly, they were most likely to frequent the Coliseum for its entertainment.

Rome, along with the rest of the Italian Peninsula, was a slave (*servus*) state, meaning approximately 30 percent of the population were slaves (*servi*). By the time of Jesus, there were between 2 and 3 million slaves out of a population of 7.5 million people in Italy. A group that large has a transformative impact on both the economy and the culture.[7] First-century slaves worked primarily in agriculture, with large crews, sometimes numbering in the thousands, working on the farms of the upper classes. Even smallholding farmers usually had one or two slaves. Many Roman slaves were prisoners of war. But they also came from families sold into slavery to pay debts or just to attempt to find a better way of life. Some hapless people were captured by slavers and sold. Others were raised as slaves, abandoned by their parents as small children.

Most likely performed agricultural work, but slaves also had a wide variety of jobs and responsibilities. They could be clerks, cooks, secretaries, and artisans, including sculptors, painters, and even respected doctors. Women slaves tended to have domestic jobs, such as maids, launderers, midwives, and hairdressers. Both male and female slaves were used as prostitutes. Extremely talented and learned slaves were given positions of accountability both in business and government. All slaves, and especially those connected to wealthy households, were given a life with regular meals, good lodging, and clothing commensurate with their station. The slaves of the upper class typically lived better than the poor free people in the city. Still, slaves were legally considered commodities, to be sold and purchased at the will of their owners.

It is surprising that most slaves in the ancient world eventually were given their freedom, typically at the age of thirty. Others had the opportunity to make money and purchase freedom at an even younger age. Slave owners believed that the possibility of freedom motivated their slaves to work harder and become more productive. These freedmen, *libertus* in Latin, and freedwomen, *liberta*, also became Roman citizens. It is believed that during New Testament times, more than half of the city of Rome was made up of slaves, freedmen, and freedwomen.

Most *libertus* and *liberta* remained attached to their owners, often performing the same services but in a patron relationship. A large number kept shops, worked as artisans, or continued with domestic duties.

> Freedmen learned from their masters how to run a shop he financed, how to practice a trade to which he apprenticed them, and how to handle his accounts. They served in the master's place in occupations below his status.[8]

On very rare occasions, freedmen became quite wealthy or were able to climb to higher social classes, some even to the ruling aristocracy.

4

KEEPING HUNGER AT BAY
A Strategy for Enduring Shortage and Famine

I suspect that we have all experienced hunger. For most of us it was very temporary. Perhaps we were scheduled to have blood drawn and had to fast until afterward. Or maybe we had to abstain from food for a longer period, perhaps a day or even several days, due to the nature of a medical procedure. We might engage in a cleansing fast for health reasons. Whatever the reason, we experienced that emptiness in our stomach as we missed one or more meals. For most of us, the hunger is temporary, ending soon enough.

Missing a meal or even several meals is significantly different from enduring a real food shortage or famine. We have seen the pictures from parts of the world stricken by famine, where children's stomachs are distended from a severe lack of protein, nursing mothers' milk is "dried up" because of the lack of nutrition, and teeth are missing from the absence of essential nutrients in diets. All animals and plants in the region have been eaten and even the bark on trees stripped to provide sustenance. A care agency provides rice, rationing two cups to a family of six. Their share must be protected from thieves who will kill for a handful of rice because their families face the same needs. Who is fed? Who is not? Food shortages might cause temporary crises. A famine can bring starvation and death to thousands, especially to children and the poorest members of society.

Dried lentils and beans will last for a very long time, providing a hedge against food shortage. They were considered food for the poor, and yet almost everyone ate them. In our time, lowly legumes are often exalted in regional cuisines and food preparation. They provide the basis for what we often call "comfort foods." Just imagine visiting southern Louisiana and not trying red beans and rice. Or missing out on Boston baked beans in the Northeast. Or eating dinner in the Southwest and skipping *frijoles refritos* (refried beans) or *frijoles charros* (pinto beans made with bacon, chilis, and sometimes cooked with a bottle of beer). Gourmet restaurants often serve the main course on a puree of compatible beans or peas.

THE AGRICULTURAL ECONOMY

The Roman economy was agricultural. There were other possibilities for income, such as mining for minerals or producing crafts, but for most of the empire, farmers and farms supplied both the food and the tax revenue needed to support it. On the other hand, the realm was not the simple agrarian culture we might imagine. A highly developed literary and philo-sophical culture coexisted in the cities with a peasant agricultural system, which coexisted in the shadow of large farms owned by wealthy senators and others from the upper echelons of society. The emperor may have been the largest landowner, but subsistence farmers with small tracts of land comprised by far the greatest percentage of land in the empire. By the first century, it is estimated that 10–20 percent of the sixty million people in the Roman Empire lived in cities. The other 80 percent or so of the population lived in rural areas and were involved in agriculture in some way.

By the first century CE, the *chora*, the countryside surrounding Rome and other major cities, had long lost its ability to feed the urban residents. Rome itself had a population of at least one million people and possibly quite a few more. It took 220,000 tons of imported grain, before loss and spoilage, to feed its people for a year. The majority of the grain was imported from Egypt, northern Africa, Sicily, and Sardinia, with additional grain sent from locations such as Gaul, Cyprus, Spain, and Palestine. Much of it was collected in the form of taxes, though some was purchased at a discounted, below-market-value price. This grain provided everyone in Rome with the bread and porridge they required for their diet.

The Roman economy was like a game. Peasant farmers needed to produce a surplus, especially of grains and legumes. A percentage of each crop was used first to feed the household, including family members, servants, and slaves. The excess part of the crop, as much as 25 percent, provided seeds for planting. Much of the remaining harvest was set aside in case bad weather or war depleted the harvest. The remainder was avail-able to sell. Surpluses commonly stayed local, sold at the local market to a miller or a baker. A merchant might purchase the surplus harvest and then transport it to an urban area. The money made from these sales enabled the farm family to purchase things they could not craft for themselves. The same was true of the grapes for wine, olives for oil, vegetables, and fruit harvested by a farm family. Some was consumed, some was stored for the future, and some was sold. Then some was taken for taxes.

The Roman state appreciated the need for the survival of the subsistence farmer, realizing that the farm family must have their surplus. At the same time, it understood the necessity to collect taxes to fund the imperial structure, senators, and the army. In addition, local officers of the state were responsible for collecting taxes as well as for the upkeep of the infrastructure that made the movement of crops, armies, and merchants possible. Farmers were by far the number-one target for tax extraction. This quote compares the subsistence farmers to sheep:

> The sheep had to be sheared, perhaps even fleeced, but not gutted. Too harsh a regime might undermine the tax-paying capacity. . . . It was a question of balance. But that balance remained heavily tilted towards the members of the most prominent families around the cities of the empire.[1]

And so, the game: the trick was to maximize tax collection without placing subsistence farmers at too great of a risk of absolute failure. A breakdown in the system would jeopardize the food supply, causing shortages and ultimately placing the economic viability as a whole in jeopardy. What could be taken from peasant farmers in tax revenue without breaking their backs and the back of the entire system?

Taxes were collected in several different ways. With taxes "in kind," grain and other foodstuffs were collected and transported straight to Rome or another urban area. But often crops were first converted to currency by the farmer at a local market, or more likely by professional merchants and traders or by the tax collector.

The 20 percent of taxes collected from the wheat farms in Egypt were the highest in the empire. A more typical tax was a rate of some 10 percent of the crop harvested. However, if *public land* was being used by the farmer, the tax rate increased to as much as 30 or even 40 percent. In essence, the farmer on public land was paying both rent and tax with the state providing the seed for the crop.[2] Fifteen percent of all the taxes collected eventually ended up in the coffers of the Roman aristocracy.

If local taxes were exorbitant because of an especially greedy tax collector, both farmers and traders found ways around the system. Farmers set up elaborate bartering systems where they could trade crops outside of established networks for the goods and services they needed. If traders and merchants were overcharged by local authorities, they could pursue the somewhat dangerous and creative alternative of smuggling. They could also stockpile produce, especially grain, until the prices were higher and taxes lower.

DEFINITION AND CAUSES OF FOOD SHORTAGE AND FAMINE

Food historian Peter Garnsey provides good working definitions of both food shortages and famine. He writes that a food shortage is a "short-term reduction in the amount of available foodstuffs, as indicated by rising prices, popular discontent, hunger, in the worst case bordering on starvation."[3] On the other hand, famine is a "critical shortage of essential foodstuffs leading through hunger to starvation and a substantially increased mortality rate in a community or region." Garnsey summarizes by saying, "Food shortages are not always serious. Famine is a catastrophe."[4]

The climate was the primary cause of food shortage. The climate of the Mediterranean Basin was and is problematic. As described in chapter 3, it is composed of countless microclimates. The usual overall climate consisted of winter rains and mild springs followed by summer heat with very little rain. October to May were the principal months for growth. But this formula was anything but consistent. One area might have received plenty of rain while an adjacent region experienced drought. The erratic nature of climate was exacerbated in both the eastern and southern regions of the Mediterranean Basin. The unpredictable nature of the climate, especially rainfall, worked against farmers.

Three crops especially were considered hedges against food shortage, and yet the failure rate of these foods was also high. Because they could be dried and stored for long periods of time, wheat, barley, and legumes were the "safety net" foods of the ancient world. Wheat was by far the favored of the three because of the high quality of the bread made with it. But it was also a more fragile plant and more likely to fail. The probability for the failure of a wheat crop could be anywhere from one in eight years to one in every four. Barley was a much heartier plant with a lower likelihood of failure: only one every twenty years or more. Barley flour does not include as much gluten, and the quality of the bread made with it was not well loved, but it continued to be an important crop as a safeguard against food shortage. Legumes had the highest incidence of failure, by some calculations as many as two years of crop failure every five.[5] But legumes provided more protein than grains, important during a food crisis.

Other natural causes for food shortage included unseasonably hot or cold temperatures, partial or complete destruction of crops by pests, and even human diseases that kept farmers from being able to bring in a harvest. A combination of several or all of these elements resulted in disaster. A plague in the region around Utica and Carthage around the year 125 BCE was said to have killed two hundred thousand people. This plague was followed by a second plague, one of locusts. The result was severe food shortage, causing even more death.

The Mediterranean Sea allowed ships to move foodstuffs quickly from one location to another, thus compensating for temporary food shortage. But what happened if storms at sea hindered the transport of staple foods such as wheat and barley? For example, the city of Rome especially depended on imports of grain, particularly from Egypt, to feed its huge population. Storms on the Mediterranean indefinitely delayed the arrival of the grain. Local sources would have been overwhelmed attempting to feed so many people, resulting in food shortages.

Human-created food shortages occurred in various ways. War was a significant one. The movement of a large number of troops into a region often overwhelmed the local food supply. Battles left many refugees moving from one location to another and caused the same problem. Farmers were often recruited as soldiers, leaving small farms without the labor to bring in crops. The problem became permanent if the farmer was killed in battle. Piracy, crop speculation, and corrupt or inefficient administration could all contribute to food shortages.

Both Athens and Rome experienced significant food shortages during the centuries leading up to the time of Paul. War, civil disorder, disease, and climate all contributed to shortages occurring sometimes as frequently as once every five years. It is notable that crisis-free periods normally were marked by successful Roman rule abroad and stable and effective government leadership at home.

Famine was different. True famines were rare and usually caused by war, especially when a city was placed under siege and its residents had no access to renewed food supplies. But if any of the causes of food shortages lasted long enough or were combined with other conditions, famine was the result.

If the severity of food shortage or famine was extreme, it would lead to significant changes in human behavior and potentially a large number of deaths. For the most part, subsistence farmers were only able to store enough of their grain and legume crops to last one to two additional years. The shortage in the *chora*, of course, became severe once reserves were exhausted. The crisis for the farmer was exacerbated if the family had to eat their livestock. Farm families counted on poultry, sheep, goats, and oxen to provide benefits in eggs, milk, wool, and work for many years. This long-term investment was lost once the animals were butchered. With a more severe shortage, families ate the fodder they had raised to feed the livestock. They next began to eat nonfood plants gathered from the surrounding countryside.

Social connections were used as a hedge against disaster. Farmers assisted families and neighbors in need with their remaining surpluses and were repaid with assistance at harvest. Wealthy farmers, especially those who were patrons of poorer ones, also provided assistance, but usually at a cost. The farmer who had been helped might be required to serve the patron as a laborer or owe a percentage of a crop after the crisis ended.

In some ways, severe shortages and famines were more difficult in urban areas (*polis*). Cities developed plans to respond to shortages, but in extreme cases of siege or because of corrupt management, reserves could become insufficient. The prices charged for food were the first sign of reaction. The costs of grains and legumes increased significantly as the shortage grew more severe. The prices of other foodstuffs also increased. At the same time, the prices for nonfood goods and services diminished as the need decreased—clay pots to store food are unnecessary when there is no food. At some point, if possible, people migrated, hoping to find "greener pastures," locations where food and work were still available. However, this option was not always available, especially for those trapped by war and siege.

Often severe shortage and famine resulted in social disorder, especially among the plebeian class. Violence and riots erupted especially if it was believed that grain was being hoarded by wealthy owners in order to drive up prices. At times, troops were used to quell riots, but the violence provided no solution to the underlying issue of hunger. More often the riots solicited a response from municipal leaders who then distributed the stores of much-needed grain to the population. In the case of famine, increased food distribution provided only a temporary solution until the stores were depleted. At that point, the people in urban areas began to consume nonnormal food products. If still available, grass, leaves, bark, and even the trees in public areas were eaten. Dogs, cats, insects, and even rats and mice were consumed. Leather clothing was targeted. Finally, in very rare cases, human flesh was eaten. All the while, hunger became starvation and ultimately resulted in the death of many.

HOW THE ANCIENT WORLD PREPARED FOR SHORTAGE
AND FAMINE: WHO SURVIVED AND WHO DID NOT?

As we have seen, plebeian farmers had strategies to survive the circumstances leading to shortages. These included land dispersal, crop diversification, storage of surpluses, and the development of relationships with other farmers and with patrons. At the same time, despite the inevitability of food shortage, most municipalities did very little to prepare. However, they did have some alternatives. Municipalities had relationships with other communities. A town could always notify a sister city when it was experiencing a shortage. The city then could sell some of its surplus to the one experiencing the shortage. Governing authorities also had some degree of oversight over imports and exports. If local supplies were plenteous, they could restrict imports, thus keeping local prices from dropping more than usual with an abundant harvest. Alternatively, when food supplies were dwindling, imports were invited.

Wealthy farmers, merchants, and those with the financial means to purchase and hoard grains and dried legumes could prepare by waiting for the appropriate prices, either abroad or at home, in order to sell and make large profits. The risk during times of shortage was the possibility of violence. It was assumed during a time of shortage that the wealthy were hoarding grains, waiting for yet a better price for their wares. The greater the shortage, the stronger possibility of mob violence. City administrators and the owners of surplus foods became targets. City leaders responded to shortages by requesting that the wealthy sell their reserves. In more extreme cases, the community might make the sale of grain compulsory. As a last resort, either the city administration or the mob opened the doors of the granaries and emptied them. Usually before the outbreak of mob violence, outside authorities such as governors intervened to assure the people were fed and violence was held at bay. If grain reserves were taken, then the owners of the grain were eventually compensated, though at a discount. Ironically, cities preferred that their wealthy grain owners sell their holdings rather than reserve foodstuffs for a future shortage or famine. After all, exporting brought tax revenue to the city.

Often it was philanthropists and benefactors who engaged in the generosity necessary to assist and even save their communities from crisis. They might advance money or grain into the market for feeding the people or sell at greatly reduced prices. But they rarely provided grain to the populace without making at least a small profit. Money was loaned with interest for the purchase of grain, or wheat was sold with the requirement of repayment, again with interest.

Because they came to the rescue of the populace, benefactors expected recognition and honor from their communities. Resolutions, plaques, banquets of honor when the food was plentiful, and even public statues were the types of honors presented to those who assisted their cities during times of crisis. The problem was that all these ad hoc responses to famine did not present a permanent solution to the fundamental issue. There were no frameworks, systems, laws, or institutions developed to assure that the ordinary citizen did not go hungry or starve to death during a food shortage, especially a severe one.

One method that the city of Rome used to deal with the issue of food was the institution of a wheat dole. Originally the dole was only for Roman citizens, and the grain was sold at a discounted price. Those eligible were contractors, freeborn, craftsmen, and business owners, all primarily from the plebeian class. Later, slaves and the poorest residents of Rome were added to the dole. Eventually, the wheat was given away instead of sold. The number of those receiving the dole fluctuated greatly, anywhere from 150,000 to 300,000 people.

Paul would most certainly have experienced municipal food shortages during his travels and time spent in cities around the northeast and northern Mediterranean Basin. Access to basic foodstuffs in the marketplace at a reasonable price certainly concerned his little Christian communities, and it must have worried him as well. There were several instances during his lifetime when Rome experienced a serious shortage. Augustus dealt with a significant shortage in 6 CE, perhaps around the time of Paul's birth and not long after the birth of Jesus, by expelling many people from Rome, sending gladiators and many slaves from the city and forcing senators and their entourages to retire to their estates in the *chora*. He then rationed grain and doubled the amount of the grain dole. In earlier shortages, Augustus purchased grain himself and gave it to Rome's residents. In 19 CE, Tiberius in similar fashion reacted decisively to a significant shortage by setting the maximum price of wheat to stop profit-taking and inflation. He then compensated traders who brought wheat into the city. Ironically, when faced with a similar shortage and protests in 32 CE, he reacted by chiding the Senate and magistrates for not dealing more effectively with the populace.[6] There were shortages during the reigns of Caligula, Claudius, and a significant one following the Great Fire during the time of Nero (64 CE). It was during the Nero's reign that Paul was executed in Rome, possibly with other Christians who were blamed for the fire. Still, despite these and other experiences, Rome typically remained unprepared for future major shortages.

Who fared best and worst during shortages? The wealthy of course had access to food, including their own reserves on lands they owned in the *chora*. During times of famine, especially caused by war or siege, even the wealthy in cities were exposed to the extreme shortages. Those escaping to the countryside fared better. The subsistence farmer likely had access to more food than the plebeian living in the city, though each situation had its advantages. The plebeians and craftspeople living in Rome accessed the dole and other distributions as long as food lasted. Though at times of severe shortage even these "safety nets" were curtailed. At the same time, the small farm owners continued to use the produce they raised. If the shortage, especially one caused by drought or marauding soldiers, was severe, then the farm family ate the wheat stored for future plantings. On those occasions when all the stored food was eaten or taken, then the farmer had no seed for future crops.

As noted above, farm families fell back on relationships, including those of patronage, both for food for the present and seed for the future. Many owners of small farms also worked on large estates during times of harvest, making them valuable to wealthy farmers and thus qualified aid. But such assistance was usually not free, and farmers faced the serious risk of falling into debt extreme enough that their land was in jeopardy of confiscation for payment.

It might seem as though farm slaves were exposed during times of shortage. And most certainly their rations were reduced. But because they were considered property, owners made sure that slaves received enough food to remain alive. As crass as it might sound to modern ears, wealthy farmers did not wish to lose their investments. Perhaps tenant farmers and wage laborers were the most exposed. Tenant farmers had access to some of the resources of the landowners and the wealthy owners had both the motivation to see tenants succeed and perhaps a contractual obligation to ensure that their tenants survived, "at least until the crop was harvested."[7] Typically wage laborers had the weakest position for survival. They usually did not own land and worked on the farms belonging to others for wages only. There was very little work during a time of shortage, and when there was work, the wages dropped, sometimes dramatically, because of the abundance of unemployed laborers. They depended especially on the generosity of the people they knew in the community.

PAUL, FOOD SHORTAGE, AND FAMINE

Paul's own ministry became a relief effort aimed at assisting Christians in Judea. The Book of Acts records a prophecy that speaks of a worldwide famine:

> At that time prophets came down from Jerusalem to Antioch. One of them named Agabus stood up and predicted by the Spirit that there would be a severe famine over all the world; and this took place during the reign of Claudius. The disciples determined that according to their ability, each would send relief to the believers living in Judea; this they did, sending it to the elders by Barnabas and Saul. (Acts 11:27–29)

The famine did not cover the entire world, but it did impact Egypt, Judea, Syria, and Greece in the years 45–47 CE. We might assume from Paul's letters that the famine was most severe in the province of Judea where Jerusalem was located. That was the focus of the relief effort.

The texts not only record that Paul took relief funds to Jerusalem but also that he actively collected money from the church communities with which he was connected. In chapters 8 and 9 of 2 Corinthians, Paul discusses the raising of funds for the Jerusalem Christians. He begins the section by bragging about the Macedonian churches, Philippi and Thessalonica, and how they were able to give so generously. Ironically, or perhaps as any good fundraiser might do, he boasts about the generosity of the Corinthians to the Macedonians (2 Corinthians 8:1–5; 9:1–2)! In his first letter to the Corinthians, Paul suggests a method of setting aside money for those in need: "You should follow the directions I gave to the churches of Galatia. On the first day of every week, each of you is to put aside and save whatever extra you earn, so that collections need not be taken when I come" (1 Corinthians 16:1–4). He further recommends that they choose representatives to take the gifts to Jerusalem and that he might personally go with them (1 Corinthians 16:3–4). He refers to these fundraising efforts in his letter to the Romans, telling them that when the project is over and he has delivered the funds to Jerusalem, he intends to visit the Roman Christians while on his way to Spain (Romans 15:25–29).

If nothing else, this survey demonstrates first the seriousness of the food shortage and famine that stretched along the eastern portion of the Mediterranean Basin. It certainly caused enough concern among the other Christian communities that the response was to raise money, especially for the poorer members of the famine-stricken region, so they could afford food. Community members were willing not only to give money but also to travel a great distance to share their collection with the Jerusalem Christians. It also shows Paul's personal involvement in the relief effort. Food shortages and famines seriously threatened the well-being and lives of many people. He wanted to assure that his young congregations did their part to alleviate as much pain and uncertainty as possible. As he writes to the Christians in Corinth, "Now as you excel in everything—in faith, in speech, in knowledge, in upmost eagerness, and in our love for you—so we want you to excel also in this generous undertaking. I do not say this as a command, but I am testing the genuineness of your love . . ." (2 Corinthians 8:7–8). Concern for the poor and those experiencing hardship became a hallmark of ancient Christianity, as important as any other aspect of discipleship.

THE LOWLY LEGUME

Along with grains, legumes were one of the most important foods of the Roman Empire. At the same time, they were one of the least favored. Legumes were deeply associated with poverty, and for a number of reasons. They were inexpensive. The vast majority of the people received their nutritional protein as well as starch and mineral salts from legumes. The wealthy ate protein-rich animals such as sheep, goats, and swine, and at the same time reviled legumes as food fit only for peasants. Sheep and goats required a large amount of grazing land, a great deal of grass, and, ironically, fodder consisting of legumes to feed a small number of people per animal. On the other hand, the same field of legumes provided protein for a large number of people. Legumes cheaply and efficiently met a nutritional requirement for most people.

In a comedy written by Aristophanes, there is a discussion about a friend who is now among the *nouveau riche*. "He became a rich man and suddenly he no longer likes lentils."[8] With a new wardrobe, a different manner of speech, and a diet with more meat and fewer legumes, the newly rich man wanted to ensure that he was no longer compared to a plebeian or craftsman. Diet became a marker of class, and legumes were plebeian food, a poor person's meat.

Ironically though, everyone ate legumes on at least occasion; most ate them daily. They may have been a marker of class, but they were also an "emblem of simplicity."[9] Many Greeks and Romans looked longingly to a humbler past, and leaving legumes on the menu helped them to experience the time when soldier-farmers who ate barley porridge and stews made with lentils or fava beans conquered the known world. The Romans compared that vision of the past with the senator who spent nights at banquets, feasting on flamingo tongue, eating hams that were molded into the shape of giant oxen, drinking wine to extreme, and then rushing to the vomitorium. Both images, to some extent, were idealized. Even in the first century, the time of Paul, philosophers and playwrights were crying for a reform of attitude in the direction of simplicity. The wealth of the empire made it difficult.

Apicius included several recipes where legumes are raised to a new level with the addition of herbs, spices, and other flavorings. It is symbolic of the significance of the legume that four important Roman families were named after legumes: Cicero the chickpea; Fabius the fava or broad bean; Lentulus, the lentil; and Pisolus, the pea.[10]

Legumes were occasionally eaten fresh, sometimes still in the pod. But they were almost always dried so they could be stored for years and prepared in a variety of ways. They were roasted, boiled, fermented, and ground into a flour, sometimes added to the flour from grains. Some legumes were grown only as fodder for cattle or to be plowed back into the ground, adding vital nitrogen to the soil.

Legumes as Fodder, Fertilizer, and Famine Food

There were three legumes primarily used to feed animals but also available to humans. Two are the *grass pea* and the *vetch* or *bitter vetch*. Both were used as fodder for livestock. The pods of the grass pea and vetch seeds were eaten by people during times of severe food shortage or famine. Both are toxic, especially when eaten in large amounts. The grass pea pods and vetches were boiled, removing some of the toxicity. Vetch seeds look very much like lentils but take two to four times as long to cook.[11] What a difficult situation, especially for the poor during a time of severe want, to have to choose between eating food that was poisonous or starving.

The *lupine* was a slightly more honorable food. Lupines have an attractive flower and were grown in gardens. They also grew and still grow wild in much of the Mediterranean Basin, especially on sunny hillsides. They were cultivated primarily as fodder but also as green fertilizer, plowed back into the ground, adding nitrogen to the soil. The lupine was actually eaten as part of a meal. They were salted or brined and could be eaten as a snack or appetizer along with olives and nuts. During times of severe food shortage or famine, lupines were ground and used as flour extenders for bread or porridge. Pliny the Elder writes that they were food for animals and only the poorest of people.[12] The Jewish Mishnah states that lupines were "good for the poor" and "good for goats."[13] The playwright Athenaeus quoting Lycophron describes a banquet where, instead of gourmet delights, the guests are served lupines: "And there danced forth the plebian lupine in lavish abundance, that companion of the paupers' triclinium (banqueting room)."[14]

The Cynics often ate lupines, in part to make a statement. The Cynics were a philosophical school that looked with contempt on the conventions of society, especially on the lifestyles of the rich and comfortable. Diogenes, one of the movement's founders, reportedly lived in a barrel and ate raw beef and octopus. His followers made lupines part of their regular diet, "just to show their disdain for decent food and perhaps so they could generate enough wind to offend people in public places."[15]

As with vetches, lupines are poisonous. They contain bitter alkaloids that negatively impact the central nervous system, causing depression, convulsions, and, in the worst case, respiratory failure. They must be boiled and then washed in running water for a week before eating. As with olives and other foods, one must wonder who it was that had the tenacity to try lupines and then determine how to make them edible. Famine most likely was the precipitating cause.

Lentils and Beans

Lentils are an extremely ancient legume and one of the first to be cultivated. Archaeologists have found evidence that wild lentils were collected for food in sites in Syria and southern Greece dating from 12000 to 10000 BCE. They were cultivated in Greece before 6000 BCE, and around the same time they began to be grown around Jericho, in Turkey, and at other sites in the Middle East. In many of these places they were developed alongside einkorn and emmer wheats, peas, and barley.

The lentil was a multiuse plant. The seeds were eaten and provided an extremely efficient source of necessary nutrients, especially with each seed composed of 25 percent protein. Lentils are actually one of the vegetables with the most protein, second only to tofu. The stems and husks of the plant were then used as fodder. As with other legumes, the lentil plant draws nitrogen from the atmosphere and deposits it as rhizobium bacteria on root nodules. Lentils were grown among the rows of wheat, fertilizing the soil and the wheat as the plants grew.

The health benefits of a diet based on both legumes and grain must have been observed or experienced as essential by ancient humans. One modern writer remarks, "Eating patterns evolved spontaneously along these lines in many parts of the world."[16] Those who ate both were healthier. Those who ate one without the other were more likely to become sick. Eating legumes and grains together was already an established diet by the first century CE. Though high in protein, lentils lack certain amino acids that were supplied by wheat and other grains. Likewise, a type of amino acid called *lysine* that aids in digesting proteins is missing in grains and supplied by legumes. The combination of the grain and legume provided the protein that ancient people needed. Dried lentils are also rich in iron and phosphorus.[17]

The first recorded recipe for lentils was written by the Akkadians around the year 1600 BCE. The Akkad was an ancient Mesopotamian empire that spread along the Tigris and Euphrates Rivers almost as far west as the Mediterranean Sea. Among a number of recipes for porridge and meat stews, there is only one for milled lentils, ground in a manner similar to wheat or barley for bread. The lentil flour was cooked with beer and served with meat. If archaeologists are right and the little seed was a prominent part of the Mesopotamian diet, then why were there not more recipes? One possible answer is that the cooking of lentils was so common that recipes for the legume were not deemed necessary to record.

Lentils were well loved in Egypt. The ancient playwright Athenaeus remarked that the Egyptian city of "Alexandria is full of lentil dishes."[18] As well as food for the living, lentils were commonly used as funerary offerings and thought to provide nourishment for the dead residing in the underworld. Large amounts of lentils were found by archaeologists in tombs and in Zoser's pyramid.[19] These findings qualified lentils as a symbol of resurrection. Eventually the Egyptians became major growers and key exporters, shipping a significant percentage of their crops to the Romans. Egyptian lentils were considered the best of all that were grown in the Mediterranean Basin.

Perhaps the most unusual use of lentils was as shipping material. During the reign of Caligula (37–41 CE), a large obelisk was moved by barge from Egypt to Rome. In all, 120 bushels (120,000 modii, or one ton) of lentils were used as ballast for the valuable monument.[20] I strongly suspect that, after the obelisk was set in place, the lentils were sold and used to feed many of the plebeians in Rome. The obelisk still stands in front of the Vatican.

The importance of lentils for diets in the Near and Middle East is illustrated by many references in the Hebrew Scriptures, the most famous being a lentil stew made by Jacob. The story is well known. Esau, Jacob's brother, was a hunter, often bringing home fresh deer meat for the family to eat. But one day, he returned empty-handed and hungry. Jacob, as the text says, was a quiet man, living in tents. He took advantage of his famished brother and sold Esau a bowl of red lentil stew and a piece of bread in exchange for his birthright (Genesis 25:27–34). The account has layers of meaning, one of which explains why the birthright was passed to a younger son instead of, traditionally, the oldest. Another meaning illustrates the story of the transition from the hunter-gatherer culture to that of the settled farmer. The family were shepherd nomads but did settle from time to time to grow crops (Genesis 26:12–14).

Lentils were an important part of the Greek food culture, along with wheat and barley, making it one of three staples of Classical Greece. They were usually cooked until they had the texture of porridge. In fact, the Greek word for porridge, *phake*, and that for lentils, *phakos*, have the same root. Lentils were also ground into flour and made into bread or added as an extender to flour from grains.

Greek philosophers desiring a return to a more rustic, simple lifestyle extolled the virtue of the simple lentil. Aristophanes defends the lentil by writing, "You who are to insult lentil, sweetest of all delicacies."[21] The philosopher Zeno promotes lentils with this somewhat cryptic passage: "A wise man acts always with reason and prepares his lentils himself."[22] Certainly someone that is wise acts with reason, and the second part of the sentence seems to honor lentils, but why prepare them himself? Perhaps because of their significance.

Romans also had prejudices against the lowly lentil, and yet, especially for the common people, they were an important part of the daily diet. Pliny the Elder found the lentil diet to be conducive "to an equable temper."[23] *Apicius* included several recipes for lentils. In fact, recipes for lentils range from very simple to quite complex. They were prepared with a bit of salt, vinegar, sumac, and olive oil; with garlic and leeks; or with just several sprigs of fresh cilantro and salt. One of the recipes in *Apicius* included pepper, cumin, coriander, mint, rue, *garum*, and pennyroyal, and then a mixture of vinegar, honey, and more *garum*. Finally, chestnuts cooked in olive oil were stirred into the stew. It was an attempt to elevate lentils to the level of the sublime.

Pliny the Elder mentions two types of lentils. There were more. These four were the most common:

1. Red lentils that came originally from Egypt are particularly good to use in soup because they easily disintegrate and make a thick potage.

2. Brown lentils are especially appropriate for side dishes and are still used in the Mediterranean to accompany duck, goose, lamb, mutton, and sausages.
3. Green lentils are best cooked, thoroughly drained, and used at room temperature for salads.
4. A lentil that is now called either the du Puy or the Beluga lentil is black, expensive, and most often used by restaurant chefs. Ancient literature describes an even greater variety of colors and sizes of lentils.

The Bean

The word *bean* in the ancient Mediterranean world meant broad bean or fava bean. Other types of beans came primarily from the Americas, but Europeans had to wait for Columbus and other explorers to bring them back some fifteen centuries later. It is unknown where fava beans originated or were first domesticated. Archaeologists found a large reserve of wild beans in Nazareth, left there between the years 6500 and 6000 BCE. Perhaps they originated in the Middle East or Egypt. Some food historians believe they were first domesticated in the area of Afghanistan and the Himalayan foothills. An alternative theory is that fava beans were domesticated almost simultaneously in both Spain and Israel. We do know that by the third millennium they were being grown in areas of Spain, Portugal, northern Italy, Switzerland, Greece, and the Middle East. Fava beans soon became a favorite in Egypt and Persia (Iran).

Despite beans' popularity, Egyptian priests refused to eat or even to look at them. History certainly provides speculation as to why. They were used in sacrifice and perhaps were considered "off limits" for that reason. Pliny speculates that beans dulled the senses and caused sleeplessness.[24] Perhaps Egyptian priests believed they should be wide awake and aware. Egyptians also connected beans with the place where the souls of the dead waited for reincarnation, calling it "the beanfield."[25] Whatever the reason, fava beans were a staple for the rest of the population.

The Jewish Talmud describes a special dish called *cholent* designed especially for the Sabbath. Beans, barley, and meat were placed in a clay pot with a lid and then buried in slow-burning coals. The stew was made before the Sabbath began so it would slowly simmer overnight without the family needing to cook. Any work, even preparing dinner, would have been considered a violation of the Sabbath rest.

As they did with other legumes, the Greeks and Romans looked down upon fava beans as food for the poor. "To eat fava beans was to become like the poor."[26] Athenaeus writes that the menu for the poor included beans, lupines, greens, turnips, *pulses*, vetches, and perhaps cicadas. Yet beans were a staple part of the Mediterranean diet with few exceptions. Along with Egyptian priests, Pythagoreans, followers of the philosopher Pythagoras, refused to eat beans. This is curious because the Pythagoreans were vegetarians and the beans would have been a healthy alternative to meat. But like Egyptian priests, they believed that beans were somehow connected to death. For Pythagoreans, the souls of the dead entered fava beans, and eating them was a form of cannibalism. There is a story that Pythagoras was pursued by assassins and apprehended and killed because he was trapped by bean fields in flower and refused to cross. Pythagoras also might have found beans to be repugnant because of their connection to politics. They were used for voting in democratic Athens; white beans for "yea" and dark beans for "nay."

Beans may have been considered lowly fare but were not always viewed negatively. A pot of beans was a dish of rustic simplicity, a food that was simple and authentic. Pliny the Elder was able to write that "the highest place of honor belongs to the bean," at the same time wondering if there was something of the souls of the dead about the fava.[27] Columella writes that beans were the food of artisans; Pliny that peasant farmers survived on them. Martial remarks that builders lived on them. These artisans, while not on the social plane of senators and equestrians, were still respected by many for their place in society.

Along with representing mortality and the souls of the dead, beans were symbolically significant and part of religious ceremonies and sacrifices. They were symbols of creation and part of the ritual offering in marriage ceremonies, with each bean representing a male child in whom an ancestor would return to ensure the continuation of the family line. "Bean pottage has a sanctity of its own in sacrifice to the gods," Pliny writes.[28] At the end of the bean harvest, June 1, on the feast of *Calendae Fabariae*, the new beans were sacrificed as an offering to the gods. Beanmeal cakes were also used as an offering. For the Feast of *Lemures* or *Lemuria* in mid-May, the father of the household would go outside at midnight and throw beans over his shoulder nine times, saying, "Souls of my ancestors, depart." Family members would bang on pots at the same time. It was a similar theme: the beans and the souls that inhabited them were snatched instead of the souls of family members. It is fascinating that Lemuria later became the original date for the Christian celebration of All Saints' Day. All Saints' was later moved to November 1.

Fava beans were sometimes eaten fresh but most often were dried and then boiled or roasted. The beans were also ground into a flour and used to make cakes or added to barley or wheat for bread. The skins on the beans can be thick, so both ancient and modern cooks recommend boiling the beans for four or five minutes, until the skins loosen, and then letting them cool. Then the skins can easily be removed. Recipes varied from quite simple to very complex. After soaking, they were cooked in stock or water or fried in oil and then eaten with salt. Leeks, onions, and garlic were added as flavorings. If available, herbs and spices provided additional flavor. Once again, with several recipes used by his cooks, *Apicius* took a simple food and raised it to the level of a Roman gourmet dish. One recipe added lovage, pepper, ginger, hard-boiled egg yolks, garum, wine, honey, and vinegar. The fresh beans were cooked and ground before the flavorings were added, turning the beans into a puree. Fresh peas were also cooked according to this recipe.

There is a disease called *favism* that can be caused by eating fava beans. It is extremely rare and is caused by eating fresh raw fava beans. Those from the Mediterranean Basin who lack a certain enzyme in their blood are susceptible to the disease, and it causes the destruction of red blood cells.

Peas and Chickpeas

As with the other legumes, chickpeas have an ancient heritage connected to the Fertile Crescent and Mediterranean Basin. Archaeological remains of chickpeas have been found in both Turkey and Syria that date from 10000 BCE. It is known that chickpeas were harvested in Greece, Israel, Jordan, Egypt, and France ranging from 6000 to 4000 BCE. Pliny describes a variety of chickpeas, one that looked like a ram's head, some that were white, and another variety that was colored black. The dove pea, also called the Venus pea, was bright white, round, smooth, and smaller than the ram's head chickpea. And as with the other legumes, chickpeas were considered food for the poor. The Latin phrase *fricti ciceris emptor*, "buyer of roasted chickpeas," was a slang phrase meaning "poor person." It was believed by some that the god Poseidon introduced them to the human race and that they were an aphrodisiac.

Still, chickpeas were widely consumed if not widely enjoyed. Plato, in his dialogue *Republic*, posed this question to Socrates: What will people eat in his ideal city? His answer, of course, was wheat and barley. And one could not do without wine, olives, or cheese. And for snacks, figs, chickpeas, and beans. Roasted chickpeas were widely consumed by the Greeks as a snack, usually at the end of a meal. They were served during the symposium part of a banquet, as Socrates suggested, along with figs, roasted fava beans, and nuts. Athenaeus paints a scene in his play of lying on a soft couch in front of a fire during the winter, sipping sweet wine and munching on chickpeas.[29] Roman vendors were known to sell roasted chickpeas at theatrical performances in the same way modern movie theaters sell popcorn. They were eaten whole, with salt or perhaps dried cheese sprinkled on them. Stalls in southern France still provide roasted chickpeas as a snack food.

Though occasionally eaten fresh and green, chickpeas were almost always dried first and then roasted or boiled. They were also ground into a flour and used for bread, cakes, or as an extender when added to wheat or barley flour. Chickpea soup was a common and cheap Roman street food. In the countryside, peasant farmers ate a simple soup, boiling the beans in water or broth until they were soft and then seasoned with olive oil and salt. The farmer with a large kitchen garden added herbs and onions to the soup. To make a *puls* or porridge, chickpea flour was cooked in milk.

Peas are as ancient as the other legumes in this chapter and were often cultivated along with lentils, wheat, and barley. They were considered a staple food for the poor, but without the stigma. For one, they did not cause the degree of flatulence that is common with other legumes. For another, they were easier to cook and disintegrated quickly into a creamy *puls* or soup.

The early precultivation history of peas is not known, though there is speculation that they grew wild in three different locations: the Mediterranean Basin, Ethiopia, and central Asia. By 7000 BCE, peas were being planted in Iraq, and then in Jericho, Anatolia, and Greece. Early cultivation also took place in Egypt.

They may not have had the same kind of social dishonor as other legumes, but they were still considered food for the poor. Millennia later, peas finally achieved a degree of honor. In 1614, green garden peas, similar to the ones we eat today, were declared by Castelvetro of France as "the noblest of the vegetables."[30] They became a favorite of Louis XIV and his court and remain popular.

Peas were eaten fresh, immature, and green, but were also dried both whole and split. The color of mature peas differed; white and yellow were the most common. As with other legumes, they were commonly used in soups and porridges. Apicius and his cooks provided elaborate recipes to make them more appealing to his gourmand friends. His instructions for pea recipes included such ingredients as sausages, meatballs, and chunks of pork shoulder. Flavorings such as pepper, oregano, dill, onion, coriander, *garum*, and wine were added as well. In one recipe, raw eggs were added and the dish was baked until the casserole set and became solid.

I strongly suspect that legumes were a large part of the Apostle Paul's diet just as they were a significant part of everyone's menu. Even as a Roman citizen, he was not a wealthy person. He only occasionally stayed with hosts who might have been wealthy, and even then, he likely ate a fair amount of beans, lentils, and peas. He might even have snacked on lupines and roasted chickpeas while on the road.

The same was true for Paul's Christian communities. They likely consumed legumes and grains as a significant part of their diet as well. I posit that they were much more familiar with a bowl of lentils than we are. And what did Paul's new Christians eat during their feasts? Was the presence of food symbolic or intended to provide real nourishment? If so, bread, legumes, and wine were always on the table.

DINNER WITH A PLEBEIAN FAMILY

The menu for this chapter is a dinner for a plebeian family in Rome, though it could be a meal eaten in many of the towns and cities in the empire. Rome had an incredible variety of foods and ingredients available, but few plebeians could afford to sample more exotic foods and flavorings except for very special occasions.

This meal with a plebeian family is presented in a different style. I describe numerous recipes for this meal, but choose one dish with legumes, one with grains, and one with meat. One of the recipes has an alternative that a poor family could not often afford, providing a comparison. The ingredients might include additional flavorings such as leeks, herbs, or even some meat. Realize that a pot of beans with sausage or chunks of lamb would have been a very special meal indeed.

MENU: DINNER WITH A PLEBEIAN FAMILY

The chickpea cakes serve as the bread for the meal. I bought lupines imported from Lebanon by a company called Tazah and fed them to a large gathering of friends with mixed reviews.

Lentils and Bulbs
Chickpea Cakes

Lamb and Lentil Soup
Posca (recipe) or Wine from the market
Cauliflower with Cumin
Roasted Onions
Almonds from the market; Pickled Lupine Beans ordered online

RECIPES

Lentils and Bulbs

Use small turnips instead of flower bulbs.

- 1–2 small turnips, washed, peeled, and cut into bite-sized pieces
- 1 cup red lentils
- 7 cups chicken stock
- 1 tsp. each of ground cumin, ground coriander,

dried rue leaves, celery seeds, dried mint leaves
- 1 tbs. fish sauce
- 2 tbs. honey
- 1 tsp. salt and 1 tsp. pepper

Boil turnip pieces until just tender. Drain and add turnips to lentils. Add the chicken stock, herbs and spices, fish sauce, honey, salt, and pepper. Bring to a simmer, cover, and cook for at least 30 minutes. Adjust seasoning and serve.

Chickpea Cakes

Eat these instead of bread. I like to use panko breadcrumbs for this recipe, which are not authentic to the first century, though any toasted breadcrumbs or even #1 bulgur will work. Serve with a dipping sauce.

- Two 15-oz. cans chickpeas
- ½ cup Greek yogurt
- 2 eggs
- ⅓ cup olive oil, divided use
- 1 tsp. each cumin, coriander, and lovage (or celery leaves or seeds)

- ¼ tsp. salt
- 4 green onions, chopped
- 3 tbs. fresh cilantro leaves, chopped
- 1 cup breadcrumbs
- 1 minced shallot

Rinse chickpeas and drain. Grind chickpeas in a food processor or with a mortar and pestle. Whisk all other ingredients, including 3 tablespoons of the olive oil. Fold in the ground chickpeas. Divide the chickpea mixture and form into patties. In a nonstick pan, cook 4 patties at a time in 1½ tablespoons of olive oil, 7 to 8 minutes on each side.

Lamb and Lentil Soup

This recipe is a variation of one given to me by Wendy McAllistar, a retired professional baker, chef, and good friend. The poorest members of society rarely had access to meat; when they did, they used it in soups and stews in order to extend its use to feed a large family unit.

- 1 lb. ground lamb
- 1 tbs. olive oil
- 1 large onion, minced
- 1 bunch scallions, trimmed and minced
- 3 carrots, peeled and chopped
- 3 cloves garlic, minced
- 10 cups beef stock
- ½ cup fresh parsley, minced

- 1 cup dry red wine
- 1 lb. red lentils, soaked and drained
- 1 tsp. each dried thyme, cumin, ground coriander, and lovage or celery leaves
- 2 bay leaves
- 2 tsp. salt
- 1 tsp. pepper

Brown and crumble lamb, drain fat except for 2 tablespoons. Add olive oil, onion, scallions, and carrots. Sauté 15 minutes until vegetables are soft, then add garlic and cook until opaque. Add stock, parsley, and the rest of the ingredients. Simmer for 1 hour. Adjust seasoning and serve.

You can remove half the soup, blend in a blender, and add back to the pot to thicken.

Posca (Vinegar and Water)

This was the drink of the plebeians, the poor, and slaves involved with working in the fields. You may not like the taste, but you should try it for the historical experience.

Use 2 tablespoons of red wine vinegar for every 8 ounces of water. A tablespoon of honey (optional) should help the taste.

Cauliflower with Cumin

I like the combination of cumin and cauliflower.

- 1 head of cauliflower, cut into flowerets
- 2 tsp. salt, divided use

Dressing:

- ⅓ cup olive oil
- 1 tbs. fish sauce
- ⅓ cup white wine

- ½ tsp. ground pepper
- 1 tsp. ground cumin seed

Bring 2 cups of water to boil. Add 1 tsp. salt. Lower heat to a simmer and add the cauliflower. Cover and steam. The cauliflower should be only partially cooked and still firm. Drain and return the cauliflower to the pot.

Meanwhile, mix the oil, fish sauce, white wine, and remaining salt, pepper, and cumin. Add to the drained cauliflower. Bring to a boil and quickly cook until the liquid is absorbed. Adjust the seasoning and serve.

Roasted Onions

Roasting makes onions sweet and mild.

- 1 yellow onion for every two people
- Olive oil
- Salt
- Herbs such as thyme or rosemary, optional

Preheat oven to 350 degrees. Place parchment paper on a baking sheet with rim. Leave the skin on the onion. Cut each onion in half. Pour olive oil and sprinkle salt on the exposed part of the onion. Add herbs should you choose. Place onions face down on the parchment paper and roast in the preheated oven for 40–45 minutes. When done, cool the onions enough that you can remove the outside skin. Adjust seasoning and serve.

Alternative: place whole onions in a charcoal or wood fire. Roast for 35 minutes or longer depending on the temperature of your coals. The outer skin will be burned black. Remove and allow to cool. Peel off the burned layers and season with olive oil and salt.

5

THE GRAND ROMAN BANQUET

A friend of mine enjoys telling the story of being a guest at a seven-course wedding banquet. She remembers sitting before an array of plates, spoons, forks, and wineglasses. The head waiter announced the different wines and the various dishes as they were being served for each course. She was overwhelmed by the formality of the meal until a waiter brought her what appeared to be a cup of coffee in a China cup. "Would you please bring me some sugar and cream?" she asked. "You might want to try it first," he responded. It was beef consommé.

A modern banquet or special meal can take a lot of forms. There are wedding rehearsal dinners, religious celebrations, Thanksgiving feasts, and simple but special meals with friends and family. For years, several friends and I gathered every three months to cook and eat together: four of us prepared the meal, two opened and poured the wine, one set the table, and one watched in expectation. There was only one rule: the cooks had to prepare their dishes in front of one another. Everyone experienced a wonderful evening filled with good food, excellent wine, and great conversation.

The expectations of the host at a special meal are straightforward. Whether simple or complex, the food should be lovingly prepared

Vase with scenes from a banquet. *Heather Rose*

85

using the best ingredients available. The hospitality must be such that the guests know that they are special.

First-century banquets were quite similar in many ways. The guest list was usually small; nine was considered the perfect size. The meal could range from being modest to quite elaborate. Either way, it still was a feast. The host was responsible for serving the best-quality food and wine possible. Entertainment was often part of the banquet, as was conversation and sometimes even drinking games. Conviviality—that is, lively promotion of friendship, as well as hospitality—was the essential aspect of the ancient banquet, just as it is for the modern dinner party or any other special meal.

THE HISTORY OF THE BANQUET

Banqueting is almost as old as civilization. Ancient records describe a variety of distinctive meals as far back as the second millennium BCE. There were religious banquets with the gods, especially if the statue of a god or goddess visited from another city. The banqueting of the king and his court was designed to reflect divine banqueting.

Any type of formal contract was normally sealed over a special meal. The meal became an actual extension of the agreement. The ritual for the feast served as a precursor for later banquets. This description from a land sale at the beginning of the second millennium BCE sounds very much like a Greek feast from the third century BCE or a first-century-CE Roman banquet:

> The eldest son of the family had the honor of offering guests water to rinse their hands and then of serving them food and drink. Bread was eaten, beer was drunk, and bodies were anointed with oil.[1]

Ancient Assyrian weddings also placed a great emphasis on feasting. The ceremony was little more than anointing the bride's head with oil. Then the couple, family, and guests enjoyed an elaborate banquet.

Even a thousand years before the first century CE, royal banquets were grand affairs. The occasion might be a treaty or military victory, the completion of a new palace, or a visit by a foreign ambassador. These meals were ruled by a strict etiquette. The feast took place in a large courtyard or an adjacent great hall. The king was always served first. If he chose, as a sign of great honor, he sent his food to a special guest. As with other very ancient feasts, these affairs were typically for men; only on occasion did the queen join the king.

Many of the ancient rituals were included as elements in later banquets. The guests were assigned seats according to rank. Their hands were washed by servants, and they were given vials of perfume to anoint themselves. They were served a dinner of grilled and stewed meats, bread, and vegetables. Desserts consisted of fruits, nuts such as pistachios, and honey-soaked pastries. Archaeologists have found many molds for these little pies and tarts.

When ancient people drank from a common cup, which was typical at the feast, they established a special bond with one another, regardless of class or wealth. Ultimately the sharing of food and the relationship it created was more important than the food itself. The king ended the occasion by offering special gifts, such as formal banquet clothing or small objects made from precious metals, to his guests.

We find an early Greek reference to the shape of a formal banquet in Homer's *Iliad*, written between 750 and 850 BCE. It describes a feast where the heroes of the battlefield eat roasted meat. After eating, the tables are cleared and wine is made available. The two activities, eating the feast and then drinking and enjoying one another's company, became the hallmark of the banquet. It most likely reflected a practice that was becoming popular in Greece and perhaps other areas of the Mediterranean.

By the seventh century BCE, other common elements of the banquet became noticeable: religious rituals, hymn singing, entertainment, drinking games, philosophical discussion, and the recitation of poetry. At that time, the practice of reclining to dine at the banquet was becoming popular. The feast remained one focused on comradery, but it was now primarily between men of shared lifestyles and backgrounds, both socioeconomic and ethnic.[2] The entertainment and drinking portion of the banquet was first called a *symposium* somewhere around the seventh century BCE in a work by the writer Alcaeus.

THE FIRST-CENTURY BANQUET

Banquets were quite stylized and formal by the time of Paul. As a Jew and a Roman citizen living in the important city of Tarsus, Paul must have attended many banquets. After moving to Jerusalem, he likely participated in feasts that were Jewish versions of the Greco-Roman banquet with variations in the rituals. He would have been familiar with every aspect of the occasion, knowing how to act, eat, and interact with fellow guests.

The banquet began with invitations. The requests for attendance set the tone for the importance of the occasion. They were handwritten and delivered to the potential guests by servants. Invitations tended to follow a standard form and, in the twenty-first century, these are purchased in card shops with blanks for the details. Feasts could be held in both public buildings, such as temples, and in private homes.

Ancient examples of banquet invitations have been discovered in dig sites around the Mediterranean, especially in the Middle East and Egypt. In many cases, we still can read who was invited, who hosted the feast, and where the feast was located.[3] The following are texts of ancient invitations:

> Claeremon requests you to dine at the banquet of the Lord Sarapis in the Sarapeion tomorrow, the 15th, at the 9th hour.

> Dioscoros invites you to dine at the wedding of her son on the 14th of Mesore in the temple of Sabazius from the ninth hour. Farewell.

> Diogenes invites you to the dinner for the first birthday of his daughter in the Serapeion tomorrow which is Pachon 26 from the eighth hour onwards.[4]

Some guests received verbal invitations. The host might see a friend, colleague, or even his patron in the marketplace, at the gymnasium, or at the public baths and invite him to the occasion in much the same way that I might ask a friend I ran into at the supermarket to drop by the house for dinner and a glass of wine. Popular or powerful individuals might receive multiple invitations and attempt to attend more than one banquet in an evening. How were choices made? One host might be well-known for his cook and kitchen, another for excellent wine and fun-loving guests.

In addition to those "party hopping" from one banquet to another, there are numerous references in ancient literature of "banquet crashers" or "parasites" (*parasitos*, those who sit at another's table). Apparently, the term *parasite* originally did not have a negative meaning, but eventually it came to mean something similar to "one who sponged on others."[5] Men searching for a fun party with a good deal of wine simply arrived uninvited to a friend's banquet after the meal was eaten. These *parasitos* were often teased and became the brunt of practical jokes but tolerated the treatment for the free wine and companionship. Sometimes they arrived with friends.

The public baths were a preferred meeting place for those who later would be attending the banquet. The baths themselves resembled a modern community center, with spaces for lectures, poetry readings, and advertisements for social events around the city. A soak in hot water, fellowship with friends, and a glass of wine and a snack helped the guests to relax and assume the correct mental attitude for the evening. After relaxing, the guests changed into formal, almost floor-length togas. Poorer clients invited to the feast borrowed formal wear from their patrons so they looked appropriate for the evening.

The size of the feast fluctuated based on the intent of the banquet. Many more attended a wedding than a dinner party to mark the birthday of a child. A feast with the emperor might be quite large, while most banquets resembled a dinner party. Available space impacted the number of guests invited. A rented banqueting room in a public space such as a temple might have a larger area for a feast. On the other hand, most banqueting rooms in homes were built for a much smaller feast. *Triclinia*, meaning "three beds," were built-in couches that could be positioned both outside and inside.

The word *triclinium* also referred to the banqueting rooms and spaces. Wealthy Roman men entertained their guests in atriums that might have mosaics for a patio floor, fountains, and pools of water with fish and plants. Tables were made of metal or even inlaid marble. When built indoors, the *triclinia* of the wealthy had frescoes decorating the walls and mosaics on the floor. One famous floor mosaic demonstrated the artist's sense of humor with images of food scraps. Another rendered different types of animals, fish, fruits, and vegetables that might become part of the menu.

A banquet for nine was considered the perfect size. All those invited appreciated the smaller group because hospitality and conversation were more easily experienced. All nine attendees could sit in the same space, uncrowded, and participate in the convivial atmosphere. In addition, sometimes male guests brought female companions (prostitutes or mistresses) with them, and of course there was always the possibility of the arrival of *parasitos*. Archaeological evidence supports the contention that dining spaces for nine banqueters was normative.

Banquets typically were all-male occasions, with the possible exception of female musicians and consorts. Rules about the presence of women began to change in the first century CE. Egyptians were more open in allowing wives to attend banquets with their husbands, and even Romans occasionally allowed reputable women at their banquets.[6]

The Feast Begins

As the guests began to arrive, a servant or slave ushered them into an entrance room or anteroom. At that point, their feet were washed. This was not a ritual washing. The streets in ancient cities were filthy, often paved with dirt, and Roman men typically wore sandals. Their feet would have been very dirty under the best of circumstances. At some banquets, guests' feet were also anointed with perfumed oil. A woman in the household washed the feet if the host did not own a slave or could not afford a servant. After washing the guests' feet, the slave or servant washed each person's right hand, the hand used to hold a cup. Then they were given a glass of wine.

The guests were next directed into the banqueting room. Whether in a room in a house or a rented room at a temple, the banqueting room was "U" shaped, with *triclinia* couches usually built against three of the walls and covered with cushions. There were three individual couches on each wall if there was an individual couch for each diner. On occasion, a guest invited a friend to accompany him to the banquet. The friend was called an *umbra*, or a "shadow." A smaller banqueting room might only hold five couches while a large one could accommodate as many as fifteen. Very large halls in grand public spaces were designed to hold multiple settings, where dining couches were grouped like several smaller banqueting rooms. The fourth wall contained the door, and the center of the room was an empty space awaiting tables of food and wine. All the diners faced the center of the room in order to promote conversation and conviviality.

Following the very ancient predecessors of the Greco-Roman banquet, assigned seating was assumed. Guests were placed according to their ranking in society. A good host oversaw seating without causing embarrassment or insult. Perhaps he made sure not to invite two or more comrades too closely associated to the same rank. The guest of honor always sat to the right of the host.

Not only were seats assigned, but some guests were given responsibilities. As might be imagined, the responsibility for planning the menu, making a list, inviting the guests, and securing the location rested with the host. He not only solicited a guest of honor but also chose one of the attendees to be the *symposiarch*. The symposiarch introduced the drinking rules, that is, the ratio of water to wine and how full the cups were to be filled. The symposiarch was expected to know the quality of the wine being served and even the purpose of the evening. Was it to inebriate guests who would play drinking games and flirt with the hired musicians, or was it to promote poetry reading and philosophical discussion?

Several servants also had special roles. Long before the symposiarch commenced his responsibilities, the *cellarius*, or wine steward, began his work. He ordered a sweetened wine, called *mulsum*, that was offered to the guests both in the entryway and during the first course. Wines used during the dinner and afterward were chosen and decanted from a seven-gallon storage container called an *amphora* into a smaller container where it was filtered and appropriately flavored with herbs. Sometimes this process took place in the room with the guests, sometimes hours before the banquet began.

Another slave or servant, the *structor* or *scissor*, was solely responsible for carving the meat. Because guests ate with their fingertips, it was essential that the meat was sliced into bite-sized pieces. It was believed that barbarians such as the Celts chose large pieces of meat to tear off the bone with their teeth; "civilized" Greeks and Romans considered it an embarrassment to soil either their faces or hands while eating. "Etiquette required that small amounts of food be taken each time and that one should always remain clean. Ovid admonished: 'Take the food with your fingers, this is the usual way to eat; but do not soil your face with your dirty hand.'"[7] For a small, informal banquet, the *structor* left the meat, other serving dishes, bread, and sauces placed on tables in front of the diners. For a large, formal feast, servants were constantly refilling the plates of the diners.

The attendees began the banquet in earnest after reclining. As we have seen, the primary pattern for the banquet was established centuries earlier, as ancient as the writing of the *Iliad*. First the guests enjoyed a meal, called the *deipnon* in Greek. By the time of Paul, this segment of the feast included a first course of appetizers and a main course with several main dishes if the host was wealthy and wanted to impress the guests. The second part of the banquet, as mentioned, was called the *symposium*, given over to drinking wine and enjoying some type of entertainment. A third course was also served during the symposium: little salty snacks, fruit, and sweet tarts and cakes. The primary purpose of these foods was to keep the guests thirsty and drinking wine.

After everyone reclined on a couch, their hands were washed again, this time both hands in order to eat. The food was brought in on tables that rested on tripods and was served in bowls and on platters. It was normative for three guests to eat from the food on one table, though that was not the only model. On occasion a larger table was placed within reach of all the guests, or each guest was given a small table for individual use. Roasts sometimes were brought into the room whole, carved at a central table, and then left for the guests.

As mentioned in an earlier chapter, there were no knives, forks, napkins, or individual plates, though this was not the only model used at a banquet. Spoons were occasionally provided for soup, but even soup was often scooped with bread and fingers. Fastidious guests might bring their own napkins, but small pieces of bread or sleeves usually sufficed to wipe greasy fingers. Again, on occasion, a guest might even use a slave's hair to clean his fingers.

Servants carried the food into the room and the meal began. The food was important primarily because it symbolized an offering of hospitality. It made an evening of fun and fellowship possible among comrades and business partners where mentors and clients enjoyed the same food and drink, even the same cup, as their students and protégés. Greeks and especially Romans loved serving and eating vegetables as appetizers. Lettuce with leeks and herbs were eaten with a vinaigrette made with olive oil and vinegar or *garum*. Cabbage was popular, as were root vegetables such as turnips. These were dipped in a special sauce. Oysters, snails, and small bites of marinated octopus were well-loved starters. Olives, tapenade, patinas, and other snacks were placed on the tables, as was the omnipresent bread. Romans especially were fond of eggs—hard-boiled, soft-boiled, even raw from the shell.

The first tables were whisked away, and new ones carried into the room laden with the next course of the feast. At one time, and especially in a Greek-style banquet, the *mensa prima*, or main course, might be as simple as a heavy soup of grains or legumes and vegetables. The point was to offer the best possible food that the host could afford with the finest conceivable preparation even if the food was simple. In that way, the focus remained on fellowship and *convivium*. But as Rome became wealthier, the dishes served at the *deipnon* of a banquet became more elaborate. A Greek-style meal with its concentration of fellowship regardless of what was served became less acceptable in first-century Rome. Guests expected fish, poultry, or some type of meat, not just for a special feast but for every banquet. Meatballs or fish cakes were common, but eventually did not suffice. Pork was extremely loved, as was pork sausage. The Romans especially preferred their meats to be boiled or baked so they became a background for the sauce. The *mensa prima* might have two parts or even three.

At the banquets of the wealthy, foods were often molded into the shapes of other foods or hidden inside other cooked animals. It was not enough to serve sausages. Rather, sausages were cooked inside the cavity of a pig so that when the servant sliced the roasted swine open, the sausages rolled onto the carving table. Fois gras was molded into the shape of small hens; chicken in the shape of a suckling pig. Other foods also found their way onto the banqueting table, including a variety of birds such as figpeckers, cranes, geese, pigeons, and magpies. Fresh and saltwater fish, lamb, goat, sow's udder and womb, kidneys, and other offal were popular. Freshly killed wild game was considered a treat. Those living close to the Mediterranean shore or in a large city especially enjoyed seafood. Shrimp and little spiny lobsters were much loved. Fish cooked in a broth, served with a sauce, or as part of a terrine provided a special treat. Freshwater eels, especially moray eels, were a favorite. Even small fish such as anchovies were grilled or baked and eaten out of hand or as part of a terrine. Wine was served throughout the *deipnon*, water mixed with the wine by the servant, individually in each cup.

The Symposium

The banquet had at least a veneer of religious ceremony. The *deipnon* began with a common cup of wine that was not mixed with water. It was passed around to guests with each one taking a sip and proclaiming a toast to the god of wine, Dionysus, with these words: *agathou daimonos*, or "good deity." The symposium began with a more elaborate ceremony. Garlands were passed around for guests to wear as though they were crowns. In addition, each guest was presented with a vial of perfume to refresh before the drinking and entertainment. At this point, the water and wine were ceremoniously mixed in a common cup. The toast was to the Zeus Savior, *Dios Soteros*. A ritual libation or offering was poured onto the floor or into a fire. Finally, a hymn or chant was sung honoring Zeus and the gods. According to the occasion, the ceremony might become either more or less complex.

Once the *deipnon* was completed, the servants took away the tables and swept the floors in preparation of the next portion of the banquet. It was usual practice for guests to toss bones, fruit cores, and soiled bread used as napkins onto the floor while eating. If hands were washed again, it happened at this time. There was always a possibility that unexpected guests arriving for the symposium increased the number of guests to the extent that couch space was not available for everyone. In such a case, the *parasitos* sat on chairs brought for them by the servants or slaves. On rare occasions the *parasitos* were made to sit on the floor.

The servants arrived with at least one *crater*, a large bowl, and ladles to mix water and wine for the symposium. It was the custom to boil a portion of the wine and then add it back to the rest of the wine before storage. Water was then added before drinking to bring it to a better texture and taste. The usual proportion was three-fifths water to two-fifths wine. But based on the purpose of the symposium, the symposiarch might require the servants or slaves to increase or decrease the strength of the wine, use larger glasses to hold more wine, or ladle more or less wine into the glasses during the evening.

Entertainment heightened by the consumption of wine was the primary purpose of the symposium. Music was the most common form or aspect of the event, and very wealthy hosts provided elaborate amusement, including entire musical ensembles with dancers and acrobats. But the most common entertainment was the "flute girl," who likely played the double flute (*aulos*, or *tibia*) and entered the room after the wine libation. The flute players were often temple musicians who earned extra money by playing for banquets. There are a large number of artistic renderings of the flute girls from the ancient world, many of them on pottery, and a great many of those displaying a symposium.

After a short time, the music likely faded into the background as the guests enjoyed other types of entertainment. There were poetry readings by the guests and riddles and other word games designed to stimulate conversation. A variety of drinking games were popular, including one called *cottabus*, where players would fling wine from their drinking bowls, a flattened vessel with two handles called a *kylix*, at a target placed in the center of the room. A toast was offered to a lover, and if the wine hit the target, then it was seen as good luck for the couple.[8]

There is no denying that many *symposia* had overt sexual overtones. Even though the flute player was usually a temple musician, she was seen and sometimes treated as a sexual object. Guests would bring courtesans or mistresses to the banquet with them. The courtesans invited to banquets were not at all like the common street prostitutes but had much in common with the legendary Japanese geishas. At a time when most Greek wives and most Jewish and Roman women were not allowed out of their homes, courtesans were well educated and sometimes allowed to study at famous philosophy schools. They were considered "refined, beautiful, and very costly."[9] Still, the mixture of women, erotic poetry, drinking games, and large amounts of wine certainly could result in sexual tension and acting out. However, it was very rare that the symposium actually became an orgy.

Music and games were not the only agendas for the symposium. Guests might read poetry they had written, whether comedic or serious.

Philosophical banquets, described later, posed questions for discussion. A question might relate to the banquet itself: "What is the nature of *convivium* promoted by the symposium?" Topics might have to do with sports, "Why did the gods create the Olympic competitions?" or politics, "Is democracy the most effective type of polity?" Other types of issues and questions were posed for discussion. Questions concerning the Torah, the first five books of the Hebrew Scriptures, were asked at Jewish banquets.

The custom was to end the banquet by giving small gifts to the guests. These might be a food treat for wives and children, a piece of jewelry, a comb, or a bottle of oil or perfume. Since the *parasitos* arrived after the meal, they were given food to eat on the way home.

It cannot be emphasized enough that the primary goal of the grand banquet was forging the relationship between guests. All guests had equal occasion to feast on the same food and drink from the same *krater*. Everyone was allowed to voice an opinion, share a poem or story, or just enjoy the entertainment. Friendship, equality, and unity were all important elements that permeated the ancient banquet. There were certainly elements of socioeconomic difference, such as the seating arrangements. Only two men reclined next to the host, and only one at the place of honor. And those who arrived uninvited for the symposium might be required to sit in chairs, but still the goals for the evening were the same.

To reiterate what I wrote earlier in this chapter: "When ancient people drank from a common cup, which was common at the feast, they established a special bond with one another, regardless of the disparity of class or wealth. Ultimately the sharing of food and the relationship it created was more important than the food itself." As Rome grew in wealth and power, the banquet became corrupted. Foods became more exotic and significantly more expensive and arrived from around the empire. Fattened pigeons and *puls* with sausage were replaced with pork stuffed with live birds, peacock brains, and flamingo tongues. Ice was carefully transported from the Alps at great expense just so wine could be cooled for the symposium.

Hosts began to segregate their guests. Wealthy, more powerful invitees were given the choice food and best wine, while others were served more ordinary fare. Perhaps the most conspicuous sign of indulgence was the use of the *vomitorium*. Feasters purged their stomachs in order to continue to eat and drink rich food and expensive wines in very large quantities. Prophets in the form of playwrights and philosophers bemoaned the corruption of the banquet and called for reforms. Even laws were passed that placed ceilings on the amount of money one could spend on the opulence of the feast.

Extravagance offered as a gift to friends became extravagance as an end unto itself. Unity and fellowship no longer were considered primary goals. The gift of community and sharing disintegrated into an evening of individual indulgence. Still, for many, the banquet and its goals remained untouched. A host provided the best he could so good friends could enjoy an evening of conviviality.

The banquet was a pastime for the wealthy. Craftsmen, laborers, and plebeians did not spend evenings reclining on couches while enjoying gourmet food, expensive entertainment, and engaging conversation. From time to time an up-and-coming freeman or bookkeeper was invited to a banquet by his mentor. He likely felt out of place and often was given or had to borrow the appropriate clothing for the event. Average people knew of such banquets and strongly desired to take part in the lifestyle. Gradually, over time, they developed their own means to access at least a version of the banquet. Their alternatives became different guilds and organizations whose dues were primarily used to provide facsimiles of banquets for its members. These and other special meals are explored in subsequent chapters.

As we have seen, the pattern for the banquet began to be established a thousand years before the first-century Greco-Roman convivium, with elements gradually added over much time. Some elements made perfect sense. Feet and hands had to be washed, not just as a sign of hospitality but also because feet and hands were dirty. Food was offered first because guests were hungry and drinking large amounts of wine on an empty stomach was a recipe for disaster. Perfume and garlands made the evening special but also provided a pleasant setting during a time without commercial deodorant or frequent baths. Reclining was a meal posture originally reserved for kings and queens and used by guests who, for a few hours, were treated as royalty. Reclining was a position of one being served.

The most essential element developed over time was the two-section form of *deipnon*-symposium. It had considerable influence on many types of meals and feasts around the Mediterranean and the empire, including the ones described in this book. The first question is a cultural one. Can we imagine Paul and members of his churches attending a banquet with its possible overindulgence and erotic overtones? Imagine a Christian in Rome participating in a libation ceremony where everyone else extolls the virtues of Dionysius and Zeus. The second question I ask is, what impact did a two-part feast have on early Christian worship? The other types of feasts and banquets in this book are examined both as providing part of the culture in which Paul and his Christian communities existed and as providing a model, even if a subconscious cultural one, for their gatherings.

SPECIAL SAUCES FOR SPECIAL FOODS
ON A SPECIAL EVENING

For a Roman, a piece of meat "was like an artist's blank canvas, to which he could apply colour and shape."[10] A sauce provided the color, shape, and flavor added to the piece of meat, or to many other foods for that matter. Sauces were often used even in Mediterranean cultures that enjoyed simple flavors and preferred their foods roasted, baked, and broiled.

As today, there were a variety of techniques for using sauces. Composed sauces were created in the kitchen and served with a particular dish. The recipes collected in *Apicius* contain hundreds of composed sauces. For example, a white sauce intended for boiled meat was prepared separately and poured over the meat immediately before the food was served. Prepared sauces accompanied fish, vegetables, poultry, and all manner of dishes.

Sauces were also added to dishes as they were cooked. Most Indian curries and stir-fried foods are prepared in this manner. *Apicius* has several recipes for foods, especially vegetables, that were cooked in sauces. One tasty dish includes carrots that were blanched, sliced, and then cooked in a cumin sauce. Such dishes were served in the cooking sauces. A similar technique was used to cook shellfish.[11]

A third type of sauce that was extremely common was one used as a condiment. Instead of being poured over the food, it appeared on the table beside the food so pieces could be dipped into it. Numerous sauces for vegetables and eggs were prepared and used in this manner. A condiment sauce could be as simple as oil with vinegar, fish sauce, or *garum*, or as complex as a homemade mayonnaise with herbs and pine nuts.

A sauce, such as pesto or Romesco, can be a simple mixture of ingredients, or it can involve several stages of preparation. As today, one began a complex sauce by making stock or reducing wine to the consistency of syrup, to which might be added *garum* or any number of seasonings. Separately, herbs, spices, and other flavorings were ground with a mortar and pestle. These were then added to the stock or moistened with the reduction. Many were quite complex both in preparation and in taste.

Ancient sauces typically were named either for the food they accompanied, as in "veal sauce," or were distinguished by their color, such a white sauce or green sauce. As mentioned earlier, a sauce might be interchangeable between different types of food. One for shellfish might end up covering carrots. A white sauce intended for pork might be delicious when napped over chicken.

Sauces were used for various reasons. They certainly enhanced the flavor of a dish, especially foods that were boiled and tasted bland. Sauces provided alternative flavorings to appetizers such as hard-boiled eggs. An egg dipped in *garum* might be more interesting than one just sprinkled with salt. Even more so, an egg dipped in a homemade mayonnaise with herbs and pine nuts was more interesting still. At a time before refrigeration, sauces were created in part to hide flavors of meat and other foods that were in the early stages of spoiling. Seasonings and sauces were used for this purpose until the last century or so.

Garum

Garum, also called *liquamen*, was by far the sauce used most often in the ancient Mediterranean kitchen. It was a salty sauce, and it tasted and smelled fishy. *Garum* was professionally produced in many places around the Mediterranean and Black Seas beginning around the fifth century BCE, and it continued to be used for almost fifteen hundred years. *Garum* was manufactured wherever salt was processed from the sea and fish were available, especially in locations where salting and preserving fish was already a thriving industry. Its use began as a condiment for the wealthy. But with mass production, it became almost universal, especially in cities and towns around the Mediterranean Sea.

Food scholars and cooks need look no further than *Apicius* to see how the Roman Empire used *garum*. Even though ancient literature makes numerous references to it, the playwrights and authors of agricultural manuals and natural histories usually just commented on its smell, which was strong and fishy. However, the recipes in *Apicius* illustrate its ubiquitous use. It was a component in almost every recipe. From savory to sweet foods, it either served as a condiment or was used instead of salt. Likewise, it provided a meaty "umami" flavor that most people still find very compelling.[12] Eventually *garum* fell from favor and was no longer produced in the Western world.

The method for making *garum* was simple. Herbs or other seasonings were scattered on the bottom of a barrel. Then fish were placed in layers, either the heads, tails, and entrails of large fish such as tuna and mackerel or whole small fish such as anchovies and sardines. A large amount of salt was then added on the fish and additional layers created: fish, salt, fish, salt. The barrel with its contents was left to ferment for two months. The resulting liquid was drained and stored in *amphorae*, large, heart-shaped, clay containers with two handles that could hold up to seven gallons. Wine and olive oil were also stored in this type of container. The remaining disintegrating fish solids were called *allec*, which researchers say also had culinary uses.[13] *Garum* was produced in a variety of quality levels depending on the type of fish used. A low-quality sauce made only with scraps from a variety of different fish was marketed to the poor and likely was the only fish many could afford. The highest quality came from southern Spain, which was given the name *garum sociorum*, or "partners *garum*," and used only mackerel.

Cooks devised variations of *garum* to keep in their kitchens and make even more complex sauces. Three combinations most frequently were used: *hydrogarum* blended *garum* and water; *oneogarum* combined *garum* and wine; and *oxygarum* combined *garum* and vinegar.

Garum probably tasted very similar to Asian fish sauce. Even the technique for making fish sauce is quite similar. When trying the recipes in this book, I suggest using either a *nam pla* from Thailand or *nuoc mam* from Vietnam in place of *garum*. I have sampled generic fish sauces purchased from grocery stores and was not impressed. Two that I do like and use are Lucky Brand Thai Fish Sauce and Red Boat Fish Sauce. Lucky Brand is saltier, but the fish flavor is not as strong. I use it for cooking. Red Boat has a much more sophisticated flavor and is appropriate for finishing a sauce or using as a condiment.[14]

Wine as an Ingredient

Wine and unfermented grape juice, called *must*, were common ingredients in sauce making. The wine itself was prepared in a variety of ways. Wine was added to a sauce or used as an ingredient in a marinade. A small amount of wine might be added to ground herbs and spices to moisten or added directly to the sauce of a cooking dish. However, Romans almost always used reduced wine when making sauces. *Defrutum* or *sapa* (*saba*) is grape must that has been reduced to the consistency of a syrup. Because must is unfermented, the sugars are not consumed by the yeasts, and the syrup is quite sweet. If the must was reduced but not to the consistency of a syrup, by one-third to one-half, it was called *caroenum*. A raisin-flavored wine was also used for sauce making, cooking, and drinking. The Romans called this type of wine *passum*. Amarone is a modern Italian wine with raisin overtones. With amarone, as with ancient *passum*, grapes are placed on racks after harvest and allowed to partially dry, condensing the sugars and giving the wine a raisin-like flavor. Amarones are expensive, and I would not use a bottle for cooking. I will provide a recipe for an inexpensive alternative in chapter 10.

Making a Sauce

Romans ate bold sauces. The examples we have, especially from *Apicius*, describe sauces "that are far from subtle."[15] They also enjoyed the balance of conflicting flavors, such as sweet and sour. In most cases, recipes for sauces simply listed the ingredients. Rarely did they describe cooking methods or tell the amounts of ingredients to be used, though standardized measuring spoons and cups existed in the first century. Many sauce recipes began with various herbs and spices, fresh or dried, that were ground with a mortar and pestle. These were then moistened with vinegar, brine, and/ or wine. This mixture formed the base of the sauce. A very large amount of pepper was added, causing modern cooks to wonder if the peppercorns were as strong as their modern equivalent. Pepper was one of those spices imported from India, so it was possible that it lost some of its potency during shipping. Still, Romans must have enjoyed very spicy food.

A primary goal of Roman cookery and sauce making was to produce a blended bouquet of flavors rather than one or two dominant tastes. This was one reason why many herbs and spices, sometimes as many as ten or twelve, were used in a single sauce. No one herb or spice stood out. It should be noted that some modern cuisines also mix numerous spices and flavorings to produce a blended flavor. For example, many cooks in New Orleans use a seasoning salt that might have eight or more ingredients.[16]

To a large extent, Roman cooking and sauce making was profoundly influenced by the Greeks they conquered. Historically, the Greeks ate and liked simpler foods, but their cuisine was impacted when Alexander the Great unified Macedonia to the north and the city-states of Greece and then conquered Persia, Egypt, part of what we now call Afghanistan, and northwest India. The armies brought home foods, plants, and spices that changed culinary Greece and eventually Rome. In culinary matters, there is an astonishing link from ancient Greece through the modern era. The sauces were simpler and much more likely to be used as dips for bread, meat, and vegetables. A vinegar-and-oil dipping sauce with mint and pickled green peppercorns and an *oxygarum* sauce with caraway, celery seeds, pepper, and parsley are two examples. A well-known garlic and bread sauce accompanied vegetables and fried fish. A sour sauce with watercress, garlic, mustard, and pureed raisins was also served. Leeks and pomegranate seeds were sometimes added. When presented with meat, fish, or vegetables, the sauce was often garnished with chopped nuts or pomegranate seeds.

As one traveled east through the kingdoms that now are part of western Turkey, the emphasis changed yet again, even though the cuisine and sauces were heavily influenced by both Greek and Roman cooking. One can detect Far Eastern, central Asian, Iranian, Anatolian, and Mediterranean influences on its food. Yogurt, cracked wheat, dips made with legumes, and fish all play a greater role in the sauces and the diet in general. Foods that tend to have a Middle Eastern reputation and origin, such as dates and figs, are more often used in preparations. Saffron, nuts, and fruits such as sour cherries were also grown in that region and incorporated into all manner of cooking and sauce making.

Ingredients for Sauces

The following is a partial list of ingredients used to make sauces.

Aromatic herbs, berries, and spices; pepper, ginger, cloves, saffron, mustard, cardamom, poppy, fennel, cumin, anise, celery (seeds and leaves), and sesame seeds; myrtle, bay, and juniper berries; mint, thyme, rue, savory, oregano, parsley, lovage, chervil, dill, coriander, and lavender.

Liquid ingredients: *defrutum* and *saba* (grape must be reduced to syrup consistency), *caroenum* (must that was reduced only by one-third), *passum* (raisin wine), *garum*, olive oil, honey, and vinegar.

Nuts and seeds: pine nuts, hazelnuts, chopped dates, dried plums, and pomegranate.

Thickeners for sauces: starch (*amulum*), eggs, crumbled bread, or dried dough (*tracta*).[17]

A BANQUET AT HOME

Think in terms of a luxurious banquet in your own home. This is the time to pull out the china, crystal, and silver that you only use once or twice a year. Light candles and open a special bottle of wine. If your guests are reclining, make sure there are plenty of cushions. Perhaps enjoy appetizers while reclining around a coffee table and move to the dining room table for the *deipnon*. Return to the less formal setting for the symposium.

MENU: A BANQUET AT HOME

Appetizers

Mulsum
Oxygarum and Romaine Lettuce
Smoked Cheese

Deipnon

Cappadocian Bread
Mint Sauce for Dipping the Bread (chapter 3)
Pork Loin and Sauce
Honey and Cumin Glazed Carrots
Chestnuts, Mushrooms, and Sauce
Wine

Symposium

Dessert Wine
Dates Stuffed with Pistachio Cream Cheese
Roasted Walnuts and Almonds, from the market

RECIPES

Mulsum

I recommend you begin simple with just the honey and cinnamon. Branch out by trying the wine with dates and date stones or with figs. You can also use several tablespoons of date syrup.

- One bottle of white wine
- ⅓–½ cup of honey

- 2 cinnamon sticks

Optional ingredients:

- 1 tbs. ground pepper
- 2 bay leaves
- Saffron threads
- 3 whole dates

- 3–4 date stones (pits)
- 3–4 figs
- 1 tsp. whole cumin seeds

Pour one bottle of wine into a pot. Heat to warm, but not to boil or simmer. Add the honey, cinnamon sticks, and any of the optional ingredients you choose. Serve hot or allow to cool.

Oxygarum and Romaine Lettuce

Oxygarum is one of the fundamental sauces and is composed of vinegar and fish sauce. Many of the recipes in this book use this combination, though it is typically hidden in a list of ingredients. Here it is used in a salad dressing.

- 1½ tsp. each of caraway seeds, celery seeds, and peppercorns
- ½ tsp. salt
- ¼ cup finely chopped parsley

- 2 tbs. honey
- 2 tbs. vinegar
- 2 tsp. fish sauce
- 1–2 romaine lettuce hearts

Crush the seeds, peppercorns and salt with a mortar and pestle or use a spice grinder. Add the parsley to the mortar and pestle and grind with the seeds. Pour this mixture into a small bowl with the honey and stir with a fork to make a paste. Then mix in the vinegar and fish sauce.

Roughly chop the lettuce. Add the *oxygarum* dressing. Adjust seasoning and serve.

Smoked Cheese

The trick with smoking cheese is to have minimal fire, but enough to cause smoke. You will need a grill with a lid.

- A brick of solid cheese, such as Halloumi, cheddar, or gouda
- 2 disposable roasting pans that will easily fit in the grill
- Ice

- Toothpicks
- Charcoal
- 1 cup of woodchips, a mellow hardwood such as apple or cherry

Thirty minutes before cooking, place woodchips in a glass and cover with water. To prepare the grill: Place 3–5 charcoal briquettes on one side of the charcoal grate. Light them and allow to become ashen coals. On the other side of the grate, place one of the aluminum pans. Fill it with ice. Drain the water from the cup of woodchips and scatter the wood on top of the coals. Stick toothpicks under the cheese to allow for ventilation and to keep from melting. Place this aluminum pan on the cooking grate over the ice. Cover the grill and half open the vents. Check when the smoke stops. Remove the lid, add more ice and ice chips. When finished smoking, remove the cheese, and when it cools wrap it in parchment paper and refrigerate.

Cappadocian Bread

Not only were the Cappadocians known for delicious romaine lettuce, they were also known for their bread. It was a luxury bread because it was made with milk and eggs. This recipe calls for a mixer. You may knead the bread without the help of your KitchenAid, especially if you are an experienced baker.

- 1 tbs. quick-rising yeast
- ½ cup warm water (approx. 110 degrees)
- 3 eggs, divided use
- 1 cup of half milk, half water
- 6½ cups white unbleached flour
- 1 tbs. salt
- 4 tbs. butter, softened
- 1½ tbs. honey
- 1 cup whole milk

Place the yeast and warm water in the bowl of a mixer. Wait until yeast begins to activate, approximately 15 minutes. It will change color and begin to bubble. Crack two of the eggs into a liquid cup measure. Beat slightly with a fork and use the water-milk mixture to fill to the 1 cup mark.

Add the flour to the yeast mixture. Add the rest of the ingredients, including the egg mixture (except for the remaining egg; set that aside).

Mix the dough with a dough hook for 5 minutes. Start at the slowest speed and then increase the speed to medium slow. Let rest for 15 minutes. Then mix the dough for another 5 minutes. The dough should be slightly sticky and springy. If it is too wet, add extra flour a tablespoon at a time during the second mix. If the dough is too dry, add water.

Turn the dough out onto a floured surface and knead for about 30 seconds. Place in an oiled bowl and cover with a cotton towel or oiled plastic wrap. If your mixing bowl is large enough, then leave it in the bowl to rise, still covering with a towel or plastic wrap. Let rise until double in size, between 1 and 1½ hours. After rising, turn out the dough onto a floured surface. Punch down the dough to allow some of the gas to escape. Form the dough into two loaves about 10–12 inches in diameter. Cover the loaves with a kitchen towel or the oiled plastic wrap. Allow to rise another hour.

Preheat the oven to 400 degrees with a pizza stone, baker's tiles, or a thick baking sheet on the middle rack of the oven. Crack the remaining egg into a small bowl and mix with a fork. Using a kitchen brush, apply the egg to the top of the bread. Slide the bread into the oven using a well-floured pizza paddle or a well-floured back of a cookie sheet, especially one without a rim.

Pork Loin and Sauce (Apicius)

This recipe originally called for veal scallopini, which is delicious with this sauce. Many people object to eating veal, so I replaced it with pork. Feel free to use veal. Chicken thighs can also be used. This might become a new favorite recipe.

- 3 pounds of pork loin
- 2 tbs. olive oil

- Salt and pepper

For the sauce:

- ½ cup raisins
- ⅔ cup red wine
- 2 tsp. dried lovage
- 2 tsp. celery seeds
- 1 tsp. ground cumin
- 2 tsp. dried oregano
- ½ tsp. ground pepper

- 2 tbs. honey
- 2 tbs. *saba* (condensed grape must)
- 2 tbs. olive oil (divided use)
- 2 tsp. fish sauce
- 1 tsp. each salt and pepper

Slice pork 1 inch thick. Then cut into bite-sized pieces. Mix with olive oil, salt, and pepper and set aside.

Heat the wine and pour over the raisins. Allow to soak for at least 30 minutes. Place all the sauce ingredients (except 1 tbs. olive oil) in a food processor or blender and run for several seconds until ingredients are chopped and mixed.

Sauté pork pieces in 1 tablespoon of olive oil until brown. Then add the sauce. Remove the pork when it has finished cooking. And boil the sauce until it is the consistency of a syrup. Add the pork back to the sauce to warm and glaze. Adjust seasoning and serve.

Note: If using veal, do not cut into pieces. Dredge in flour before cooking.

Honey and Cumin Glazed Carrots

- 1½ lbs. carrots, peeled and cut into large matchsticks
- 2 tsp. cumin seeds, roasted and ground
- 3 tbs. honey
- 1 tbs. sweet wine
- 2 tsp. fish sauce
- 1–2 tsp. olive oil
- 1 tsp. salt
- ½ tsp. pepper

Boil the carrots until partially done. Mix together the cumin, honey, sweet wine, and fish sauce. Use the olive oil to oil a baking dish and add the carrots. Pour cumin-honey mixture over the carrots and mix until all carrots are covered. Add salt and pepper. Bake at 350 degrees until carrots are tender. Adjust seasoning and pour any remaining glaze mixture over the carrots. Then serve.

Chestnuts, Mushrooms, and Sauce

I do not have access to chestnuts where I live so I order them online from Blanchard and Blanchard. We have porcini (boletus) and chanterelle mushrooms in the mountains above our town. Foraged porcinis and chanterelles are perfect for this recipe.

- 6 oz. chestnuts
- 1 tbs. olive oil
- 8 oz. cleaned and sliced mushrooms, baby portabellas or porcinis and chanterelles
- ½ peeled yellow onion, cut into half rings
- 1 tbs. each finely chopped parsley and mint
- 2 tsp. fish sauce
- ¼ cup white wine
- 2 tbs. *saba*
- 1 tsp. each salt and ground pepper

Sauté the chestnuts in a dry skillet for several minutes. Add 1 tablespoon of olive oil and the mushrooms and onions. Continue to cook until mushrooms have released their moisture.

In a bowl, mix the parsley, mint, fish sauce, white wine, and *saba*. Add this mixture to the skillet. Then add the salt and pepper. Continue to sauté until the liquid ingredients form a syrup. Adjust the seasoning and serve.

Dates Stuffed with Pistachio Cream Cheese

Date stones can become one of the ingredients for your *mulsum*. Save the stones and add them to the wine as it is heating. Leftover dates also can be added to your *mulsum*.

- 18 dates
- ½ cup cream cheese or a creamy goat cheese
- ¼ cup shelled pistachios, finely ground

Remove the stones from the dates. Combine the cheese and ground pistachios and spoon ½ tablespoon into the cavity left by removing the stones.

6

GROWING UP JEWISH IN TARSUS

How many of us have experienced being with a group of people whose values, culture, and beliefs are radically different from ours? How did it feel? For an evening or even for several weeks it might be an interesting experience or even exciting. Then again, it might feel isolating or even off-putting. Perhaps we long to rejoin the group of people with whom we feel comfortable, people like ourselves. What if we lived as part of a minority culture for most of our lives?

Paul was a Jew who grew up in a large Gentile city in the midst of the Greco-Roman world. A sizable Jewish population existed in Tarsus, but still his friends and companions were part of the minority. He most likely attended Jewish banquets of the type described in the last chapter. But was he invited to Gentile *convivia*? He spoke and wrote in Greek instead of Aramaic. He read the scriptures in Greek instead of Hebrew. When he quoted Hebrew Scriptures in his letters, he used the Greek translation. His life in the minority must have influenced how he saw the church and understood the gospel message.

PAUL AND THE CITY OF TARSUS

"I am a Jew, from Tarsus in Cilicia, a citizen of an important city" (Acts 21:39a). Paul was right. Tarsus was one of the more important cities in the Roman Empire. Even in the first century, Tarsus was an extremely ancient town, having been established thousands of years earlier. Some scholars believe it might very well have better claims than Damascus for being the oldest city in the Western world.

Tarsus was the capital city of the province of Cilicia, itself an important region in the northeastern Mediterranean. It sits in what is now southwest Turkey, in an area known as Asia or Asia Minor in the ancient world. Only ten miles from the coast of the Mediterranean Sea, it was located on the shores of the Cydnus, a navigable river that permitted trade ships to dock near the city. Just to the north, a web of important roads came together allowing spices and other goods from India and the Middle East to move north to Ephesus and then to Greece and Macedonia. The road system for the movement of trade goods became extremely important during the winter rainy season when travel by boat became very difficult and dangerous. The broad plain in eastern Cilicia was ideal for farming, especially flax, and provided range land. The city was known for producing excellent-quality linen from the flax and goat's hair. These materials were used to produce a very fine fabric that was perfect for making high-quality tents, which was Paul's occupation.

The city purportedly had a large population, somewhere between seventy and one hundred thousand. There are literary references to beautiful broad avenues, bridges, marketplaces, promenades that ran through the city and along the river, numerous public baths, fountains, a gymnasium, and a stadium. Unfortunately, most of the architectural glory is buried beneath a modern city of three million people; as such, very little archaeological exploration is possible. Remains of the foundation of a colossal marble temple still exist, but the temple itself is totally lost.

The city had a reputation for being a great center of learning. Along with promenades and fountains, there were numerous schools for rhetoric and a very large library rumored to have two hundred thousand volumes, including a sizable collection of scientific works. Students studied philosophy, linguistics, and poetry, all of which were considered foundational to a well-rounded education. Some believed that the schools in Tarsus rivaled those in Athens and Alexandria in prominence and learning. One of the scholars from Tarsus, Athenodorus, became the principal tutor for Augustus, thus guaranteeing favored status for the city.

Over its long history, Tarsus was conquered a number of times, including by the Hittites and Persians. Even before the arrival of the Greeks, Tarsus was already adopting aspects of Greek culture. Alexander the Great arrived in the year 333 BCE and reportedly almost died after swimming in the Cydnus River. One story tells that he nearly drowned in the current; another that he became seriously ill from its very cold water.

After the Romans took control, the city became involved in the political struggles resulting from the murder of Julius Caesar. The result was that Mark Antony assumed control and began to reside in Tarsus. It was during that time that Cleopatra visited him, sailing up the Cydnus River in a barge, dressed as the reincarnation of Aphrodite, the goddess of love. It initiated a very famous and scandalous love affair, to which some historians contribute the famous couple's demise.

By the time of the birth of Paul, the city was composed of a mixture of the original Anatolians (the relatives of Hittites and Persians from millennia earlier), Greeks, and Romans. Also, Jews made up a sizable portion of the population by the first century. Tarsus was considered a "free city" instead of under direct Roman rule. To be a citizen of a free city was a high honor, in some cases more significant than being a Roman citizen. Paul claimed his citizenship in the important city of Tarsus in Cilicia along with his Roman citizenship (e.g., Acts 22:3, 25–27). A Tarsus citizenship must have been considered quite significant.

THE DIASPORA

Paul was a *diaspora* Jew from a family of diaspora Jews. The diaspora Jews lived outside of Palestine and especially beyond the region around and in Jerusalem. Significant challenges faced Jews in the diaspora. They were no longer part of a community where the belief in and worship of the one God permeated almost all aspects of life. Diaspora Jews did not live within proximity of the Jerusalem temple with all that it meant. First-century Jews were required to travel to Jerusalem three times a year for the great pilgrimage feasts of Passover, Pentecost, and Tabernacles, which were celebrated with sacrifices, temple liturgies, and great festivities. Even the poorest Palestinian Jew attempted to participate in at least one of these festivities. The temple was also the center of ritual life. Sacrifices were made for sins, and ritual purification was required for cases of defilement. Jews brought offerings of first fruits from the herd and crops during the summer. In addition, they had to pay a temple tax of one-half shekel, the equivalent of fifty to seventy-five dollars. Jews living in the diaspora might make a pilgrimage to the temple only once or twice in their lives.

The movement of Jews away from Palestine actually began with the Babylonian captivity many centuries before the time of Jesus and Paul. Babylon conquered Judah in the years 587–586 BCE, and a large percentage of the Jews were taken from their homeland and resettled, many as slaves and servants. In a somewhat hasty turnabout, Cyrus the Great of Persia then conquered the Babylonian kingdom in 539 BCE, allowing the

Jews to return to their homeland. But some stayed behind. Perhaps they had started successful businesses, or perhaps the new rulers, much like the old ones, appreciated their administrative acumen. From that time, many Jewish people chose to leave Palestine for a variety of reasons, many for economic opportunities. By the first century, the majority of Jews lived in the diaspora. It is estimated that as many as five to six million Jews lived outside of Palestine, most of them, but certainly not all, in the Mediterranean region. Easily 10 to 15 percent of the population of the large cities along the Mediterranean coast were Jewish. The percentage in Alexandria, with an ancient Jewish population, was much higher.

Diaspora Jews reacted or adapted in different ways. Many attempted to wall themselves off from the surrounding cultures. Peoples in ancient times tended to live in ghettos, areas with other people like themselves:

> The Jews were normally organized as a distinctive community, governed by its own laws and institutions, and often contended, sometimes successfully, for equality with the full citizens.[1]

Having like-minded neighbors enabled Jews in a foreign land to practice their religion: eat a kosher diet, study the Torah, keep the Sabbath, and attend synagogue, if there was one. Most Jews in the diaspora also continued to pay the half-shekel temple tax, sent to the temple in Jerusalem every year. The problem with isolation and freedom was that the surrounding population might and did eventually come to resent their Jewish neighbors.

Other diaspora Jews became Hellenized to a varying degree, adopting many of the customs of the surrounding Greco-Roman culture, including dress and education. Some completely dropped their Jewish practices and beliefs or remained Jewish by birthright only, completely blending into the surrounding culture.

Many, if not most, of the diaspora Jews no longer spoke or read Hebrew and Aramaic, the everyday language of those who lived in Palestine. The Hebrew Scriptures, the Old Testament, were translated into Greek, beginning in the third century BCE and finishing in the year 132 BCE. The Greek translation was called the Septuagint or LXX. So even in most diaspora synagogues, scripture readings were in Greek instead of Hebrew.[2] The Jewish philosopher Philo provided an example with his writings. As Meeks describes, the dilemma of being a Jewish scholar in a Greek world "can be sensed on almost every page of Philo. He writes an elegant, rhetorical Greek; it is doubtful whether he knew any more

Hebrew than he might have found in some handbook interpreting biblical names. He read Plato in terms of Moses, and Moses in terms of Plato."[3]

The synagogue in the diaspora was a way Jews remained grounded in their Jewishness. But it was a very different synagogue than what modern Jews experience. The surrounding culture understood the Jewish people as members of a *collegia* or *synodos*, common words for a club, guild, or association. In many ways, the synagogue functioned similarly to a *collegia*. Both had religious and social functions. Both enjoyed wealthy benefactors and officers who, because of their financial support, were given honorary titles and special seats at worship and other gatherings. Especially important in the ancient world, the synagogue and other *collegia* provided for the burial of its members who died.

There were differences between Jewish and other *collegia*. All Jews were members of the synagogue by virtue of their birth, so there were no enrollments or admission requirements. In addition, in the case of conflicts or petitions to city magistrates, the officers of the synagogue served as spokespersons for the entire Jewish community.

As with other *collegia*-type organizations, the ownership of facilities was not always necessary. Spaces were sometimes leased for meetings, or the synagogue met in a house owned by one of the members or purchased one for the sole purposes of membership. One synagogue, until the membership was large enough and it obtained sufficient financial backing, met in a small house with benches against the walls. Over time, they were able to build a grand facility, but not for centuries.[4]

The synagogue had several purposes. It was a place where shared prayers were offered and, even more important for the first-century Jew, corporate study of the scriptures took place. Even in the synagogue, the Torah used for worship and for study was from the Greek Septuagint (LXX).[5] The synagogue space became the setting for meetings and for training Jewish children. Community meals and celebrations were also held there. Synagogue life provided an anchor for many Jews in a difficult environment where the surrounding culture caused a significant temptation to adopt a Hellenized lifestyle.

The diaspora synagogue allowed Jews to live out their worldwide mission: "I have given you as a covenant to the people, a light to the nations" (Isaiah 42:6; also see Isaiah 2:2–4; Genesis 12:1–4). After all, they were a visible Jewish presence in the midst of a very non-Jewish Greco-Roman culture. Philo believed that the laws of the Jewish people attracted and would win the attention of all.[6]

The diaspora provided a progressive presence that appealed to many non-Jews who encountered a synagogue. Hellenistic Judaism no longer focused on the temple, sacrifices, and the Jewish priesthood. The separation in distance and culture from the temple and Palestinian Judaism was too great. The result was that Gentiles who considered converting focused on their deep appreciation for the Jewish ethical standards and monotheism. This group, called *proselytes*, were baptized, and the males were circumcised. A full conversion required "more personal sacrifices and behavioral changes."[7] Because of the rigors of the Jewish ethical lifestyle and the requirement of circumcision, many began this path but never became *proselytes*. Further, a group of Gentile "God-fearers" were often attached to synagogues. They were Hellenists "drawn from the heathen into adherence to the Jewish community [who] pledged themselves to confess belief in the one God and to observe a minimum of ritual commandments (Sabbath observance, the dietary laws)."[8] God-fearers were able to continue their full non-Jewish public life without the same restrictions as proselytes. In addition, many were in position to give sizable donations and even provide a house to be used as a synagogue. Furthermore, no demands were placed on God-fearers to undergo circumcision. Palestinian Jews, and especially Pharisees, disapproved of God-fearers.

It is unknown how Paul became a Roman citizen. Quite possibly his father or grandfather provided some type of service to the Romans or might have served in the Roman army. However, Jews did not typically choose army service because their observance of the Sabbath made military life difficult. Fighting in a battle or even moving to a new location with one's battalion was considered work for Jews and forbidden on the Sabbath. Roman citizenship also could be purchased for a high price.

This was Paul's situation in life, his *sitz im leben*. He and his family lived in a large Greco-Roman city that had a sizable but minority Jewish population. His schooling likely occurred both in one of the many well-respected schools of rhetoric and at the synagogue. As such, Paul honed his verbal and debate skills while learning the scriptures. Different opinions exist about his education based on an analysis of his letters, with some believing that they show him to be quite a scholar and others simply an ordinary student. He wrote with what is known as *koine* Greek, the language of the common people, rather than the refined Greek of classical literature. He attended a synagogue where prayers and scriptures were read in Greek. But even more important, he likely absorbed the strong sense of the synagogue's mission to Gentiles. Both Greeks and Romans probably attended the synagogue as proselytes and God-fearers with he and his family.

Paul must have been quite comfortable in the Greco-Roman world, and yet, at the same time, he was also a devoted Jew. I speculate that his experiences of eating, praying, and studying with Gentiles eventually colored his theology of freedom and his willingness to envision Christian communities where Jews and Greeks were equally part of "one body," each with important roles to play. But first he moved to Jerusalem and studied with the great rabbi Gamaliel, becoming a zealous Pharisee, one who likely became distraught with the very laxness that was part of his Tarsus synagogue, a zeal that easily carried over to his initial attitude toward the first Christians.

In the first chapter, I remarked that Paul was a person of the *polis*. The people who dwelled in the countryside were much more conservative, slow to change. Cities were the places where new things were experienced. In the ancient world, this was also true of religion. In that first decade after Jesus's death, we see Christianity leaving the village and moving to the city, especially the Greco-Roman city. Major changes were taking place among the new followers of Jesus, especially with their relationship to Judaism. Most of the new followers were urban Gentiles. Paul became a Christian near the beginning of this movement of transition from *chora* to *polis*, Palestinian countryside to Greco-Roman city. And his background as a diaspora Jew and a Jerusalem rabbi must have helped him with his role.

THE SABBATH FEAST

Home feasts are a hallmark of ancient and modern Judaism. Of these, the Sabbath feast is the most important.[9] Even in the diaspora, keeping the Sabbath and celebrating it with a special meal provided Jews with a sense of identity. It offered them a connection to other members of the community and, at the same time, differentiated them from the culture at large. As with other traditions and practices in the diaspora, the Sabbath feast united them with Jews still living in Palestine and bonded them with the Jews of the past.

Unlike other special meals, the Sabbath feast truly focused both on family and on neighbors and friends. It was not, as we experienced with the *convivium*, a meal for male friends and colleagues. Most of the other feasts in this book focused entirely on men. As an exception, feasts in the *chora* to celebrate the harvest or occasions such as Saturnalia involved the entire household or community. And as with some feasts, the purpose of the Sabbath feast was not philosophical discussion or costly entertainment. The

Sabbath feast truly was for family first and foremost, involving the women of the household and children.

The Sabbath feast was a celebration. It infused a day of rest with prayers, foundational theology, and special food shared among family and friends:

> The weekly day of rest merged with the Jewish understanding of Creation, the Exodus from Egypt, and the sovereignty of God. First-century Jews believed that God's creation was good and that its goodness should be enjoyed and celebrated. . . . Moreover, the Jews believed that God remained active in creation. The delivery from slavery in Egypt was the primary example. The inheritance of the Promised Land was another.[10]

The command for the Sabbath rest is found most explicitly in the Ten Commandments (Exodus 20:11; Deuteronomy 5:12–15; see also Genesis 2:2). It was not intended as onerous regulation, a compulsion for people to refrain from work against their will. Rather the requirement for a weekly day of rest was found within the ideal of relationship, and especially the covenant relationship with God. In essence the commandment said: spend the day resting and contemplating the wondrous gifts God has given to you, including the gift of creation. And enjoy!

This was the context for the feast. It was one of the ways that the ancient Jews set the Sabbath apart and kept it holy. As with other special meals, the Sabbath feast had rituals connected to it, some of them similar to those of the surrounding cultures and some unique. In fact, the meal really was and is a combination of religious ceremony and family feast.

For ancient Jews the day began at sunset and so that was the start of the Sabbath observation. Usually, the extended family and other friends and neighbors gathered for the Sabbath meal. They performed the practical rituals such as the lighting of lamps and washing of hands. These everyday rituals were accompanied with prayers, bringing a religious element to the meal even before it began. The meal started, as was common for all Jewish meals, with the blessing and sharing of bread. Broken and shared bread was and still is a symbol of unity and fellowship. The host also offered a separate special prayer for the Sabbath called a *Kiddush*. This expanded on the theme of thanksgiving that is central to the Sabbath. It also set apart the Sabbath day from the other days of the week by praying that it will be kept holy.

Thinking about the prayers for the diaspora, Sabbath gives rise to an interesting question. What language was used for the prayers? For that matter, what language was used in the synagogue? We know that scriptures were read from the Greek LXX in most diaspora synagogues. We also strongly suspect that all instruction and discussion about the Torah took place in Greek simply because most in the diaspora no longer fluently spoke Aramaic or Hebrew. It makes sense that even the prayers were spoken in Greek as well.

The same situation existed in most homes, where both semitic languages had been dropped by the family generations, if not centuries, earlier. The family was acquainted with the prayers, but they knew them in Greek and not in Hebrew. I have been unable to find convincing evidence to confirm the home prayer language, but one of the ways in which even the sincerest, practicing Jews assimilated was to drop Aramaic and Hebrew and use Greek.

The feast continued after the Sabbath prayer. Because of the special nature of the meal, special foods were prepared and served. Meat or fish might find its way onto the table, and if not meat, then poultry. If the family could not afford those luxuries, perhaps they added a pigeon or small piece of lamb to a vegetable stew or *puls* to give it flavor. Likely the service scheme unfolded similarly to the banquet. The meal began with appetizers the host family could afford: vegetables, hard-boiled eggs, and dips made from olive oil or *garum*. Almonds and fruit would make the first part of the meal special for a poorer family. Then a main course was served. Finally, the wine was blessed with a prayer offering thanksgiving for God's creation, which allows for the growth of grapes and vinting of wine. Sweet or salty foods were then served. Perhaps family and friends remained around the table to eat dessert snacks, drink wine, and discuss the events of the week.

CELEBRATING THE SABBATH WITH FAMILY AND FRIENDS

It is unfortunate that we have dropped the practice of the Sabbath feast. Followers of Jesus likely stopped sharing a Sabbath meal when Christianity moved from Palestine and Jerusalem out into the greater Roman Empire and Gentiles became disciples and church members. Perhaps those early Christians, especially Jewish Christians, considered the weekly gathering for worship that included a meal with blessings for the bread and wine as a new Sabbath feast. But eventually that meal was dropped as well, with only the remnant of eating bread and sipping wine remaining through the centuries.

There is renewed interest in Sabbath rest among all types of people: Jews, Christians, non-Christians, and those who identify themselves as "spiritual but not religious." With fast-paced and hectic lives, many people are looking for ways to intentionally slow down and take the opportunity to see and give thanks for the world in which they live. Some incorporate turning off electronic devices. Others use their Sabbath for long walks or uninterrupted time with family. For those without a religious connection and perhaps for those with one, the day and time are not essentially important. Sabbath time might be Wednesday afternoon or Saturday morning, as long as it is not interrupted by housecleaning or calls from work.

But what about the weekly Sabbath feast? Is it possible, in a fast-food, fast-paced world, to set aside weekly time to cook for family and friends? The dinner does not have to be elaborate. Even in the ancient world, the meals could be "potluck" with neighbors bringing food to share. For non-Jews, the rituals might not be necessary but they certainly would set the meal apart as special. Candles at meals always mark them as exceptional occasions. We see candles at restaurants and use them for birthdays and wedding anniversaries. Why not for our own Sabbath meal? Consider this suggestion. Turn off the television. Hide the iPhone. Light candles. Begin serving Sabbath meals to your family. Invite friends to be part of the experience. See how your life might be changed.

YEAST AND BREAD

Food writers agree that the three principal foods of the Mediterranean Basin, then and now, are bread, wine, and olive oil. Maguelonne Toussaint-Samat in her book *A History of Food* calls them the "three sacramental foods" or the "fundamental trinity." She quotes Jean-François Revel, who called bread and wine "those two pillars of consumption in Western civilization."[11]

Bread truly was the fundamental food for much of the world. It still is in many places. The word for *food* in numerous languages is equivalent to the word *bread*. In the Lord's Prayer, Christians pray for "daily bread," meaning bread and their daily food. As we saw in chapter 4, the largest concern of the populace during times of food shortages was gaining access to the grain needed to make bread and porridge, which some would say is just liquid bread. In the ancient Anglo-Saxon world, the word for the *lord of the manor* is best translated as *loaf guardian*, and for the lady, *loaf kneader*.

Bread was life in a way that twenty-first-century people do not understand. Bread was absolutely the essential food in the world of the Roman Empire. When the bread was gone because of famine or poverty, life itself was in jeopardy. The hoarding of grain during times of need resulted in riots because the people knew starvation was at hand. Over 50 percent of the calories for the average person came from grains and legumes. For many people, grains and legumes were their principal sources of protein. Bread was necessary and eaten at almost every meal. In some cases, as mentioned earlier, it also served as a plate and as a napkin for wiping hands during meals.

Simply defined, bread was the end product of baking a mixture of a cereal flour, especially wheat flour, with a liquid such as water at a steady, high temperature. It was a very ancient food that depended first on the domestication of cereal grains. Gluten helps the flour/water mixture to form a "cohesive loaf."[12] It is estimated that the domestication of grains began in the Fertile Crescent around 7000 BCE. The growing of grains also marked the beginning of settled agriculture.

Porridge was most likely the first use of grains for food. Flat cakes were the next step toward hot loaves of risen bread. Flat cakes began with little more than flour, water, and perhaps a pinch of salt and, in time, the addition of olive oil. The dough was flattened and cooked on hot coals, large hot rocks, and eventually on a hot griddle. The shape of the flat cakes fluctuated somewhere between thick tortillas, pita bread, and bean cakes. Remember that recipes for pita bread include yeast and those for flour tortillas use baking powder, so the comparison is close but not totally accurate.

Yeast is a single-celled fungus. These cells are so small that literally hundreds of millions will fit in a teaspoon. The discovery of yeast is a historical mystery. There is the wonderful story of the Bedouin woman who, after making her dough, walked away, and forgot about it. She returned to find that it was bubbling and smelled funny. She cooked it anyway and discovered that it tasted good.

Several prerequisites for making bread were required. Each seed of grain was encased in an outer sheath of chaff that was protected by an additional inner sheath of chaff. After cleaning off the outer chaff, the grains were heated:

> The first thing that had to be done when clean grain was needed was to separate the edible part of the grain from the husks surrounding it. In the case of wild types, the seed and chaff are reluctant to be parted, and it was therefore necessary to toast ("parch") the ears to make the chaff brittle enough to be loosened.[13]

Once parched and ground into flour, the grains could be used to make bread. With time, some grains were genetically modified to grow without the tough outer shells. This grain could be threshed without the addition of heat.

The next jump was to combine the yeast and the flour. Archaeologists tell us that dough with yeast was likely first created in Egypt. The Egyptians brewed beer with barley, relying perhaps without knowing it on the natural yeasts that were present on the outside of the barley grains. As fate had it, bread was often baked in the same space where beer was brewed. With a large amount of beer brewing constantly in an industrial-type space, the amount of yeast in the air in the room was significant enough to attach itself to the bread and initiate the process of rising. Alternatively, a clever brewer may have wondered what would happen if he or she replaced the water for making the dough with the brewed beer. The result was a different kind of bread that was light, fluffy, and filled with holes.

The process happens like this. The starchy center of the grain of wheat, called the *endosperm*, contains the gluten-forming proteins. The grains of wheat are milled, ground into flour. When a liquid is added, such as water or milk, the yeast, which is a living organism, feeds on the sugary starches of the flour and produces carbon dioxide gas and a small amount of alcohol. When the two elements interact, yeast and dough, the result is a spongy mass of tiny gas bubbles that causes the bread to rise. Each gas bubble is also enclosed in an elastic skin of gluten, which after milling is part of the flour. When heat is applied, the gluten becomes firm and holds the bread in its risen form.[14] It is fascinating that Romans initially resisted leavened bread, believing that it was not healthy to eat.

The way most people baked breads was in earthenware vessels or molds. The Assyrians mixed wheat and barley flour, heated large earthenware vessels with embers and hot stones, and then added the dough. The vessels were sealed and placed in the ground to bake. The Egyptians also used casts, pouring the dough into them and placing them in an oven.

The next important historical jump was the creation of the bread oven. The Greeks developed a "true" bread oven, one that was dome-shaped with an opening in the front. Fires were started in these ovens early in the day, heating the inside to a very high temperature, some speculating as high as eight hundred degrees. The coals were removed and the oven was ready to use, to bake bread and other foods.

With some modification, these types of ovens are still used. They are popular among restaurants that make "wood-fired" pizzas and breads. Wood-fired ovens are used by bakers around Europe to produce truly excellent bread. I saw a number of these ovens for sale while touring Greece several years ago. They looked perfect for backyard use. Unfortunately, I am certain that I could not have found an airline that would let me carry the oven back to Colorado, at least at a cost I could afford.

By the first century, these ovens were universally used. Farmers, rich and poor alike, had bread ovens in their courtyards or outside their homes. In a small town, an oven might be kept in a neighborhood courtyard and shared by several families. But such an oven was not practical or even safe in larger towns or cities. Homes were built very close together. The plebeians lived in high-rise buildings, structures with several floors of apartments, where even a hibachi-type grill for cooking simple dinners posed a significant fire risk. The density of the buildings was such that a fire could quickly spread and burn a sizable percentage of the city. Most of the ovens in the cities were used by entire neighborhoods and operated by professional bakers.

After the dough was made, the woman in the household in charge of baking took it to the oven. Families sometimes marked their dough so they knew which loaves belonged to them. Other foods, such as beans in a clay pot, were taken to the oven for cooking as well. There are communities in the Mediterranean Basin that still have neighborhood bread ovens today. Paid employees prepare the oven each day and bake the bread.

Alternatively, the households in a neighborhood could rely on professional bakers who owned and operated large bread ovens as a business. As with modern bakeries, they prepared bread and sometimes other baked foods and then offered them for sale. This was likely the model most often used in the largest cities such as Rome and Athens.

Milling is the process of grinding wheat into flour. Different varieties of mills existed by the first century. Most were based on rotary wheels, where a top stone was turned against a stationary mill stone while the grain passed between the two. Either humans or animals turned the stones. By the time of Paul, professional millers used water wheels. Running water turned a wheel against the mill stone. The water wheel was considered a great advancement. It became the normative technique for milling grain for the next eighteen hundred years.

The Greeks and then the Romans realized that the art of baking and that of cooking other foods was quite different. Those wealthy enough employed or owned slaves that specialized in either one or the other, but not both. They also realized that the best cooks and the best bakers in the empire came from different regions. The Greeks believed that the best bakers were from Lydia and Phoenicia. The Romans especially sought after Greek cooks, but when it came to bread, they preferred bakers either from

Greece or from Cappadocia, the region that now is central Turkey.[15] Cappadocia, already famous for producing a type of lettuce similar to romaine, was also famous for its bakers. Cappadocian bread was softer, with a nice texture and flavor, formed by using milk, sometimes with the addition of eggs, instead of water for its liquid.

Bakers in Gaul discovered what the Egyptians had realized much earlier: that beer yeast present in the froth of the fermenting liquid made a light, delicious, well-risen bread. A number of Gauls immigrated to Rome as bakers. At the same time, Greek bakers were experimenting not so much with the taste of bread but with its shape and appearance. By the time of the emperor Augustus, in the year 30 BCE, there were 329 bakeries in Rome run by Greek bakers, many of which employing assistants from Gaul. Around the same time, bakers in Rome formed a *collegium* with very stringent regulations, in essence creating a type of caste system for bakers. A baker was required to retain his occupation for life. Likewise, the sons of bakers had to follow their fathers in the profession. A monument was erected in honor of the famous baker Vergilius Eurysaces after his death, thus demonstrating the significance of those *collegium* members who supplied bread for the city.

I suspect that most people, when they have an image of first-century bread, think of a flat bread that looks and tastes a lot like pita. Certainly, flat breads were made and usually cooked over hot coals, in hot ashes, or on a spit or griddle. But by the first century, a very large variety of breads were being baked around the Mediterranean. *Picene* bread was the traditional Italian style made in earthenware pots broken after baking to extract the bread. *Panis boletus*, or mushroom bread, was baked in a round mold that allowed the rising dough to come over the top in the shape of a mushroom. The pan and top of the dough were covered with poppy seeds. *Strepitikiosartos* was a bread made with pepper added to the dough. *Cappadocian* bread was made with milk and a lot of salt and had a soft crust. *Torta* was a large round loaf divided into quarters. Large *torta* loaves were preserved by the volcano in Pompeii. *Panis secundarius* was the favorite of Emperor Augustus. It was a brown bread, likely whole wheat, heavier and considered healthier than the popular white bread. Numerous additional types of bread included:

- *Eskharites*—a loaf baked over a brazier and "anointed," dipped in or covered with a sweet sauce.
- Egyptian emmer bread—a sourdough bread made with emmer flour.

- *Nastos*—a loaf with a filling.
- *Panis militaris*—two different types of Roman army bread, one for marching and one for camp. Both were biscuits that had to be soaked before eating.
- *Panis adipatus*—a type of pizza containing pieces of bacon and made with bacon fat.
- *Cybus*—a cube-shaped bread with aniseed, fresh sheep's cheese, and olive oil.
- *Criban*—a bread containing cheese curd.
- *Panis lomentus*—bread made with flour of dried and ground fava beans.
- *Panis mustaceus*—a bread baked in the form of a ring with a laurel wreath laid on top. It included cumin, aniseed, and must in the dough. It was the traditional bread to serve at wedding feasts.

One ancient writer states that there were seventy-five different varieties of bread. Just this short survey convinced me that he must be right. Popular ingredients added to the dough were grape must, wine, milk, or eggs. Spices such as cumin, pepper, caraway, fennel, sesame, and poppy seeds were also commonly included in the bread dough.

Cultivating Yeast

In the 1980s and 1990s, I was a fan of the television cooking shows sponsored and sometimes produced by the Public Broadcasting Service (PBS). I especially remember watching a show that changed my understanding of bread. Until that time, I had experience baking a simple white bread, whole wheat, a rye loaf with caraway seeds, and Italian bread sticks. Making all these loaves began by opening a packet of instant-rise yeast, a product not available in the first century. The show was part of a series by Julia Child called *Cooking with Master Chefs*. Nancy Silverton was the guest chef, and she made a variety of stunningly beautiful loaves. But what impressed me was where she found the yeast. Silverton used a half pound of grapes that she placed in a cheesecloth bag. The grapes were lightly crushed with a rolling pin and then submerged in a mixture of flour and water. It so happens that two varieties of yeast are actually present on the outside of the grape skins. This yeast slowly began the process of fermentation when added to flour and water.

Fruit skins are one of the sources ancient bakers utilized for yeast to add to dough. Other sources were also used. As already described, the froth in the top of brewing beer is rich with yeast. It was removed from the beer and added to the flour and water mixture. Pliny the Elder describes six additional ways of culturing yeast. One was using millet flour kneaded with grape must. The technique was similar to that used by Nancy Silverton, where the unfermented, unpasteurized grape juice was rich with yeast from the skins. After fermentation began, the millet/must mixture was treated like a sourdough starter.[16] A similar technique used the bran of the wheat kernels. This flour was kneaded, soaked in white wine must for three days, formed into cakes, and dried in the sun. When it was time to use them, they were soaked in water and boiled with refined emmer flour. Bread then was made with this flour and the yeast cakes. This technique was said to make excellent bread, but the yeast did not last long. Pliny describes other techniques, including the use of dough balls made of barley and water and a yeast culture made with chickpea flour and used with barley bread.

By far the most common yeast was simply prepared by boiling unsalted flour with water to a porridge and leaving it to ferment and absorb existing yeast in the air.[17] Pliny recommends allowing it to ferment until just beginning to become sour, producing a sourdough-type bread. Once any of these techniques were used, then a portion of the previous day's risen dough was set aside before baking and mixed with fresh dough. In this manner, the yeast lasted a very long time.

Baking First-Century-Style Bread at Home

While writing this book, I pondered how to present recipes that best replicate first-century-style breads. At the same time, I realized that your level of baking skill and experience will vary greatly. But I believe that some of the recipes should be as authentic to the first century as possible. The first issue must be the use of yeast. Some of the bread recipes will use a standard active dry yeast, primarily because I want average home cooks to try baking their own bread. We will also experiment with methods of cultivating our own yeast starter. Silverton and her grape yeast were apparently the tip of a trend. Many world-class bakers and home cooks are experimenting with using yeast that they have cultivated.

The second issue involves the cooking medium. A modern convection oven is not the same as a brick "fired" oven. I have experimented with pizza stones and different pans in order to produce what I believe to be a loaf of authentic first-century-style bread. Then I discovered the use of a cast-iron Dutch oven to bake bread. A preheated Dutch oven becomes very hot and, when the lid is used, holds in moisture. The result is a crusty bread with a nice, chewy interior.

The third issue is personal. I live in the mountains of Colorado, and my house sits exactly seventy-five hundred feet above sea level. The techniques and even the measurements of ingredients at that altitude are quite different than they are at most other places. In short, I have had to translate my experiences and recipes so that a person living at a much lower altitude can use a similar technique with the same outcome.

One method of bread making that especially intrigued me came from a bakery and restaurant in San Francisco called Tartine. With the help of friends, the baker/owner developed a practice for home bakers that results in a rustic, country-style loaf that is very similar to his own bread. He introduced many home cooks to using a Dutch oven as their bread oven. The technique for making Tartine bread is described in a book named after his bakery. One can also find many videos online where he and others describe and demonstrate how to make this style of bread. The recipe was also published in the *New York Times*. The yeast he uses to create a starter or starters is cultivated naturally from the air and the wheat itself. It is not a fast process; it takes fourteen days on average to create the starter.

In an online response to the article and recipe printed in the *New York Times*, one seasoned home baker named Doug wrote this:

> I have been baking this bread for years with this (Tartine) method. When people ask me for the recipe, I have to tell them that it is not so much about a recipe, but a way of life. . . . If you want to make your life better, bake this bread.[18]

DIASPORA SABBATH FEAST

You should try a Sabbath feast with family and friends, either using the special menu selection described below or any recipe choices in the book. The point of the meal is to slow down our lifestyles and give thanks for the ways God works in our lives, for the people who mean so much. For your Sabbath feast, have a bowl, a pitcher of water, and towels handy. Place candles on the table. Remember that the washing of hands is symbolic at your meal. Your family and guests likely arrived with clean hands. If not, a sink and soap are available. First-century guests arrived with dirty hands and there was no sink available. The host begins with this prayer:

Blessed are you, Lord, our God, King of the Universe, who sanctifies us with his commandments, and commands us concerning washing of hands. Amen.

After everyone has washed their hands, the hostess or someone else lights the candles and uses this prayer:

Blessed are you, Lord, our God, King of the Universe, who sanctifies us with his commandments, and commands us to light the candles of the Sabbath. Amen.

The following are the traditional prayers to begin the meal. The first is the Sabbath kiddush. The second is the one used specifically for the bread:

Blessed are you, Lord, our God, King of the Universe who sanctifies us with his commandments, and has been pleased with us. You have lovingly and willingly given us your holy Sabbath as an inheritance, in memory of creation. The Sabbath is the first among our holy days, and a remembrance of our exodus from Egypt. Indeed, you have chosen us and made us holy among all peoples and have willingly and lovingly given us your holy Sabbath for an inheritance. Blessed are you, who sanctifies the Sabbath. Amen.

Blessed are you, Lord, our God, King of the Universe, who brings forth bread from the earth. Amen.

The host then takes the bread and holds it during the blessing. After the blessing, each person at the table tears off a piece and eats it.

After the meal is finished and the table is cleared, the wine is blessed. The host holds a glass of wine in hand and uses this prayer:

Blessed are you, Lord, our God, King of the Universe, who creates the fruit of the vine. Amen.

You might want to recline on cushions and eat with your fingers. Or sit around a formal dining table and use your best china and silverware. One path is more authentic; the other more comfortable. But what really matters is that you and your guests enjoy the spirit of Sabbath.

MENU FOR A SABBATH FEAST

Capturing Yeast for Country Bread
One-Pot Chicken
Bulgur Pilaf with Parsley and Raisins
Chickpeas and Eggs
Olive Tapenade
Broccoli and Olives
Honey-Almond Dip
Apples, Pears, and Other Fruit for Dipping, from the market
White Wine, Pistachios, from the market

RECIPES

Capturing Yeast for Country Bread

My son Robert, who is an actor and a musician, makes bread from his own starter. He has become an extraordinary baker and pasta maker. It is proof that good things come to people who take their time, slow food at its best. Your own starter will become your leaven for many loaves. Of course, you can purchase starter online or from a local bakery. Or, if you are lucky, a friend who makes sourdough will give you some starter. Measurements are given in grams. It will be helpful to have a good set of kitchen scales.

STARTER

- 1,000 grams each of white-bread flour and whole-wheat flour, divided use

Mix the flours together. In a 3-cup mason jar, mix 100 grams of warm water with 50 grams each of the flour mixture. The water should be approximately 80 degrees. Mix thoroughly and cover with a kitchen towel and leave in a warm place for 2–3 days or until the mixture begins to bubble. Once the starter is active, begin regular feedings. At the same time each day, discard all but 50 grams of starter and feed it with 50 grams warm water and 50 grams of the flour mixture. After about a week the starter will rise and fall predictability and take on a slightly sour smell.

LEAVEN

Take 100 grams of the starter and mix with 200 grams of water. Stir with your hands as if they were a whisk. Add 200 grams of the flour mixture and combine well. Cover with a towel and let rest for 12 hours or until it begins to bubble. You are now ready to bake your bread.

FEEDING THE LEAVEN

If you refrigerate the starter, you should feed it every week. Feed it more often if you leave it on a kitchen counter. Remove all but 100 grams of the starter. Add 50 grams of bread flour, 50 grams of rye flour and 100 grams of water. Stir with chopsticks until the flours are completely combined with the water and starter.

We keep our starter in a 4-cup mason jar with a lid.

One-Pot Chicken

- 2 tsp. each ground cinnamon, cumin, and coriander
- 1 tsp. salt
- 1½ lbs. chicken thighs or breasts, cut into bite-sized pieces
- 2 tbs. olive oil
- ½ yellow onion, chopped
- 3 garlic cloves, crushed
- 1 tsp. grated ginger root

- 2 cups chicken broth
- 1 cup white wine
- 2 cups canned chickpeas
- ¾ cup pitted Mediterranean olives, such as Kalamata
- ½ cup raisins
- 3 tbs. honey
- ½ tbs. cinnamon
- Additional salt to taste

Place cinnamon, cumin, coriander, and salt in a bowl. Add the chicken pieces and mix until covered by the spices. In a hot skillet, add the olive oil, then sauté until brown. Remove the chicken. Add the onion and sauté. Then add the garlic, ginger, broth, and wine. Add the remaining ingredients and the chicken. Cover and simmer until finished. Season and serve.

Bulgur Pilaf with Parsley and Raisins

Bulgur is parched wheat. It works very well as a side dish with stews. You can leave out the raisins if serving with one-pot chicken, which already includes raisins. You can also use pomegranate seeds.

- 1 cup coarse-cut bulgur, #3
- 2 tbs. olive oil
- ½ medium onion, chopped
- ¼ tsp. ground cumin
- ¼ cup slivered almonds

- ⅓ cup raisins, or a dried fruit of your choice
- 1½ cups stock or water
- ⅓ cup finely chopped parsley
- 1 tsp. salt

Using a fine mesh strainer, rinse and dry the bulgur. When dry, pour olive oil into a hot pot. Add the bulgur and slightly toast. Add the onion, cumin, and slivered almonds and continue to stir. Then add the raisins and the stock or water. Bring the liquid to a simmer. Stir in the parsley and salt. Cover and cook for approximately 20 minutes. Adjust the seasoning and serve.

Chickpeas and Eggs (Apicius)

- Two 15 oz. cans of chickpeas, rinsed, or 22 oz. dried chickpeas, soaked overnight
- 1 tsp. lovage, celery leaves, or celery seed
- 1 tsp. pepper
- 2 tsp. grated ginger

- 2 hard-boiled eggs, peeled and chopped
- 2 tsp. fish sauce
- ¼ cup red wine
- 2 tbs. honey
- 2 tbs. red wine vinegar

Cook the chickpeas in four cups of water until the beans are soft and much of the water has evaporated. While beans are cooking, grate the ginger and chop the eggs. Carefully pour the beans and remaining water into a blender or food processor and puree. Return the beans to the pot. Add the remaining ingredients, as well as additional water if needed, and cook until flavors blend together. Adjust the seasoning and serve.

Olive Tapenade (Cato)

A fast way to remove the stone in an olive is to press the flat side of a knife on the olive. This loosens the skin and makes it easy to remove the stone. Use Mediterranean olives like Kalamata or Castelvetrano.

- 1 cup mixture of black and green olives, stems and stones removed
- ¼ cup olive oil
- 2 tbs. red wine vinegar
- 1 tsp. ground coriander seed

- 1 tsp. ground cumin seed
- 1 tbs. fennel seeds
- ½ tsp. rue
- 1 tbs. finely chopped mint leaves

Rinse the olives and then chop them into small pieces. Place the olives in a jar or a small bowl. Mix in the rest of the ingredients and pour over olives. The oil mixture should just cover the olives. Set aside to allow flavors to mingle. I recommend placing in the refrigerator for 12 to 24 hours. Bring to room temperature. Add salt if needed and serve.

Broccoli and Olives

Pliny the Elder writes about broccoli: how to grow it and how to eat it. Apicius never mentions broccoli. Unlike Pliny (and me), he must not have liked it.

- 2 tbs. olive oil
- ½ to 1 head of broccoli, cut into flowerets
- ½ red onion, cut into thin half moons

- 2 cloves of garlic, minced
- 1 cup Kalamata olives, sliced in half
- ⅓ cup white wine
- ½ tsp. salt

Pour the olive oil into a large skillet with a lid. Sauté the broccoli and onion. When onions are soft, sweat the garlic and add the olives. When the garlic is opaque, pour the wine into the pan. Add the salt, then place the lid on the skillet. Cook until the broccoli is tender. Uncover, adjust the seasoning, and serve.

Honey-Almond Dip

Use fruit that is easy to dip. Apples and pears are good. The dip can be adjusted to the size of the gathering as long as the ratio of honey to almonds is 1:1. Serve with whole fruit so guests can cut the fruit themselves. Alternatively, add lemon juice to the fruit to keep it from turning brown. And beware, the honey almond dip is habit forming.

- ½ cup honey, heated in the bottle with simmering water
- ½ cup pine nuts or slivered almonds
- ⅓ tsp. salt
- Assorted fruit for dipping or simmering

Begin heating the honey in a pot of simmering water. Then roast the nuts in a skillet on low heat. Remove when the nuts begin to turn brown. Crush the nuts with a mortar and pestle, or use a food processor. Leave chunky. Place the nuts in a small bowl. Add the honey and the salt, and stir with a fork.

7

FOOD FIGHTS IN ANTIOCH

The Church in Crisis

In a perfect world, the act of joining with family and friends over good food should always build a sense of unity and community. Participants share in the generosity and hospitality that is offered by the hostess and host. The atmosphere is one of celebration. I have enjoyed many special meals that were shaped by these ideals: Thanksgiving feasts, holiday brunches, wedding rehearsal dinners, unplanned meals with friends, and backyard cookouts. Whether for four people or forty, the experience exemplified what is best about a feast.

But the world is not perfect. A special meal is also tied to culture and history. The second glass of wine can reveal conflicts, both new and old, among those at the table. The stress of a holiday feast can remind the participants of past times that were not happy. How difficult it is to enjoy a well-prepared meal when animosity and anger are as tangible as a moist slice of turkey with gravy.

In many ways the church in Antioch was an amazing development for the first generation of Christians. Antioch was third largest city in the Roman Empire and had a thriving community of those who followed Jesus as disciples. It must have seemed like that perfect feast: a community of Jews and Gentiles celebrating unity and hospitality at every meal and with each work of mercy. The reality was different. The feast that promoted unity and fostered goodwill would eventually separate people based on different backgrounds and cultures. Greeks and Jews came to realize that it was often difficult living in community, especially at the table. The church in Antioch became a fertile setting for conflict.

PAUL AND HIS JOURNEY TO ANTIOCH

Paul's journey took years. It began with his mystical experience on the road to Damascus. Clearly the event had a powerful impact on him and greatly influenced everything that followed. His encounter with the risen Lord knocked him to the ground and left him blind. A voice in the light confronted him about his persecution of the new Jesus sect and changed his life forever. Paul himself connects the way his calling set his life on a new trajectory: "[God] was pleased to reveal his Son to me so that I might proclaim him among the Gentiles" (Galatians 1:13–17; see also 1 Corinthians 15:8).

Paul had been a follower of Jesus for approximately eight years by the time he arrived in Antioch. He was not a new Christian or an unexperienced evangelist. He had taught and preached in Damascus where his message almost had him killed. His experience in the Nabataean Kingdom likely was not successful, but we know little about his time there. He went to Jerusalem for a short time, where, because of his past, the Christian community had a difficult time trusting him. Paul made several references in 1 Corinthians about receiving the Jesus tradition in Jerusalem. Then he stayed approximately two years in his hometown of Tarsus, likely with a successful ministry, before moving again (1 Corinthians 11:23; 13:3). It was in Tarsus that Paul met Barnabas.

It was after several years in Tarsus that Barnabas invited Paul to move to Antioch:

Then Barnabas went to Tarsus to look for Saul, and when he had found him, he brought him to Antioch. So it was that for an entire year they met with the church and taught a great many people, and it was in Antioch that the disciples were first called "Christians." (Acts 11:25–26)

We can be certain of several things before his arrival in Antioch. He taught, preached, and lived this new direction in his life with great zeal. He utilized the skills and knowledge he had accumulated up to this point: his use of his training in rhetoric and logic; his understanding of Hebrew Scriptures, especially the Greek translation or Septuagint (LXX), gained from his childhood and at the feet of Rabbi Gamaliel; and his experience with both diaspora and Jerusalem Jews as well as a wide variety of Greeks, Romans, and other Gentiles.

ANTIOCH ON THE ORONTES

Antioch, located in the northwest corner of the province of Syria, now in the farthest southwest reaches of Turkey, was the third largest and third most influential city in the Roman Empire. It sat on the Orontes River, not far from the Mediterranean coast. The river opened into a seaport known as the Seleucia Pieria. It was one of the principal harbors in the eastern Mediterranean. Antioch also was strategically located on the overland route connecting Asia Minor, Syria, and Palestine, so the city and its seaport served as a hub for trade caravans from eastern countries, from which all types of goods were shipped around the Mediterranean Sea. Antioch was famous for trade long before the first century. Wealth from trade made the city a target for Alexander the Great. After he occupied it, Antioch became a center for the spread of Hellenistic culture throughout Syria and the East.

From 300 BCE, the city was a mixture of Macedonians, Greeks, and native Syrians. A large number of Jews appeared at approximately the same time. They arrived both as veterans of the army who were granted land around Antioch as a reward for service and as prisoners that had chosen the wrong side in conflict. After the premature death of Alexander the Great, the land he had conquered was split between his generals. This should have been a workable solution to foster rule and oversight. Instead, the generals and their armies waged battles over the actual boundaries of their territories. This was especially true of the conflict between the Seleucid Kingdom that controlled Syria, Persia (present-day Iraq and Iran), and Asia Minor and the Ptolemaic Kingdom, which included Egypt. Control of Palestine was a major target of conflict. Not only were Jewish mercenaries and prisoners taken to Antioch, but those Jewish citizens wishing to avoid war migrated to Antioch and to other cities in the Mediterranean Basin.

With both the presence of Greeks and wealth made through trade, Antioch became a center of culture and sophistication. Its crossroads and seaport connected the city both to the Eastern world of Persia and to India and the Mediterranean Basin cities, especially the Greek communities in Asia Minor, Greece, Macedonia, and Alexandria in Egypt. Such a successful and influential trading center provided the rest of Syria with the means to trade its goods, especially wine, grain, leather, and dried fruit.

The Romans occupied Antioch and Syria in 64 BCE. It became the military headquarters and capital of Syria. Antioch was also a special project of the Romans, who focused a significant amount of resources on enlarging and beautifying the *polis*. It enjoyed a succession of emperor benefactors, including Julius Caesar, Augustus, and Tiberius. King Herod, anxious to show his support of the Romans, also assisted the city with new construction projects. Additional resources were used to enlarge the seaport and improve the road system. These improvements, along with the security provided by the Pax Romana, the "Peace of Rome," made available through enhanced security and military presence, increased the commercial influence that Antioch was already enjoying. At the same time, the already large Jewish community continued to grow and enjoy the support of and its good standing within the city. The increasing instability of life in Jerusalem made migration to cities such as Antioch desirable. The city was prepared to accept Jewish immigrants, and the atmosphere was appropriate for their economic success. Likewise, in Antioch, Greek-speaking synagogues enticed a number of Gentiles who found Jewish monotheism and its high ethical standards an attractive alternative to the pantheon of gods and goddesses provided by Greek and Roman religions. This was the Antioch where Barnabas brought Paul in the year 44 CE.

Antioch and the Christian Movement

The first Christians found Antioch a fertile venue for their message. The city already embraced a diverse population with a variety of religions. There were the Greek gods and goddesses, but also mystery religions that emphasized death and salvation in a way the mythology of the pantheon did not. It was likely that, very early on, the new followers of Jesus continued to observe some version of Judaism, remaining part of the Greek-speaking synagogues and participating in Jewish festivals. But quickly following the Christian community's formation, "Christianity burst its Jewish framework and reached the Greeks."[1] With the growing number of Greek converts, the question was eventually asked: "How Jewish must Gentile converts become?" From the point of view of history, it makes sense that Antioch would be the Christian community where the "circumcision issue" came to the fore.

Circumcision was not the only issue. Early Christians enjoyed common meals, called *agape feasts* (love feasts), also called the *Lord's Supper*, the *breaking of bread*, and meals of thanksgiving (*Eucharists*). The meals were essential elements of the Christian communal life: "They devoted themselves to the apostles' teaching and fellowship, *to the breaking of bread* and the prayers" (Acts 2:42, emphasis mine). The new communities of Jesus followers had to determine how Jewish and Gentile Christians would eat these meals. The question may seem insignificant to the modern reader, but it essentially would define the nature of the church as a community and how it came together to worship.

The emerging issue was whether Jews could eat with Gentiles and, if they did, what they could eat. Many Jews considered it difficult, if not impossible, to eat with Gentiles and not become ritually defiled. The issue was even more complex when considering what food to eat. Would the diet be Greco-Roman, with the inclusion of pork and shellfish, or would it be Jewish and kosher? One option was that Jewish Christians and Gentiles would eat at different tables. But this solution undermined the very principle of the unity and community-building aspect of table fellowship, or agape love meals. Another solution was to have corresponding meals in different parts of the house, with each location serving a different menu. Again, while the solution might have worked, the opportunity for the feast to construct a sense of coalescence would be lost. Other alternatives were to have one shared meal where everyone ate only kosher food or to have totally separate communities with separate home churches, one for Jewish Christians and one for Gentile Christians.

The community in Antioch took a progressive approach, one that seemed consistent with the diversity of the broader community and with the makeup of the young church itself. One can infer from a reading of Paul's letter to the Galatians that the church in Antioch simply chose to eat together. And since it most likely included a meal in the form of the two-part banquet, *deipnon* and symposium, their worship began with food, flanked by the blessing of bread and wine, and then continued with discussion, readings, singing, and other features.

How lax were the Jewish Christians? They were eating with Gentiles, but were they also eating nonkosher foods? They might easily identify and avoid pork and shellfish, but were they mixing milk dishes with meat? Was cheese placed on the table with a stew of lamb or goat? The answers are unknown. But what we can discern is that the Jewish Christians were in the habit of eating with the Gentiles, maybe even the same food, and that Barnabas and Paul were joining them in table fellowship.

To complicate matters, the Jerusalem Christian community heard rumors concerning the lax behavior in Antioch and sent a delegation to investigate. What they found, first and foremost, was that Gentile followers of Jesus had not been circumcised. The question was raised, and a debate erupted among the members of the Christians in Antioch. The solution was to send a delegation to meet with the leaders in Jerusalem. The meeting is commonly called the Jerusalem Conference. Barnabas and Paul were included among the representatives.

Apparently, the discussion became quite heated, with Pharisaic Christians strongly in favor of circumcision and the adoption of a kosher diet for new Gentile Christians. But the ultimate decision was to allow Gentile converts to remain uncircumcised and to place food restrictions on them instead. James, the brother of Jesus and head of the Jerusalem Christian community, summarized the decision:

> Therefore, I have reached the decision that we should not trouble those Gentiles who are turning to God, but we should write them to abstain only from things polluted by idols and from fornication and whatever had been strangled and from blood. Moses has had those who proclaim him, for he has been read aloud every Sabbath in the synagogues.

⌒

> For it has seemed good to the Holy Spirit and to us to impose on you no further burden than these essentials: that you abstain from what has been sacrificed to idols and from blood and from what is strangled and from fornication. If you keep yourselves from these, you will do well. Farewell. (Acts 15:19–21, 28–29)

The mention of "blood" and "what is strangled" are not-so-veiled references to a kosher diet. Before meat could be eaten, all blood had to be removed from it. In addition, the prohibition not to eat meat sacrificed to idols made it almost impossible to purchase meat in the cities of the Roman Empire. Much of the meat sold at markets originated from animals that first were sacrificed to the gods and goddesses in local temples.

Paul must have been furious with this decision. We know from his letters that he strongly disagreed with the food limitations. Paul refused to encumber his church communities with such restrictions, emphasizing instead being conscious to the sensibilities of others. His theology placed a high premium on unity, and especially in the case of table fellowship. His letters describe an understanding of the Christian community based on the metaphor of a body, and not just any, but the Body of Christ. Now certainly his letters exhibited years of reflection on his understanding of the church, and their foundation is probably in the Jerusalem experience. But, for Paul, the community that followed Jesus was one where dividing walls no longer existed: "There is no longer Jews or Greek, there is no longer slave or free, there is no longer male and female; for all of you are one in Christ Jesus. And if you belong to Christ, then you are Abraham's offspring, heirs according to the promise" (Galatians 3:28). The emphasis in this passage was baptism, with special interest in the Jew and Greek being equal in their unity in Christ. Paul would say, no longer are just Jews and Jewish

Christians considered Abraham's offspring; all who are baptized into Christ are Abraham's offspring. Paul continued to write about the unity of those who are part of the community, a unity not to be separated by anything, including issues of circumcision and food. "So we, who are many, are one body in Christ, and individually members of it" (Romans 12:5; also see Ephesians 2:14; 4:1–16; 1 Corinthians 12:14–27).

At the time, it must have appeared to Paul that the counsel had adopted what has been called a "two-track" model for acceptance as a follower of Jesus. The first track, or the superior track, was the Jewish model. This track included circumcision and the food regulations as described in the Torah. The second and inferior track was for Gentile converts. They could share the same table but only with restrictions, as long as kosher food laws were not violated. Otherwise, they had a "separate but equal" status. But for Paul, "separate but equal" meant no equality at all.[2] So it was in this context that Paul angrily erupted at his friends Barnabas and Peter. The precipitating cause was the arrival of yet another delegation from Jerusalem, apparently to discern whether the Antiochene Christians were abiding by the will of the Jerusalem council. Perhaps they were following the new procedures, but they also continued having meal fellowship with one another. Upon the arrival of the delegation, the Jewish Christians, including Peter and Barnabas, immediately separated themselves at table from the Gentiles. Paul recounted the occurrence in his letter to the Galatians:

> But when Cephas (Peter) came to Antioch, I opposed him to his face, because he stood self-condemned; for until certain people came from James, he used to eat with the Gentiles. But after they came, he drew back and kept himself separate for fear of the circumcision faction. And the other Jews joined him in this hypocrisy, so that even Barnabas was led astray by their hypocrisy. But when I saw that they were not acting consistently with the truth of the gospel, I said to Cephas before them all, "If you, though a Jew, live like a Gentile and not like a Jew, how can you compel the Gentiles to live like Jews?" (Galatians 2:11–14)

Paul lost the food fight in Antioch. From Professor Raymond Brown, "To Paul this attempt to compel the Gentiles to live like Jews violated the truth of the Gospel!"[3] Luke describes a disagreement causing the ministry of Barnabas and Paul to split, the conflict involving who to take with them on a missionary trip (see Acts 15:36–41). But it is highly suspected that the disagreement over table fellowship and Paul's theology of a unified church, especially as reflected in the passage from Paul's letter to the Galatians, ultimately caused the split. Even though Paul visited Antioch several more times, the city never again played an important role in his ministry.

The issue of food and circumcision continued to have an important and unsettling role in Paul's ministry as an evangelist. For Paul, the issue of regulations was never simple. It was grounded in the truth of the Gospel and the nature of the Christian community. On these issues Paul was uncompromising. For him, they were foundational.

SPICES MAKE THE WORLD GO ROUND

Herbs are easy to understand. They are the leaves of plants—they just happen to not be poisonous and to taste good. Even more than that, they make our food taste good. The question of spices is more difficult. The Oxford English Dictionary says they are "one or other of various strongly flavoured or aromatic substances of vegetable origin obtained from tropical plants, commonly used as condiments."[4] Several issues are raised by this definition. Not all spices are tropical. In fact, some spices were grown in the Mediterranean Basin in places that are still hot and humid, but not tropical. And plants other than spices can be aromatic and of vegetable origin, such as herbs. With that said, the rest of the definition is helpful. It should be added that, whereas herbs are fresh or dried leaves, spices are the dried versions of the other parts of plants: roots, rhizomes, bark, flowers, fruits, and seeds.

Access to spices was often connected to conquest. In chapter 2 I mentioned the role of Alexander the Great on changing the culinary tastes

Roman Spice Ship on way from Egypt to India. *Heather Rose*

not only of the Greeks but also eventually of Romans and the rest of the empire. The ancient Greek diet was known for simple, straightforward food. The fishermen along the coastline ate grilled and boiled fish, and shepherds who kept herds of goats and sheep ate meat and cheese. Farmers raised olives and grapes. Barley was used for *puls*, porridge, and cakes. Everyone ate vegetables, fruits, and legumes. Hard wheat, which is best for bread, did not grow well in Greece, so it was imported from Africa. These foods formed the foundation of the ancient diet—that is, until Alexander the Great.

Alexander was from Macedonia, north of Greece. Born in 356 BCE, he was one of Aristotle's students. He ascended to the throne of Macedon at the death of his father, Philip II, in 336. He first unified Macedonians with the various city-states of Greece, and then, within two years, he committed to wage war on Persia, traditional enemies of the Greek people. In the year 333 BCE, he conquered the western portion of the Persian Empire, Syria, and then the Egyptian Empire in 331. In the process, he and his armies encountered two very different and complex culinary traditions. Both the Persians and the Egyptians had access to fruits and foods that were little known to the Greek people. Foods, especially those served at banquets, were heavily flavored with spices from India and sauces. Tables at these meals were covered with expensive fabrics and featured appointments of glittering gold and silver. The guests were given expensive perfumes at the occasion of a feast, and everything smelled of exotic incense. It was said that the royal ovens were large enough to roast whole camels.[5]

Alexander's conquests did not stop with Egypt and western Persia. His armies continued to move through the rest of the Persian Empire and into northwest India. There he and his men became acquainted with even more spices and an altogether different cuisine. Eventually they withdrew from India, taking their newfound knowledge of spices and foods with them. The Macedonians and Greeks remained in control of Persia, Egypt, and the Middle East for several centuries. The overland trade routes from India to Persia and the water route from India to Egypt were expanded to the Mediterranean Sea and to Greece.

As one might imagine, the impact of the cuisines on Greek food was significant. Seeds and cuttings for new fruit trees and vegetables were brought back to Greece to be added to the gardens and orchards of farmers. New trade routes brought spices. No longer were the meals considered simple and wholesome but gradually took on a complexity with new flavorings and a very different vision of banqueting. Over time, the culinary landscape of the country changed considerably.

Eventually the Romans conquered Greece and much of Alexander's kingdom. The wars with the Greeks were said to be vicious and the victors not always generous with those they defeated. But the Romans did not destroy the culture of the conquered Greeks, instead adopting much of it completely. That was certainly true of the culinary culture. The Roman diet had been quite similar to the earlier Greek one, with a simple emphasis on fruits, vegetables, grains, and occasionally fish from the sea and meat from the flock. But just as the Persians, Egyptians, and the people of the kingdoms of northern India introduced the Greeks to a much more sophisticated diet, so the Greeks did for the Romans. By that time, the Greek cuisine, especially that of the rich, and the *triclinium* of the banquet were an exotic hybrid of Mediterranean simplicity and Eastern exotic complexity. High-ranking soldiers and politicians brought this new type of cuisine to Rome with them. Greek cooks and chefs, especially from Athens, became as sought-after a commodity as servants and slaves.

Such was not always the case. It might have been a similar story in Carthage. After a series of wars, the Romans conquered the kingdom and great city in 147 BCE. Carthage was leveled. Centuries of the ancient culture were destroyed, along with its highly developed cuisine. As one scholar wrote, "The Romans had not come to Africa to exchange recipes but to rob and plunder mercilessly."[6] In exchange for terminating a culture, they gained control of the Carthaginian lands of present-day Algeria, Tunisia, and Libya, thereafter referred to as Africa, and the Carthaginian colonies in Spain, Sicily, and Corsica. One can only wonder what Roman cuisine would have been with the overlay of the Carthaginian food culture.

Spice Trade

For millennia, spices were used and traded. In the third millennium BCE, the Syrian civilization of Mari recorded using cumin and coriander seed to flavor beer. The Greeks used spices such as cumin, sesame, coriander, and saffron to enliven their food. But these were local spices in a sense, ones that were available or obtained through trade around the Mediterranean Basin. Alexander the Great's conquest fomented change. The ancient trade routes became safer and were extended to the west. For example, the Silk Road, a route from China to India and then Afghanistan, was opened to the Mediterranean Sea. Cargoes were loaded onto ships in cities such as Antioch that lay along the eastern shore of the Mediterranean and transported to Mediterranean countries and city-states. The Silk Road made the cities along the route rich from trade and taxes. As municipalities became financially powerful, an emphasis was placed on elements of culture, including architecture, the arts, learning and the fertile exchange of ideas, and gastronomy.

A second ancient route was used to bring incense, sap from trees dried into a hard resin, to the eastern shore of the Mediterranean. Frankincense and myrrh were harvested and processed in the area of the southern end of the Arabian Peninsula, the modern countries of Yemen and Oman. The resins were used as incense in religious ceremonies and in homes at special occasions; to make perfumes; as part of burial rituals; and for embalming. The Incense Route went overland by camel across the Arabian Peninsula to the Mediterranean. Nabataean merchants acted as "middlemen" in the trade of the incense resins to the Mediterranean. They did not actually become involved in the transport, but their capital city of Petra provisioned the caravans, watered the camels, and taxed the goods. The trek took sixty-two days to complete. It is estimated that, by the beginning of the first century CE, the annual export of frankincense stood at approximately 1,675 tons and required 11,000 camels.[7] The Incense Route remained a major trade route for centuries until it was replaced in the first century CE by sea routes, over which Roman traders in ships took delivery of frankincense and myrrh on their return trip from India to the Red Sea.

The Romans did not create the sea routes that brought back spices from India. These existed long before the first century CE. The Egyptians, controlled by the Macedonian Ptolemies, explored the Red Sea along the African coast to Ethiopia and along the Arabian Peninsula. They were not alone. These waters were sailed by Egyptians, Ethiopians, Phoenicians, Arabs, and most likely sailors from India. All were involved in trade. Spices such as pepper, cloves, cinnamon, and nutmeg that finally arrived into the Mediterranean Basin first were controlled by north African and Arab middlemen. That is why Pliny still believed that cinnamon was a product of Ethiopia. It is also why the cost of spices was so exorbitantly high. With a reference to the high cost, Antiphanes wrote in the fourth century BCE, "If a man should bring home some pepper he's bought, they would propose a motion that he be tortured as a spy," alluding to the reality that a common person with the money to buy pepper must have received the funds through illegal means.[8]

"The Romans were not the first Europeans to eat pepper, but they were the first to do so with any regularity."[9] Once the Romans conquered Egypt, they usurped the maritime Spice Route. In doing so, the flow of spices into the Mediterranean and especially to Rome increased significantly, especially with larger ships and knowledge they gained concerning the nature of the sea routes. A sailor, Hippalos, was the first to determine that the journey from the top of the Red Sea to India was shortened considerably by understanding the monsoon winds. Great ships with capacity for both rowing and sailing held up to five hundred tons of cargo. Compared to ships before that time, they were immense, "behemoths of ancient navigation . . . a small universe in [themselves] . . . equivalent to several ships of other nations."[10] Each boat also traveled with soldiers on board to battle pirates if necessary.

The ships began their journey from one of several ports along the Egyptian coast. Some of them took a route along the African coast, stopping at ports to trade for incense, ivory, ebony, skins, slaves, exotic animals, and gold. Those going to India turned north at what was called the Cape of Spices, at Africa's easternmost point, where modern-day Somalia seems to reach for the southernmost stretch of the Arabian Peninsula. The ships then turned east toward into the Arabian Sea and India.

By careful observation and experience sailing on trading vessels, Hippalos realized that the monsoon winds followed an annual pattern. During the summer, the prevailing winds came from the southwest, hard, wet, and occasionally quite furious. By late August, the winds began to diminish and all but died during September. From November to March, the prevailing winds completely changed direction, becoming dry and predictable from the northeast. At least 120 to 200 spice ships left during the early summer for India, arriving to the Cape of Spices some twenty to forty days later.

Nineteen ports of call lined the western coast of India, all of them destinations for trade. Pepper and other spices were the primary commodity, though silks from China, valuable gemstones, and animals—including parrots, tigers, and even elephants that were used in Rome's arena—were also transported. Romans traded manufactured goods such as glassware, works of art, metalwork, Mediterranean coral (much loved in India for magical properties), Mediterranean wines, gold, and silver. One can be assured that glassware, wine, and coral did not pay for many tons of pepper. Gold was the principal element of exchange, causing a significant trade deficit. Archaeologists continue to find large numbers of gold and silver Roman coins along the western coast of India. For centuries, Rome discharged its trade deficit through taxes, tributes, and booty from newly conquered lands.

After loading their ships, sailors and soldiers waited until the wind changed direction. Some ships might stop along the southern shore of the Arabian coast to obtain frankincense and myrrh from Yemen and Oman.

Once through the Cape of Spices, the ships retraced their route to one of the port cities along the Egyptian coast. The cargo was offloaded onto camels, and the caravans crossed the desert to the Nile River. The shipments were removed and packed onto barges to float downriver to Alexandria. From there they were shipped to Rome or one of several major trading cities on the Mediterranean. All in all, the pepper and other valuable goods were transported some five thousand miles from India to Rome.

Three Spices of Influence

The influence of a more complex cuisine with a strong emphasis on spices had great significance but did not convert all Romans. First, changes in food culture had little impact on the plebeians and common laborers. Their diet stayed the same. Some of the more successful tradesmen might have access to pepper, at least on occasion. But the financial ability to purchase ginger or saffron, unless given as a gift from a patron, remained out of reach. A few patricians both before and during the first century regretted the loss of the simple diet that fed Rome on its path to conquering most of the known world. But the vast majority of wealthy Romans readily accepted the new culinary culture with its heavy use of spices.

This is an example from a play by Plautus (254–184 BCE) describing how a "fashion-conscious cook" preferred spices to herbs:

> *Cook*: I tend to flavor my meals very differently from other cooks. Others put herbs on my plate. They give weeds to their guests, as though they were cattle. And they flavor their weeds with other weeds. They put coriander, fennel, garlic, and parsley on sorrel, cabbage, beet and orache.[11] Then they cover it with half a pound of laser [silphium]. They grind common mustard that makes the grinder's eyes water before he's finished grinding. When these lads do their cooking, they don't spice their food with seasonings. . . .[12]

Not everyone agreed with our fictional cook. In his writings and in practice, the statesman and farmer Cato the Elder resisted changes to the simple culinary practices of the past and verbally disparaged the innovative and luxurious cuisine of the Greeks. Eventually laws were put in place, sumptuary laws, that supposedly limited the amount a family could spend on luxury foods, even for weddings and other major feasts. At the time of Emperors Augustus and Tiberius, an extravagant banquet or food for a feast day would cost the same as the price of a slave (2,000 sestertius or "HS"), about the same price as a car today. And that was the top amount allowed by the sumptuary law. But these regulations were rarely followed by even the most law-abiding Roman citizens. With tongue in cheek, Athenaeus in his play *The Deipnosophists, or Banquet of the Learned,* named three men out of many thousands that actually observed the law strictly.[13]

PEPPER, THE KING OF SPICES

Instead of surveying all the spices available to the empire, I will concentrate on just three very influential ones: pepper, cinnamon, and silphium.

Pepper undoubtedly was the king of spices. Other than salt, it was and still is the most-used flavoring in the world, both for cooking and as a condiment on many tables. Unlike other spices, when introduced to the West, pepper experienced immediate acceptance and changed the culinary landscape. It originated in India, and by the first century was heavily imported to the Mediterranean Basin.

Pepper, or *piper nigrum,* is a tropical climbing vine, a parasite in the forests of India. When cultivated, it was done so alongside plantation trees, especially betel, palm, and mango. The trees gave the stems of the pepper plant the support needed to grow and climb. The seeds were harvested after turning red, when they were not quite completely ripe. They were left in large piles on the ground for several days and allowed to slightly ferment in the sun. Then they were spread and left to dry, still in the sun. The skin became black and developed wrinkles on the surface.

White pepper simply is black pepper that is left on the plant longer before harvest. The seeds are soaked until the outer skin is easily removed. Ironically, even though the cost was almost twice that of black pepper, white pepper is less aromatic and has weaker pungency and flavor. Green peppercorns are simply unripe seeds that are preserved by drying or bottling in vinegar or brine.

Misunderstandings about the nature of how pepper was grown and harvested existed because of the great distance between India and Rome. It was believed by Pliny the Elder that the pepper plant resembled the juniper plant and that the fruit developed in small pods, much like beans. At the same time, Pliny debunked a common myth that ginger root came from the pepper tree.

Pliny was not fond either of the taste of pepper or of the empire's attraction to the small, spicy seeds:

It is remarkable that the use of pepper has come so much into favour, as in the case of some commodities their sweet taste has been an attraction, and in others their appearance, but pepper has nothing to recommend it in either fruit or berry. To think that its only pleasing quality is pungency and that we go all the way to India to get this! Who was the first person who was willing to try it on his viands or in his greed for an appetite what not content merely to be hungry? Both pepper and ginger grow wild in their own countries and nevertheless they are bought by weight like gold or silver.[14]

Pliny remarks that the Romans spent at least 100 million HS per year on imports, including silks and resins for incense, but primarily on spices.[15]

A different variety, the long pepper, was also much loved in the Roman Empire. Grown in India, it has a spike approximately two and one-half inches long that is covered with seeds about the size of poppy seeds. The long pepper has a hotter and sharper flavor with a bit of sweetness.[16] Yet eventually it was not imported as often because it held more moisture and was inclined to mold. By the seventeenth century, long peppers were replaced by chili peppers from the Americas that were easier to grow in the warmer European countries and could be dried. Long peppers are still much used in Asian countries.

Black pepper with its strong flavor continued to be the most popular of the varieties that were available. Its popularity was reflected in its cost. In his *Natural History*, Pliny writes that one pound of black pepper cost four denarii. White pepper sold for almost twice as much, at seven denarii. Long pepper was priced at almost four times as much as black, fifteen denarii.[17] One denarius was equivalent to a day's wage for a laborer. Considering an eight-hour day and a minimum wage averaging $9 per hour, a denarius was worth approximately $72. In contemporary US dollars, one pound of black pepper was valued at $288, a pound of long peppers at $1,080.

Because of pepper's popularity, counterfeit pepper was sold to the Roman Empire. Pliny writes that both Alexandrian mustard seed and juniper berries were sold as pepper. When stored with pepper, juniper berries reportedly absorb some of its spicy pungency.

Pepper was mentioned first in Greek literature around 400 BCE by playwrights Antiphanes, Eubulus, and Alexis, and it found its way into a Hippocratic text. The closest thing to a first recipe we have is a mention by Diphilus of Siphnos in the third century BCE. He recommended pepper with scallops.[18] By the first century CE, pepper was used in most dishes, that is, by those who could afford it. It seemed to matter not if the recipe was for savory or sweet foods. *Apicius* called for it in no less than 452 recipes. One can only wonder how often its use was simply implied. If a family could afford pepper, they used it liberally. As such, pepper became a symbol of power and virility, in part because of its powerful and aggressive flavor, but also because of its cost. The wealthy and powerful were the ones most likely to be able to afford it.

In many cases, pepper was used in addition to other spices and herbs and provided heat to the blended flavor. Cooks utilized a mortar and pestle to grind pepper and other small seeds. Salt and then the larger ingredients such as chopped herbs were added to the mortar as well. Moisture in the form of olive oil, wine, *garum*, or *defrutum* added flavor and assisted in crushing the mixture.

CINNAMON, SPICE OF MYSTERY

The producers of cinnamon went to great lengths to protect both its origin and its means of cultivation through deception and myth. *Cinnamomum verum* is a tree indigenous to Sri Lanka. Both the inner bark of the tree and the oil from the bark were used as a spice.

Those who cultivated cinnamon gave great attention to the root stock of the trees because the best flavor came from the straight shoots that grew from the roots. The shoots were allowed to grow to a height of between five and six feet before they were cut. The outer bark was then removed and the inner bark loosened with metal rods. The next step involved making an incision around the bark and then down its length to strip the bark from the wood. At this stage the prepared cinnamon bark was allowed to dry. Later the inner bark was trimmed and cut into shorter lengths to prepare for selling.

There was often confusion between cinnamon and cassia bark because of similarity in appearance and flavor, though cinnamon is a superior product. Most countries today require that the products are clearly labeled as to whether they are cinnamon or cassia, though not the United States. The term *cinnamon* legally can and is applied to both cinnamon and cassia. Ground cinnamon most likely is a mixture of the two.

Ancient Greeks and Romans had the same issues. Arab traders were reticent to admit which product they were selling or its place of origin. In fact, purveyors of cinnamon purposely shrouded their product in mystery, if for no other reason than to drive up the cost. One story told that the nests of the mythical phoenix were made of cinnamon and that the birds were extremely dangerous to approach. Those who were harvesting waited at the base of the mountains where the birds were located, hoping some of the cinnamon might fall when the phoenix dropped its prey, which would be a large animal such as a pig or cow, into the nest.[19] Another story, told by Greek writer Theophrastus, was that the cinnamon trees grew in valleys made dangerous by the presence of deadly snakes. Workers protected their hands and feet when harvesting the valuable bark in the valley. Once they had safely extracted the wood from the valley, they divided it into three portions, one left behind for the sun. The harvesters saw the sun's portion immediately burst into flames as they prepared to leave. Theophrastus explained that the story was a fantasy used to increase the cost of the product.

A third and similar story told that cinnamon came from Ethiopia and was dedicated to Jupiter, the sun god. The cinnamon bark was not to be harvested without agreement with the god, requiring the sacrifice of "forty-four oxen, goats and rams," all of which increased the price.[20] The cinnamon was then divided equally between the traders and the god. Even the location of cassia was hidden in mystery. The story was that cassia grew in the middle of swamps protected by winged serpents and bats with claws.[21] No wonder the price of cinnamon fluctuated greatly, selling for as much as 1,000 denarii.

Pliny the Elder, first-century natural scientist that he was, refused to believe the fanciful stories surrounding cinnamon, but he misunderstood where it was grown. Pliny and others assumed that, because the spice arrived either overland on spice routes through Arabia or over the Red Sea after a sea journey from India, the origin of cinnamon must be Ethiopia:

> Inasmuch as *cinnamomum*, which is the same thing as cinnamon, grows in Ethiopia, which linked by intermarriage with the Cave-dwellers. The latter buy it from their neighbors and convey it over the wide seas in ships that are neither steered by rudders nor propelled by oars or drawn by sails, nor assisted by any device of art.[22]

Most cinnamon was used for incense and perfume. Even though other food cultures both within and to the east of the Roman Empire heavily seasoned their foods with it, the Romans only occasionally used cinnamon for desserts and for savory stews and did not make great culinary use of it for several hundred years. It was an important ingredient in *mulsum*, a sweet wine flavored primarily with cinnamon and sometimes with other spices. *Mulsum* was consumed as an aperitif, a pre-dinner drink intended to stimulate the appetite. The taste is very similar to mulled wine.

SILPHIUM, THE SPICE THAT IS NO MORE

If the description of cinnamon was filled with mystery and legend, the story of silphium ended tragically. Silphium was an extremely popular spice in ancient Greece and in Rome. The plant, belonging to the fennel family, came from Libya in the region around Cyrene. The Roman name for silphium was *laserpicium* or *laser*. When cut, the roots and stem produced a resin with a strong and desirable flavor. The stem was also reportedly delicious, but it was eaten locally and not exported. The tragedy was that the harvest practices and high usage of such a popular spice caused it to become extinct between 50 and 70 CE.

Ancient writers compared the harvesting of silphium with mining concessions. Harvesters cut a ration based on what had already been gathered and what remained. The gatherers were not allowed to cut at random or to harvest more than their concession allowed because of rapid spoilage. The resin from the stem tended to have a watery consistency, so it was mixed with a small amount of flour in a jar in order to stabilize it. The Libyan harvesters were contracted to sell all their product to the Greek-speaking kingdom of Cyrene, which brought the kingdom great wealth. An ancient painting on a Greek vase shows Battus, the king of Cyrene, supervising the preparation of silphium for export. Another sign of appreciation for the product that made them rich was the imprint of the image of the silphium plant on coins that remained in use for hundreds of years.

Both the nature of the plant and the very system of harvest and trade helped bring about its demise. The plant was never cultivated. Ancient writers tell us that it did not respond well to such attempts. In addition, the spread of other crops into areas where silphium grew caused it to die out. But the plant and its resin were worth their weight in silver, which also led to its extinction. Instead of selling to Cyrene as required, some harvesters and traders discovered they received better prices by smuggling the spice to Carthage. At the same time, the wealthy in Rome discovered silphium and used it in record amounts without considering its future.

An effort was made to find a replacement spice as harvesters and traders began to realize they had shrinking supplies. A plant with a similar resin was found in Iran, and it was named *Median silphium*, now called *asafetida*. The taste was not quite the same, supposedly harsher and with a flavor more like fermented garlic. It is still used today, primarily when preparing Middle Eastern and Indian cuisines. It is available in Mediterranean and Middle Eastern markets or online. Asafetida is frequently found in powder form, but it can also be purchased as a resin rock or in liquid form.

As access to the spice decreased, efforts were made to use smaller amounts. Silphium had a strong flavor, and only a small amount was necessary. The cost was so extravagant that even the wealthy Apicius recommended the cost-effective alternative of placing a silphium resin rock in a glass jar with fifty or so pine nuts and then sealed, infusing the nuts with the flavor. Cooks could then use a few of the pine nuts. Supposedly the last true silphium stem to be found was sent to the emperor Nero for his culinary enjoyment.

First-century cooks applied silphium to a wide variety of dishes. It was frequently an ingredient in sauces, rubbed into meats and poultry, added to vegetables (especially root vegetables), and even used with delicate foods such as fish and shellfish. Ingredient amounts are not often included with ancient recipes, but cooks most likely only added a pinch, and even that had already been diluted by mixing it with bean or wheat flour.

SILPHIUM: THE REST OF THE STORY

On September 23, 2022, *National Geographic* published an article describing the discovery of a small patch of what is believed to be silphium in the foothills of Mount Hasan in what is the Cappadocian region of Turkey.[23] In 1983, Professor Mahmut Miski from Istanbul University was led to the patch by two young boys. Miski continued to study the plants, and after almost thirty years of study, Miski began to suspect that the plants were actually silphium, the valuable spice from antiquity. As with the ancient plant, the root, stalk, and resin contain a large number of medicinal compounds, some with cancer-fighting, contraceptive, and anti-inflammatory properties. In addition, ancient descriptions of the plant were consistent with the ones found by Miski. Ancient Greeks and Romans were unable to transplant the plants or grow them from seed. Miski and Istanbul's Nezahat Gokyigit Botanical Garden also found it hard to grow and finally used cold temperatures and a large amount of water to germinate seeds in a greenhouse. The plants in the field sprouted and grew up to six feet when snowmelt from Mount Hasan and heavy, cool spring rains watered the plants. Somehow seeds from the plant migrated from Cyrene in Libya, North Africa, to Cappadocia in Turkey. Both were Greek colonies. Perhaps seeds were dropped or purposefully planted after plants were shipped from one colony to another.

Since archaeologists have not discovered a sealed jar marked *silphion*, scientists and culinary historians are unsure if these are the well-loved plants from the past. Miski decided the next best approach was to use what he found to prepare ancient dishes. Sally Grainger, who worked as the head pastry chef at London's Atheneum Hotel and earned a degree in ancient history, traveled to Turkey to test the spice. She is a coeditor of an English translation of Apicius's first-century cookbook. Like many of us who enjoy preparing ancient dishes, she always used asafetida when the recipe called for silphium: "Finding the original silphium, and experiencing ancient recipes afresh with it, is a kind of the Holy Grail."[24]

She prepared a half dozen dishes from *Apicius* with both silphium and then with asafetida. The gathering of botanists and culinary experts was amazed at the difference. The food with silphium as an ingredient or as part of a sauce was described as complex, rich, and delicious, with an intense and delightful smell. Unfortunately, there are only six hundred plants known to be in existence, three hundred of which are in greenhouses.

THE FEAST IN ANTIOCH

For this meal, it will be interesting to separate your community into two groups. I recommend that half of the guests play the role of Jewish Christians and eat a kosher meal and the other half eat a Gentile meal. Have the groups eat either in separate rooms or on opposite sides of the same room. After the meal, come together and discuss the food and the experience of the rift between the two groups. You may choose to use the meal liturgy in chapter 13, but to enhance the split, have each group give thanks and pray on its own.

Kosher Feast Menu

> Boletus Bread
> Olive Oil and Pepper
> Chicken, Mushroom, and Date Stew
> Asparagus with Eggs Cooked in Red Wine
> Salad Platter from chapter 3

Gentile Feast Menu

> Boletus Bread
> Olive Oil and Pepper
> Athenian Pork and Cabbage

Asparagus with Eggs Cooked in Red Wine
Sausage Links and Pine Nut Sauce
Salad Platter from chapter 3

Symposium

Poached Pears
Mix of Nuts, from the market
Halloumi Cheese, from the market
Fresh Seasonal Fruit, Figs if they are in season, from the market

RECIPES

Boletus Bread

Boletus is Latin for mushroom. This bread was baked in a tube so the dough rising over the top made the loaf look like a mushroom. It was covered with poppy seeds. The insert for a first-generation bread machine might work well to replicate this effect. As an alternative, you may use standard bread pans. The recipe calls for a mixer. You may knead the bread without the help of your KitchenAid, especially if you are an experienced baker.

- 1 cup plus 1½–1¾ tbs. warm water (approx. 110 degrees), mixed use
- 1 tbs. quick-rising yeast
- 5 cups white unbleached flour
- 1½ cups whole wheat flour

- 1 tbs. salt
- 3 tbs. olive oil
- 1 tbs. honey
- 3 tbs. poppy seeds, divided use
- 1 egg, whipped with a fork

If using a mixer with a dough hook: combine yeast with 1 cup of 110-degree water in the mixer bowl. Leave until yeast begins to activate. Add the flours and the rest of the water, salt, olive oil, honey, and 1 tablespoon poppy seeds. Mix for 5 minutes; let rest for 15 minutes; mix for another 5 minutes. The dough should be slightly wet. If the dough is too damp, add flour 1 tablespoon at a time. If too dry, add water 1 tablespoon at a time.

Use a plastic bench scraper or large spatula and scrape dough onto a floured surface. Briefly knead and place in an oiled bowl. Cover with a kitchen towel (not terry cloth) or plastic wrap and let rise until doubled, approximately 60 to 90 minutes, depending on the temperature of your kitchen.

Punch down the risen dough and turn out onto the floured board. Knead briefly and divide into two loaves. Rub the bread pans with oil or butter and cover with 1 tablespoon poppy seeds. Place the loaves in bread pans.

Preheat oven to 400 degrees.

Cover the loaves and let rise another hour. Using a kitchen brush, spread half of the egg on top of the loaf and cover with the remaining poppy seeds. Slide the loaves, one at a time, into the preheated oven.

Cook for 30–35 minutes or until nicely browned. Remove the loaves from the oven and release to cool on a rack for at least 2 hours.

Chicken, Mushroom, and Date Stew

I love dates and they pair well with chicken.

- 2 lbs. boneless chicken thighs or breasts, cut into bite-sized pieces
- 3 tbs. flour
- 1 lb. baby portabella mushrooms, cleaned and sliced
- 12 dates, pit removed, cut into small pieces with kitchen scissors
- 1 tbs. olive oil and extra to garnish

- 4 cups of chicken stock
- 1 tsp. ground cumin
- 2 tsp. ground coriander seed
- 1 tsp. dry, ground mustard seed
- 1 tsp. dried mint
- 1 tsp. lovage or celery leaves
- 2 bay leaves
- ½ tsp. asafetida (optional)
- 1 tsp. each salt and pepper

Prepare the chicken, mushrooms, and dates. Place the flour in a bowl and mix in the chicken until all pieces are covered with flour. Pour olive oil into a hot Dutch oven. Brown chicken, add mushrooms, and continue to sauté. Add chicken stock and bring to a boil. Add the dates. Meanwhile, mix together the spices and herbs. If using whole seeds, grind them with a mortar and pestle or spice grinder. Keep the bay leaves whole. Add spices and herbs to the chicken. Reduce heat to a simmer. Adjust as needed.

Cook until thickened. Season and serve.

Athenian Pork and Cabbage

Cabbage and pork make a nice pairing. This recipe includes asafetida, an exotic spice.

- 1 lb. pork stew meat
- 2 tbs. olive oil
- 1 leek, white and light green section
- 1 cup chicken stock or water
- ½ head of cabbage, sliced thin and then chopped
- 2 tbs. dried coriander leaf

- 1 tbs. dried rue (optional)
- ½ tsp. asafetida (optional)
- 1 tsp. salt
- ½ tsp. pepper
- 2 tbs. honey
- 2 tbs. red wine vinegar
- 2 tbs. water
- 1 tbs. chopped, fresh cilantro

Lightly brown the stew meat in olive oil. Add the leek and cook until translucent, then add the stock. Bring to a simmer and add the cabbage, coriander, rue, asafetida, salt, and pepper. Cover and cook until the meat is tender and the cabbage is wilted.

While cooking, mix the honey, vinegar, and water. Uncover and stir in the honey mixture. Add the fresh cilantro immediately before serving.

Asparagus with Eggs Cooked in Red Wine (Galen)

Galen was a second-century-CE doctor, surgeon, and philosopher. As with many other ancient doctors, he also wrote about food. Prepare the asparagus by bending it until it breaks off the tough end. Save the tough ends; they can be used for soup.

- 1 egg per person
- 1 lb. asparagus, prepared and then cut into 2-inch pieces
- 2 tbs. olive oil, mixed use

- 2 tsp. thyme
- ½ tsp. salt
- 1½ tsp. pepper

For 4 to 6 eggs

- ¼ cup red wine
- A pinch of salt per egg
- ¼ tsp. pepper per egg

- Additional olive oil to drizzle over finished dish

Remove eggs from the refrigerator and leave on the counter. Heat a pot and pour in ½ cup of water. When the water boils, add the asparagus. Cover and turn off the heat. Let the asparagus sit until it is crisp-tender. Drain the water. Heat the pot again and add 1 tablespoon of olive oil. Add the asparagus and briefly sauté in the hot oil. Add the thyme, salt, and pepper. Remove the heat and cover to keep warm.

For the eggs, use a large nonstick skillet with a lid. Heat the skillet, but not too hot. Add the remaining oil. Then crack the eggs, careful not to break the yolk, and place in the skillet. Once the eggs begin to set, pour in the wine and cover with the lid. Allow the eggs to steam but do not cook too long. After several minutes, remove the lid and see if the eggs have finished cooking. If not, place the cover back on the skillet and continue to cook. When finished, the whites of the eggs should be solid and the yolks still runny. Add the salt and pepper. For each serving, plate some of the asparagus and carefully place the egg on top. Drizzle olive oil over the finished dish. The yolk makes the sauce.

Sausage Links and Pine Nut Sauce

- 4 sausages, make or buy Italian sausage in casings
- Water or wine to cover

Boil sausages in water or wine for 20 minutes. Remove from the liquid; cut into quarters and finish cooking by sautéing or grilling until sausages are cooked through and lightly charred on the outside. Use the pine nut sauce, from the eggs and pine nut sauce recipe in chapter 8, as a dip for the sausage.

Poached Pears

You can garnish the pears with chopped, lightly roasted almonds or with sprigs of mint leaves or with both.

- 3 pears
- ½ bottle red wine
- 1 cinnamon stick
- 20 peppercorns
- ⅓ cup heavy cream

Cut the pears in half and use a melon ball scooper to remove seeds and core. Bring the wine, cinnamon stick, and peppercorns to a simmer. Add the pears and poach until soft. Remove the pears and carefully remove the skins. Return the skins to the poaching liquid and bring to a boil. Cook until the wine mixture has the consistency of syrup. Strain and allow the sauce to cool to room temperature.

Serve the pear halves with the syrup and top each pear half with some of the thick cream (without the cream for the kosher version).

8

BANQUET WITH THE
GODS IN EPHESUS

While researching material for this book, I befriended a man named Paulo who moved to the United States from Brazil. After several conversations, we began talking about the various issues the Apostle Paul faced with food and dining in his fledgling congregations. Paulo had a very good working knowledge of the New Testament, and our discussions, though often brief, were spirited and thoughtful. One day I raised the question, "In this day and time, who has to worry about food, especially meat, which was first sacrificed to a god or goddess?" (See, for example, Acts 15:19–21; 1 Corinthians 8:1–13.) It appeared to me that issues such as whether the food was first offered to a god are obsolete problems. "Not so," replied my friend. "It is a real concern in Brazil. There are many practitioners of voodoo, people who take it quite seriously." For Paulo and others in his native land, the questions with which Paul and his young congregation grappled are quite real: What if the food in the market, the dinner at someone's house, or the meat ordered at a restaurant was first part of a voodoo ritual?

Those of us who live in the United States might commonly consider other issues related to our meat. For example, was the animal genetically modified? Was it grass-fed or corn-fed? Was it given steroids or antibiotics? We might wonder if biblical texts regarding food might instead teach us lessons that can be applied to other topics. Perhaps issues of meat and other foods should be dropped from serious New Testament study. Then the question, does it matter? Paulo would answer, "Yes." Pagan religions most certainly raised issues for the young Christian communities, especially regarding food and food culture. The issues of food and culture may raise different questions that deserve our study.

Temple of Artemis in Ephesus. *Heather Rose*

EPHESUS AND THE TEMPLE OF ARTEMIS

Because of its location on the Cayster River and its good harbor, Ephesus was an important city for commerce, religion, and governance. As such, Ephesus became the most important city in Asia, also called Asia Minor, the area now known as western Turkey. With both a harbor and crossroads for north-south trade routes, it was ideally situated for trade. By the first century, Ephesus had a population of approximately 250,000.[1]

Asia had several reputations. First, it was known as a land of pleasure made possible by wealth. Because of this, its people, especially its men, were considered soft, even though they had a history of producing fierce warriors. From Sallust in *Catiline*:

> That lovely country and its pleasures soon softened the soldiers' warlike spirits. This was where Roman soldiers first learnt to make love, to be drunk, to enjoy statues and pictures and embossed plate.[2]

A somewhat more complete picture emerges from Cicero: "The income from other provinces is scarcely enough to make it worth our while to defend them, but Asia is so wealthy, so fertile that in the richness of its harvest, the variety of its produce, the size of its herds and flocks and the quantity of its exports, it exceeds every other country."³ Several beautiful rivers from the mountains formed harbors and bays along the Mediterranean. The cities of Asia, such as Pergamum, Miletus, and Ephesus were built around these rivers and harbors.

The history of Ephesus reveals a strong Hellenistic background. The Greeks drove out the original residents, Anatolians, and colonized the location. For the next thousand years, the city often changed hands: to Lydia, then Persia, and then back to the Greeks. Ephesus sided with Sparta, a Greek city-state, against Athens, only to be given back to the Persians. After only fifty-four years as a Persian city, it once again became a Greek colony, this time conquered by Alexander the Great in the year 334 BCE. Ephesus was restructured and received an influx of new citizens, some of them Greek settlers and others from around the Mediterranean Basin. The rebuilding of a temple for Artemis was a priority.

Eventually the Romans conquered all of Asia, but in a rather puzzling decision, Rome bestowed the Asian cities to the king of Pergamum, a port city to the north of Ephesus. When the last of the line of the kings of Pergamum died, he bequeathed his kingdom, including Ephesus, back to Rome.

An ancient Greek myth described how Amazons, a tribe of women warriors, founded the city of Ephesus. From them came the worship of Artemis, the goddess of the hunt. More believable is the account that the Anatolians who lived in western Turkey before the Greeks worshiped a fertility goddess. That goddess later was called Artemis by the Greeks and Diana by the Romans. The mythology of Artemis describes her as the goddess of the hunt, a fierce warrior. But more significant for Ephesus, she was also the goddess of fertility, yet ironically a virgin. The most sacred of the statues displays the goddess with many animals and plants surrounding her feet. In addition, there are twenty-four round objects on the goddess's chest. Traditionally, scholars believed the orbs were multiple breasts symbolizing fertility. More recently, some experts believe them to be ostrich eggs, also signifying fertility, and still found today in many Greek churches. They might also be fruit, yet another fertility symbol.⁴

The followers of Artemis were zealous evangelists for their goddess. They believed that she acted as a savior and had the ability to control cosmic powers. From time to time, her followers took the main statue from the temple and traveled around the Mediterranean Basin using it as a tool for evangelism, showing the image and extolling the virtue of their goddess. The result was that a sizable number of her followers lived outside of Ephesus.

It is a well-known tradition from the second century CE that John the apostle was connected to Ephesus. A local Turkish town named Ayasoluk is derived from the Greek *Agios Theologos* (holy theologian), a name given to John by the Eastern Church. One variant of this tradition is that he came to Ephesus with Mary, the mother of Jesus. Another was that he died and was buried there.

The beauty of the city impressed its visitors. The Temple of Artemis was resplendent. It was larger than the Parthenon and apparently much more ornately decorated. "In comparison with the Parthenon of Athens, the temple was bigger broader, taller, and more elaborately decorated with gilded, exaggerated detail."[5] Along with the temple, Ephesus had a large outdoor theater that provided marble seats for some twenty-five thousand people. The Book of Acts recounts the theater as being the place of conflict between Paul and the silversmith Demetrius. A large crowd gathered at the theater and began to chant, "Great is Artemis of the Ephesians" (Acts 19:23–31). The city had an important library, third only to the libraries in Alexandria and Tarsus. There was also a temple believed to be dedicated to the Egyptian god Serapis.

Ephesus thrived economically. The *polis* owned a very large amount of land, the *chora*, which surrounded the city. The land generated revenue for the city in many ways, one of which was grazing land for sheep. Ephesus and all of Asia was recognized for its herds and especially its wool, much of which was dyed and shipped to Rome. The lands around the city and north to Pergamum were also acknowledged for the wines they produced. The wines were good, though not quite to the standards of many of the best wines of the empire. Interestingly, they were made with seawater and had a salty taste. Ultimately, Miletus produced better wool and Pergamum the better wine, but Ephesus created money. Of all the cities in Asia, it was the financial center.

Not only was the temple beautiful, but it was also an important aspect of the economy. A very large and significant bank resided among its columns, a financial institution used by people from around the empire to receive loans and deposit money. The bank also received legacy gifts and private donations and generated revenue from property and other real estate investments. It also had money to assist the poor and those unable to pay debts.

Along with its bank, the temple helped the economy through tourism. As one of the Seven Wonders of the World, the temple was visited by large numbers of pilgrims, who also worshiped by making a sacrifice. Souvenirs such as reproductions of the goddess and the temple were made and sold by silversmiths in booths outside the temple proper. Archaeologists have found several of these workshops as part of the ongoing digs in the ancient Ephesus area. Paul's conflict that eventually caused him to leave the city began with one of these silversmiths. Interfering with tourism likely was his crime.

The feast day for Artemis was an imposing affair and centered on a grand procession. The large golden statue of the goddess covered with veils was taken from the temple along with many of the gifts that had been given over the centuries, "including, gold and silver and precious woods and silks, and jewels beyond imagination."[6] Young children in costume danced around the statue and ran between the columns lining the thoroughfare, the temple priests following the statue dressed in their most glorious vestments. Of course, there were feasts. The food for the wealthy must have been resplendent, but everyone enjoyed a festival meal.

One can only wonder what the Jewish and fledgling Christian communities felt about such occasions. Both the great temple and the feast surely overwhelmed the entire city. The golden statue was reminiscent of the golden gods of Hebrew Scripture, the image that the commandment warns against, "You shall not make for yourself an idol" (Exodus 20:4–6). But again, both diaspora Jews and the new Christians in Ephesus and other Greco-Roman cities certainly were accustomed to pagan temples and this type of festival day. Before conversion, the Gentile Christians most certainly participated.

The worship of Artemis was not the only religion in the city. As already mentioned, there was a community of diaspora Jews and the fledgling Christian community. There were also a number Greek and Roman gods and goddesses worshiped, including Zeus, Athena, Aphrodite, Apollo, Poseidon, and Dionysus. The Roman hero and imperial cults were well represented and important to the community because of both favor and monetary gifts from Rome. Many of the Egyptian gods were worshiped as well, especially Isis and Serapis. Perhaps this diversity inadvertently assisted the young Christian community. Cities with a larger number of religions tended to be more accepting of the variety and the introduction of new faiths. Along with those just briefly listed above, Ephesus also housed a number of Eastern and mystery religions, but none of them had very many members. In the eyes of the greater community, Paul's fledgling Christian Church initially fell into the same category, simply one new religion out of many.

It is interesting to note that, with only occasional conflict, the Jewish population in Ephesus was well accepted. This, on the other hand, caused issues for the newly founded church.

PAUL IN EPHESUS: GREAT SUCCESS
AND GREATER DESPAIR

The Book of Acts recounts how Paul accompanied his friends and coworkers Priscilla and Aquila to Ephesus. He only stayed a short time but was able to speak at the synagogue and even generate interest during his explanation that Jesus was the Messiah the Jews were expecting. The city so impressed him that he decided he must return. During his absence, a Christian evangelist named Apollos from Alexandria arrived and taught the young, small congregation. By all accounts, Apollos was an eloquent speaker and knowledgeable of the Hebrew Scriptures. Apparently, there were gaps in his understanding of the Christian Gospel and his baptism because Acts relates how Priscilla and Aquilla "took him aside and explained the Way to him more accurately" (Acts 18:26).

Paul did indeed return, most likely in 53 CE, and stayed somewhere between two and a half to three years. By that time Apollos had moved to Corinth. The Book of Acts tells the story of great successes mixed with some possibly expected failures. Paul taught at the synagogue for three months before some there began to vehemently disagree with his message and forced him to leave. He quickly replanted in a lecture hall, owned by one Tyrannus, where he ultimately taught and drew large crowds for two years. Visitors to Ephesus, of which there were many, often searched for novel experiences. Hearing a lecture describing a new religion, or at least a new take on an ancient religion, attracted at least some of these travelers. At the same time, Paul worked at his craft as a tent maker. As was the custom, his shop likely became an extension of his lectures in the hall. Customers, other tent makers, even traders and those in Ephesus for business would find Paul at his shop to listen to him speak and ask questions about the new religion.

The Book of Acts describes Paul's success with dramatic images. Not only did his lectures and teaching produce many converts, but we are told about miracles of healing where even clothes Paul touched had healing powers. Finally, representing the apex of his successes, his message reached many of the practitioners of some type of dark magic in Ephesus, who confessed their change of heart and burned books worth fifty thousand silver coins. This action alone brought much attention to Paul and his message.

Paul's relationship with the congregation he started in Corinth began disintegrating. The issues engulfing that community demanded his attention, first with a letter and then, at some point, a personal visit. The exact order of events that followed is a bit of a mystery. What we do know is that Paul's ministry in Ephesus also began to crumble. Acts tells the story of Demetrius, one of many silversmiths who made statues of Artemis and the temple. These statues were sold to pilgrims, many of whom took them home and worshiped them in household shrines. Apparently, as Paul's message became more successful, sales of statues dropped. The account continues with Demetrius fomenting a riot that ended with citizens filling the theater and chanting, "Great is Artemis of the Ephesians." Two of Paul's traveling companions were brought before the angry mob. A speaker from the Jewish community attempted to speak and explain the situation but was shouted down. Paul wanted to stand before the huge crowd and defend not only himself but also his message, but he was restrained by his followers. Finally, a city official quieted the enormous mob, sending them home, and recommending to Demetrius and his colleagues that filing a lawsuit was more appropriate. At this point, the Book of Acts becomes silent.

It is Paul who gave us hints of what followed and how the situation became much worse. Most likely he was arrested and sent to jail, at least for a time. If so, it was different from his other jail experiences where a reminder that he was a Roman citizen brought quick release. He described how the experience in Ephesus impacted him in his first and second letters to the church in Corinth. In the first letter, he wrote of struggle in his decision to stay in Ephesus until Pentecost, "for a wide door for effective work has opened to me, *and there are many adversaries.*" There might have been more ministry, but only after struggle: "I die every day! That is as certain, brothers and sisters, as my boasting to you—a boast that I make in Christ Jesus our Lord. *If with merely human hopes I fought with wild animals at Ephesus, what would I have gained by it?*" (1 Corinthians 16:8–9; 15:31–32a, emphases mine).

It appears that between the first and second letter to Corinth, Paul's situation deteriorated. The second letter speaks of deep despair, of being crushed almost to the point of death:

> We do not want you to be unaware, brothers and sisters, of the affliction we experienced in Asia; for we were so utterly, unbearably crushed that we despaired of life itself. Indeed, we felt that we had received the sentence of death so that we would not rely on ourselves but on God who raises the dead. He who rescued us from so deadly a peril will continue to rescue us. (2 Corinthians 1:8–10)

Some scholars believe that this experience was one of such despair that it might have been a second turning point in his life. Though not comparable to the road to Damascus, it still caused him to reevaluate his own faith and trust in God during times of crisis when solutions were not easy to see.

Somehow, he left Ephesus. The texts do not tell us how. He never returned. He bypassed his one opportunity to stop and visit the Christian community he helped form but instead sailed to nearby Miletus and asked the leaders from Ephesus to visit him there. He talked about his trials and tears in Ephesus. He declared that he was not responsible for the blood of any of them. He told them he would never see them again, and they prayed together with much weeping and grieving (Acts 20:15–24, 36–38).

THE FEAST OF SACRIFICE

The worship of nearly all ancient religions focused on sacrifice. In most cases, the sacrifice included a feast. With most sacrifices, the meal was an essential element of the sacrificial act, not just a superfluous activity after the offering of the animal, though there were some types of sacrifices in which there were no meals.

Sacrifices were offered for a variety of reasons. The calendar included certain days of feasts or celebration when they were required. A family event such as a wedding or the blessing of a field before planting were considered appropriate occasions, as were some acts of piety or just the desire to eat meat. The animals to be sacrificed were taken from the herd or barnyard. These included oxen, sheep, goats, pigs, pigeons, geese, and chickens.[7] The offering of wild animals (including those that were hunted), fish, and small birds that were trapped were prohibited at the altar. Wild animals were believed to already belong to the gods, while animals from the flock and barnyard were raised or purchased by the family. Said another way, a devout person offered only from his or her own belongings.

The offering of animals on the altar truly was a *sacrificial act*, especially for farmers, since animals represented future food and income. Goats produced milk. Sheep yielded wool. Barnyard birds, such as chickens and geese, laid eggs. Cattle pulled carts and plows. Those living in the *polis* spent money purchasing the animals for sacrifice. For this reason, Greeks, Jews, and other peoples of the empire typically could afford to eat meat only on the occasions of a sacrifice. Only the very wealthy could afford to sacrifice an animal apart from religious festivals, which meant only they ate meat regularly.

The Romans became the exception. Along with the wealth of the empire came a different pattern of sacrifice. Instead of only being butchered for ritual purposes, many animals were killed for the sole purpose of sale in the market without any connection to religious ceremony. This assured that Romans, especially the wealthy, had greater access to meat on a regular basis. Typically, large animals were used when Romans offered their sacrifices. The reason for sacrifices differed as well. With the Greeks and other Mediterranean peoples, sacrifices were part of public or private religious celebrations. But an important reason for Roman sacrifices was to discern the will of the gods and see the future. In this way, the altar assisted Roman individuals and families when making crucial decisions.

Why animals and why sacrifice? Romans and the Greeks before them believed that all living creatures had a life-breath, an *anima*, and that the crucial moment in sacrifice, as in any death, was the *last breath*. This breath was identified with the soul and its return to the intangible world of gods and spirits. When the priest killed the animal at the altar, the deity "absorbed the liberated *anima* and was strengthened by it."[8] Likewise, those involved in the sacrifice ate the meat, and they too were strengthened by it.

Sacrifice could be made anywhere by anyone. The following is an example of a prayer offered on a farm to purify the land. It is recorded in Cato's *On Agriculture* and calls for offering three animals: a pig, a ram, and a bull. The prayer is called a *suovetaurilia*:

Father Mars, I pray and beseech you that you be gracious and merciful to me, my house, and my household; to which intent I have bidden this *suovetaurilia* to be led around my land, my ground, my farm; that you keep away, ward off, and remove sickness, seen and unseen, barrenness and destruction, ruin and unseasonable influence; and that you permit my harvests, my grain, my vineyards, and my plantations to flourish and to come to good issue, preserve in health my shepherds and my flocks, and give good health and strength to me, my house and my household. To this intent, to the intent of purifying my farm, my land, my ground and of making an expiation, as I have said, deign to accept the offering of these suckling victims. . . . Father Mars, if something has not pleased you in the offering of those sucklings, I make atonement with these victims.[9]

Andrew Dalby in his book *Siren Feasts* describes an outdoor sacrifice that was part religious ceremony and part picnic. For the sacrifice, a sheep was purchased, a cook hired, and a small country shrine rented for the occasion. Couches and small tables were transported and baskets of food carried by servants or slaves to the shrine. Incense cakes and water jugs were part of the procession to the sacrifice. Finally, wine was included as an essential element of the preparation and the feast.[10] The head of the family took responsibility for the rituals and the sacrifice. On occasion, senior politicians in cities performed the function of priests.

Certain arrangements were made for a temple sacrifice. A suitable animal was chosen, the temple reserved, and a flute player hired. On the day of the ceremony, the animal was decorated with garlands and flowers, and, if the family was very wealthy, the horns of the animal were covered with gold leaf. The ritual of sacrifice was complex. The first part of it involved the priest inspecting the potential offering for its acceptability. The priest began by chanting, "Be off, profane ones," asking those not invited to leave the area. He also inspected those in attendance to ensure they had bathed and were dressed appropriately. He next demanded, "Hold your tongue." Two rituals followed. For one, a special flour, called *mola salsa*, was sprinkled on the head of the sacrificial animal. Then a libation, or offering, of wine was poured over it.

Prayers were offered either by the priest or by the head of the family. The prayers included an appeal to the god, then a description of the greatness of the god or some other divine compliment. A prayer of thanksgiving was offered for past support, healings, good crops, or whatever the occasion for the sacrifice. The prayer concluded with a request for renewed assistance. The animal then becomes the focus with the words, *Do ut des*, or "I give that you may give."

It was important that the animal die peacefully. Running or struggling was considered an extremely bad omen. The animal was first hit on the head with a large hammer. When it fell, the "knife holder" cut its throat. After the essential "last breath," the belly of the animal was sliced open and the entrails were carved out and burned on the altar with a large piece of fat as the gift to the gods. The offal was also examined for answers to the petitioner's prayers. The rest of the animal was then carved, with part given to the priest and the rest to the family for the feast.

Paul and Sacrificial Meat

It was acceptable to sell the uneaten portion of the meat in the marketplace if all could not be eaten at the meal. Most people in the market considered sacrificial meat as "especially health-giving because of its holiness and was highly esteemed."[11] As noted earlier, Jews and Christians were the exceptions, as they found sacrificial meat to be problematic. They believed that the presence of the pagan idols permeated the meat. In addition, for Jews the meat still likely contained blood, making it unacceptable. Many early Christians abstained from sacrificial meat, or even questionable meat in the marketplace or served in someone's home, believing the sacrifices contaminated the meat or somehow connected the Christian to both the pagan rituals and the pagan feast afterward.

Paul's position resulted from his strong belief in a robust Jewish monotheism: God is one, "yet for us there is one God, the Father, from whom are all things and for whom we exist" (1 Corinthians 8:6a). Jews were required to repeat the words of the *Shema Israel* daily for their entire lives, "Hear, O Israel: The Lord our God, the Lord is one" (Deuteronomy 6:4–9). Paul concluded that belief in the only one God gave Christian communities the freedom to eat and drink whatever they wanted.

Based on Paul's letters, we can assume that this was his position at the Jerusalem Conference. The conference concluded that Christians, including Gentiles, must abstain from things polluted by idols (sacrificial meat), from whatever has been strangled, and from blood (Acts 15:20). All three of these would have been repugnant to conservative Jews, even many Christian Jews. But for Gentiles? Paul likely believed that his rigorous monotheism superseded all these restrictions, especially the ones put in place by the Jewish Christian leadership in Jerusalem. Based on his letter to the Corinthians, he concluded that, because of the belief in the One God, "no idol in the world really existed," which made any meat or other food restrictions unnecessary (1 Corinthians 8:4). Chapter 12 includes a more thorough examination of Paul's beliefs about food and idols.

The Sacrificial Feast

The structure of the meal itself was similar to if not the same as the banquet described in chapter 5. After a toast to the deity from a common cup, likely with a celebratory reflection regarding the occasion of the sacrifice, the meal was presented and eaten. The sacrificed animal was the emphasis of the main course. After the meal, tables were cleared. A second toast was offered to the deity, this time with a ritual libation poured on the ground or on a fire. Participants sang a hymn appropriate to the occasion and drank wine while eating small amounts of salted or sweet foods. Even at an outdoor meal, unless the group was too large, family and friends reclined on couches.

Animal sacrifices were not the only type. Wheat and barley cakes were presented for sacrifice on a variety of occasions, including weddings. Offerings of first fruits, grains, beans, wine, and even milk were also common. Wine was used for a libation (drink) offering. A votive offering was a promise of future payment to the gods based on the outcome of the sacrifice. The votive typically was a terra-cotta figurine or a small model of a temple. As an example, a votive could be offered in connection with a prayer to be successful in a battle. With that result, one-tenth of the spoils taken from the enemy were given to the temple as a fulfillment of the vow. Archaeologists have found many votive figurines and models on the grounds of Greek temples, especially at the temple of Apollos, the god of war, in Delphi.[12]

The families making sacrifices had numerous options regarding where to hold the feast. When the sacrifice was at a house in the countryside, the feast was held in the home's dining facilities. As described above, sacrificial meals were also held outdoors, combining the prayers and offering with an occasion that felt like a picnic or cookout. Cities had halls with rooms specifically designed for banqueting, including sacrificial meals. These buildings included kitchen facilities for the preparation of the feast. The dining rooms were arranged as a *triclinium* with couches along three walls for reclining and eating.

The usual practice was to eat in the temple. In Greece, the dining facilities were built on the temple precincts, typically along the outer wall, away from the temple and altar. Roman temples more likely integrated dining facilities with the temple itself. On some occasions, the temple rules prohibited taking the sacrificial meat off the grounds, requiring that the feast was eaten within the temple precincts.

The movement from sacrifice to meal was experienced as the movement from one aspect of the same event to another. It expressed the two facets of the sacral sacrificial festival, from communication with the gods to celebratory contact with other people, all within the same context. Archaeological evidence indicates that temple grounds provided facilities for indoor and outdoor dining. Temporary structures and seating were erected for fair-weather dining and large, overflowing feasts. Such facilities would have been used for large public festivals as well.

Temple dining facilities were also used for other purposes. Temples served meals to pilgrims, sometimes using leftover meat and other food from private sacrifices. Pilgrimages to temples were a common experience. As we have seen, the Temple of Artemis in Ephesus was a known pilgrimage destination. So was the temple at Delphi, where people from around the empire sought advice from the oracle who dwelt there.

MEET THE PIG

Pork was by far the most popular meat in the first century. Other meats certainly were eaten and enjoyed, but for many reasons, the pig reigned supreme at the dining table. Jews, of course, avoided pork and certain other foods because of religious prohibitions described in the Book of Leviticus.

The practice of Mediterranean people was to eat meat sparingly and only at the time of a sacrifice, with Rome, as mentioned, being the exception. As with the Greeks, the Roman diet was simple, composed of grains, usually in the form of *puls* and bread, fresh or dried fruit, and vegetables. As Romans became wealthier and money poured into the capital from conquered nations, the connection between butchering animals and sacrifice at the altar declined. Fresh meat became a more prominent part of the diet, eventually for all Romans, even for the poor. It began gradually. In the year 328 BCE, Marcus Flavius distributed meat to the poor in honor of his mother's funeral. Centuries later Caesar gave away meat at each of his triumphal processions. Finally, in the year 270 CE, the emperor Aurelian made meat part of the regular distribution to the poor, along with loaves of bread.

Sheep, goats, and pigs were domesticated at approximately the same time, around the year 7000 BCE. Domestication of these wild animals paralleled the development of agriculture in the Fertile Crescent and southern Europe. Large fields of cultivated barley and wheat attracted animals. At first, the neophyte farmers considered the arrival of game basically at their doorstep an unexpected benefit of growing crops. Instead of hunting for game, the animals came to them. The next step was capturing and domesticating the animals, especially the goats, sheep, and pigs. They soon realized the benefits of the different animals: sheep provided wool; goats gave milk that was used to make cheese; and pigs had large litters that provided a steady supply of meat.

In the ancient world, as today, meat was cooked via two different methods, called "dry" and "wet." Roasting, grilling, and frying were the techniques used for dry cooking, while wet cooking involved braising, steaming, poaching, and boiling. With dry cooking, the heat reaches the meat by convection, that is, through the air or through contact with a hot pan. Wet methods allow the transfer of heat through a liquid. Even with steaming, it is the hot liquid, converted into a hot vapor through boiling, that cooks the meat. Dry procedures are especially useful for tender cuts because the meat can be prepared quickly. On the other hand, wet techniques work very well with tough cuts because the long exposure to a hot liquid breaks down the connective tissues that make some meat sinewy and gristly. Long before the first century, cooks knew which types of cooking techniques to use with different cuts of meat, though sometimes they instead chose a specific technique to produce a particular flavor. Chopping a cut of tender meat and then adding it to soup is an example. Dry and wet techniques were also combined. A tough cut of meat would first be fried in a skillet until it was browned (dry cooking) and then added to a stew to finish cooking (wet cooking).

Of all the barnyard and herd animals, only pigs were raised solely for the purpose of providing meat for the dinner table. As mentioned, the other meat animals provided wool and milk, and once birds and cattle became part of the barnyard, eggs became an important source of protein, and oxen were used as beasts of burden. What pigs produced was more pigs, sometimes as many as twelve in a litter. They grew fast and provided more edible meat than the comparable young of other domesticated animals. The woodlands were the natural habitat for pigs. They were attracted not only to the crops of ancient peoples but also by piles of refuse and household waste. They also ate grass and other wild foods.

Pigs and swineherds came to have important places in Greco-Roman mythology. For example, the infant god Zeus who became the chief of the gods was nursed by a sow. When Odysseus returned to his home after war and his numerous adventures, his swineherd and servant Eumaeus was one of the very few to assist him.

By the first century, two different types of pigs were bred. "Sty" pigs, kept penned most of their lives, were bred to have short legs and live in a small space. The Romans raised sty pigs, studying them in captivity to determine the best methods of breeding and rearing. Roman farmers also tested various methods of fattening pigs, experimenting with foods that might influence the flavor of the meat. One technique was to force-feed styed pigs with dried figs and honeyed wine. These pigs furnished wealthy Romans with the luxury meats and charcuterie they wanted for the banquet table.

Longer-legged pigs looked more like their ancient ancestors and wild boar cousins. Not only did they have longer legs, but they were smaller and had stiff hair. They lived on wild foods, foraging in the forest, eating acorns and beechnuts, the fruit of beech trees, and were kept by a swineherd. Long-legged pigs from Gaul and other areas of the Roman Empire, including Lycia and Asia, provided Romans with excellent hams.

How to Eat Pork like a Greek or a Roman

For most ancient food writers, including the famed Apicius, the word "meat" was synonymous for pork. It was said that every part of the pig was eaten, except the bones and eyes. Actually, the bones with the attached scraps of meat were used to flavor soups and stews. Homer gives the advice that beef is roasted and pork boiled: "The pot boils while the pork melts in its juice."[13] Contra Homer, many pigs also found their way to the spit, the roasting oven, and into sausage casings. As with other animals, pigs were sacrificed in religious ceremonies and then the meat eaten at the sacrificial feasts. The remaining pork, including the internal organs, was sold at a meat market.

Suckling pigs, small pigs that still live off their mother's milk, were considered a delicacy by the Greeks. The pig was stuffed with herbs and then roasted. For special feasts, the suckling pig was first fattened with grape must, which contained the stems, skins, seeds, and unfermented juice. To keep it moist, the small pig was first wrapped with caul and then cooked. Caul is a thin layer of fat that surrounds the stomach and intestines. It has the appearance of a spider web and easily adheres to the meat. It renders as the meat cooks, meaning that it slowly bathes the meat with fat to keep it moist. Apicius describes a larger suckling pig to be roasted whole, stuffed with an incredible array of fillings. His chefs recommended pieces of roasted chicken, thrushes, figpeckers, pork sausages, dates, bulbs (small turnips could be used), snails with the shells removed, mallow, beets, leeks, celery, boiled sprouts, coriander, peppercorns, and pine nuts. Fifteen hard-boiled eggs were not to be forgotten, and several good dashes of *garum* were added. Finally, a sauce of pepper, rue, *garum*, *passum*, honey, and olive oil was applied to the meat after cooking.[14] All the ingredients, especially the birds, sausages, bulbs, and eggs, were to be prepared ahead of time so they were only warmed during the cooking of the pig.

As with the Romans, Greek diners were fond of the pig's head and the internal organs, especially the tongue. The ears, jaw, cheek meat, and snout were considered delicacies. These and organ meat, such as the liver and heart, are called "offal" and are still considered luxury food in many places in the world. In most cases, organs such as the tongue and heart had to be boiled very slowly over a long time in order to break down the connective tissues. Sometimes they were served in the stock produced by the long simmering. Because most types of offal are high in natural gelatin, the resulting liquid was gelatinous as well, becoming solid when cooled. Then it was sliced and served, sometimes with small chopped pieces of meat enclosed in the gelatin. Slowly simmering the head gave the broth a very rich flavor. It also cooks another favorite piece of meat, the pig's cheeks.[15] Even the brain, sow's womb, and udders were considered favorite treats. The womb typically was stuffed and then cooked. Some Roman writers considered the womb and udders of a sow, especially one that recently miscarried, to be especially delicious. Offal sometimes was ground, mixed with meat, and used to make sausage. Liver sausage was and still is popular with many people. It was believed that offal was not sophisticated but good for the commoners.[16] It later became sought after by Roman gourmets, especially when the animals were force-fed and the liver took on the characteristics of foie gras. Offal is not often eaten in the United States but still much loved in most of the world. A local Mexican restaurant near my home makes the most wonderful tacos with beef tongue that is simmered for a very long time in a spicy broth.

Techniques for extending the life of meat without refrigeration were known and practiced. Some cuts of pork such as ham were salted to extract the moisture, which enabled them to last months or even years. German hams from the Westphalia region were salted then smoked. Italian butchers brushed hams with olive oil both before and after smoking them and then steeped the meat in vinegar. This was meant to imitate the preparation and flavor of wild boar. Hams were sent to Rome from Asia and Lycia, especially from the region south of Ephesus. Of all the hams, Romans especially loved the ones from the acorn-fed pigs in the forests of Gaul. An account by Athenaeus illustrates how hams were always served at Gaulish banquets: "The bravest man was given the upper part of it, and if any other man disputed his right to it, the two of them fought to the death in single combat."[17] The truth of the account is doubtful, but clearly the point was that the Gauls took their ham very seriously. Hams from acorn-fed pigs in the wooded areas of the Iberian Peninsula (Spain and Portugal), called *Jamon Iberico*, still are considered among the best in the world.

Ham was cooked in a variety of ways. As with modern cooks, Greeks and Romans found that it tasted quite good when prepared with fruits. Two delicious recipes from the first century are a ham and fig pie and a fricassee of ham with apricots. Ham was often carved at banquets in front of the guests, sliced into bite-sized pieces, and then served with dipping sauces. Ham and ham bones were also added as a flavoring to soups, stews, and vegetable dishes for additional richness. However, instead of ham, the gourmet Apicius preferred using pig brain or pork belly.[18]

Turning large cuts of pork into sausage was another technique for extending the life of the meat. Charcuterie, including sausage making, was a refined art even two thousand years ago. The Gauls often competed with cooks in Italy with their large variety of sausages and blood sausage. There are basically three categories of sausage, two of which were made in the ancient world. First, "fresh sausage" was made to be cooked and eaten relatively quickly. The flavored meat of these sausages was usually stuffed into pig intestines but sometimes was kept loose so it could be fried, boiled, or added to other recipes, such as a stuffing for birds and roasted pigs as described earlier. Modern examples include uncooked bratwurst, Italian sausage, or even breakfast sausage without casings to be fried as patties. Fresh sausages can be boiled, grilled, baked, roasted, or smoked. Sometimes a combination of cooking techniques was used. For example, bratwurst is often partially cooked by boiling and then finished by frying or grilling. Several recipes for this type of sausage are included and can be prepared with or without casings.

The second category is "cured sausage." Raw meat was mixed with salt, then flavorings, and stuffed into intestine casings. These sausages were kept in a cool place for a month or more, depending on the type of sausage. Because the casings are porous, the salt draws out the moisture and causes the meat to dry. Sometimes the sausage was also smoked indirectly, again prompting the moisture to be drawn from the meat. Cured sausages were made quite large because, as the moisture evaporated, they shrank considerably and could lose up to 50 percent of their weight. Cured sausages were intended for long storage and then sliced before eating. The technique is essentially the same as curing ham. Different types of salami are examples of cured sausages.

Friends and I have made both fresh and cured sausages and enjoyed the end product. The cured sausage we made was a variety quite like pepperoni. A recipe for fresh sausage is included below. Farmers made simple sausage for their families and to sell at market. Sausages were also imported. Medium and large cities had shops, like modern charcuteries, specializing in making and processing all types of cured meats, including sausages. The stalls must have been filled with hams, cooked offal, and long strings of cured sausages.

A third type that is common today but, according to my research, was unknown in the first century is sausage made from meat that has already been cooked. The meat is ground with a variety of spices and flavorings and then stuffed into the casings. Frankfurters, bologna, and mortadella are examples. These can be heated or eaten at room temperature.

By far the most famous sausage in Roman times and still made all over the Mediterranean Basin is Lucanian sausage. Roman soldiers encountered this smoky sausage in the Lucania district of southern Italy at some point in the third century BCE. They brought it home, and sausage makers in Rome began duplicating it. Despite the recipe's age and fame, the first recipe was not written until *Apicius* in the first century CE. Making it requires an entire host of ingredients, primarily herbs, spices, and berries such as bay berries. At several stages of processing, *garum* was added. Entire peppercorns and pine nuts were essential as well. Instead of fennel seed, common both in ancient and modern sausage, cumin was a primary flavoring. Once the casings were stuffed, the Lucanian sausages were hung in the chimney and applewood smoke used to give additional flavor.

Sausages were made not only with pork but with other food products as well. Fish sausage was popular. Sometimes intestine casings from very large fish were used to hold the sausage. Nonmeat sausage, such as that made with cheese and leeks, was also popular. The casings were not always necessary, and in fact a sausage recipe could easily be converted to one for meatballs.

Both blood sausage and blood pudding were popular. Initially blood foods were seen as a way to use the blood and the small bits of meat and offal. In the *Odyssey*, Homer mentions using the pig's stomach as a casing for fat and blood. It was boiled, and once it was cooked and the blood solidified and turned black, it was sliced and grilled. The recipe from *Apicius* for blood sausage called for egg yolks, pine nuts, onions, and sliced leeks. These ingredients were mixed with raw blood and ground pepper and stuffed into casings. Then it was boiled in wine and *garum* to cook.[19]

Forcemeats were another category of meat preparation. Finely ground fat was added to pork or many other meats, including fish and shellfish. Pork fat typically was used because of its neutral flavor. Forcemeats were used to make pâtés, terrines, and, when stuffed into casings, sausages. *Apicius* has many forcemeat recipes, including ones for shrimp, lobster, squid, pork liver, cooked pork brains, chicken, peacock, and mussels. Apicius has almost as many recipes for sauces to serve with the forcemeats as he did for all other types of food. He also recommended using forcemeat as a stuffing for birds and pork wombs.

Controversies over the Treatment of Animals

Even in the first century, controversy surrounded the humane treatment of animals raised to be eaten. Plutarch writes, "Animals must be killed with pity and sorrow, and should not be teased and tortured as happens a great deal at present."[20] He describes many methods of what would seem like torture in order to make the blood thicker or the udder from a sow taste better. Birds such as cranes and swans were not exempt.

Those with a gourmet inclination disagreed. Both geese and small pigs were force-fed grains and figs to make their livers swell in much the same way that foie gras is made today by stuffing live geese. Pigs were also made to drink mead, honey wine, until intoxicated and then suddenly slaughtered, their preparers believing that the liver tasted significantly better. Other smaller animals simply were drowned in wine.

Health Issues with Pork

Despite their love for the taste of pig, first-century people knew that if pork was not cooked completely, it would cause illness. It had to be thoroughly cooked or it was "disturbing to digestion."[21] Indeed, pork can be infested with parasites, especially *Trichinella spiralis*, a type of worm that causes cysts to develop in the flesh of pigs. If the meat is not thoroughly cooked, the parasites can be passed onto humans, the cause of a serious illness called *trichinosis*. Cured hams and sausages are safe because the process kills the organism.[22]

A FEAST WITH THE GODS (WITH GOD)

It is time to enjoy your own sacrificial feast. The format still is the two-part banquet similar to the one in chapter 5, with a *deipnon* and a symposium. Because of the religious setting, the prayers and hymn deserve special attention. They are addressed to gods that most modern readers will discount completely. With each prayer, an alternative is presented of the type that might have been used by a Christian in the first century.

Even though temples and other facilities had kitchens where cooks prepared the sacrificial meal, it is also appropriate to grill or roast the meat.

Begin the meal with the host or hostess explaining the reason for the celebration. It can be a special day, such as a birthday or a wedding anniversary or the celebration of a religious or national holiday. The feast itself can be a reason for the celebration.

Raise a glass of wine, and have each person make this toast before drinking: "To the Good Deity," "To our God who is good," then enjoy the meal.

After the meal, take a moment to clear the dishes and bring out a pitcher or flagon of wine. At first-century feasts, the wine was served with a pitcher or ladle from a large bowl called a *krater*. A punchbowl or some other bowl certainly is appropriate.

If you have them, pass around garlands of leaves or flowers for everyone to wear. You may also pass colognes and perfumes around the table. Then offer a toast to the god or goddess to whom the sacrifice was offered. The following is a toast to Zeus: "*Dios Soteros*," meaning "God our Savior," words that also would be appropriate for both Christians and Jews.

After everyone repeats the toast, a small amount of wine, the ritual libation, would be poured on the ground in the first century. You can easily pour some into a different wineglass, the pitcher or flagon, or, if outside, onto the ground. Finally, you can sing or read a hymn in unison. This one is dedicated to Artemis. Any Christian or Jewish hymn is also appropriate:

> Hymn to Artemis
> Muse, sing of Artemis, sister of the Far-shooter, the virgin who delights in arrows, who was fostered with Apollo. She waters her horses from Meles deep in reeds, and swiftly drives her all-golden chariot through Smyrna to vine-clad Claros where Apollo, god of the silver bow, sits waiting for the far-shooting goddess who delights in arrows.
> And so, hail to you, Artemis, in my song and to all goddesses as well. Of you first I sing and with you I begin; now that I have begun with you, I will turn to another song.[23]

Following the hymn, sit or recline with your guests and enjoy the wine and desserts.

THE MENU

Deipnon

Slow-Cooked Pork Roast
Pork Bread
Garlic-Herb Olive Oil
Lucanian Sausage
Chickpeas and Sausage
Wine

Symposium

Dessert Wine (Port or Madeira would work)
Hard-Boiled Eggs and Pine Nut Sauce
Seasonal Fruit, especially Melons, from the market
Mint, Yogurt, and Honey Dip (for the fruit)
Smoked Cheese (see chapter 5)

THE RECIPES

Slow-Cooked Pork Roast

- 3½ lbs. pork roast
- 2 tsp. each of salt and pepper
- 2 large apples, sliced
- 3 tsp. ground cumin
- 3 tsp. ground coriander

- ⅓ cup apple cider vinegar
- 2 tbs. honey
- 1 tsp. fish sauce
- ¼ cup olive oil
- ½ cup chicken stock

Remove large pieces of fat from the pork roast. Rub all sides of the pork with salt and pepper and place it in a slow cooker or large clay pot. Combine the remaining ingredients and pour over the pork. Cover and cook on low or at 275 degrees if using the oven. Cook 2 to 4 hours or until done. Remove the pork from the cooker and allow it to cool. Remove the apple pieces and pour the remaining sauce into a saucepan; boil until it begins to thicken. Pour sauce over the meat to keep it moist. Adjust the seasoning and serve.

Pork Bread

My friends Larry and Barb Walton developed this recipe. They are first-class home bakers. They advise that any leftover dough can be used to make twentieth-century pizzas.

- 2 cups shredded pork, from the previous recipe
- 1½ tbs. salt
- 7½ cups all-purpose flour, plus extra for dusting

- 3½ cups warm water, appx. 100 degrees
- 1 tbs. quick-rising yeast
- 1 egg
- Peppercorns

Take the shredded pork and spread it into a thin layer on a large cooking tray. Place in a 380-degree oven for about 15 to 20 minutes, until the meat is no longer moist and beginning to become crisp. Remove and set aside to cool.

In a large bowl, combine salt, flour, water, and yeast. Stir with a wooden spoon until there are no dry bits. Cover and allow to rise for at least 3 hours. After rising, make individual bread loaves by rolling approximately 8–10 ounces of dough into a rectangle. First sprinkle the counter or cutting board with flour to avoid sticking. Also sprinkle flour on top while rolling with a rolling pin. Repeat for four or more loaves. When the loaves are flat, thin, and well-shaped, add a thin layer of crisped pork onto the dough along one side. Beginning with the side with the pork, roll to make a cylinder-shaped loaf. Repeat for more loaves.

Beat an egg with a fork and brush onto the top of the rolled loaf. Crush peppercorns and sprinkle on top. Bake at 400 degrees, on a heated pizza stone or cookie sheet, until the loaves are golden brown, 25–30 minutes. Allow to cool to room temperature and slice. Serve with a garlic-herb olive oil for dipping.

Garlic-Herb Olive Oil

- 1 clove garlic, minced
- ½ tsp. salt
- 1 tsp. thyme
- 1 tsp. oregano
- ¼ cup red wine vinegar
- ½ cup olive oil

In a small mixing bowl, mix all the ingredients. Remix immediately before serving to emulsify.

Lucanian Sausage (Apicius)

The recipe for Lucanian (Latin: *Lucanica*) sausages originated in the southern area of the Italian Peninsula, in a province now known as Basilicata. Varro wrote about the sausage, saying that Roman soldiers stationed there loved these sausages. Lucania is still made there, though the recipe is much simpler and contains fennel seed. Feel free to add a tablespoon or two of fennel seed to this recipe should you choose.

- 5 lbs. ground pork, with fairly high fat content
- 1 tbs. ground pepper
- 2 tbs. ground salt
- 1 tbs. each dried savory, cumin powder, dried rue leaves, dried parsley, dried thyme, dried sage
- 2 tbs. fish sauce

- 2 bay leaves, ground extremely fine, optional
- 1 tbs. whole peppercorns
- ½ cup toasted pine nuts
- 1 tbs. crushed myrtle berries with a mortar and pestle or spice grinder, black skins removed
- 1¼ cups water

Place all ingredients in a large mixing bowl. Mix with your hands until everything is combined. If you have the tools and experience, stuff the sausage into pig intestines. Otherwise keep the sausage loose. Smoke the sausage in a manner similar to smoking cheese if it is loose or on a grill or smoker if stuffed. It is not cured, so it must be refrigerated or frozen.

Chickpeas and Sausage

Use the sausage you just made!

- 1½ lbs. Lucanian sausage, or Italian sausage from the market
- ½ yellow onion, diced
- 2 cloves garlic, minced
- Two 15 oz. cans of chickpeas, rinsed

- 6 cups chicken stock or water
- 2 tsp. each ground oregano, fennel seeds, ground coriander
- 1 tsp. each salt and pepper

Sauté the sausage in a steep-sided skillet at medium heat. When cooked, remove the sausage and drain it on paper towels. Pour out all but 1 tbs. of the rendered sausage fat. Sweat the onion in the sausage fat. Then add the garlic and cook briefly.

Place the chickpeas into the skillet and pour in the chicken stock. Return the sausage to the skillet and add the oregano, fennel, and coriander. Season with salt and pepper. Cook until chickpeas begin to break apart. Add water if necessary. Use a hand emulsifier, if you have one, to process half of the beans. Adjust seasoning and serve.

Hard-Boiled Eggs and Pine Nut Sauce

A winning combination.

- 12 eggs
- ½ cup of pine nuts or almond slivers
- 1 tsp. dried lovage or celery leaves

- ⅓ cup red wine vinegar
- 2 tbs. honey
- 1 tsp. salt
- ½ tsp. ground pepper

Hard-boil the eggs. Place the eggs in cold water until they are no longer hot. Dry and set aside. For the sauce: Lightly toast the pine nuts or almond slivers. Add the lovage and crush with a mortar and pestle, or use a spice grinder or Cuisinart food processor. Place the crushed nut mixture in a small bowl and cover with vinegar. Allow to soak for 45 minutes. Add the honey, salt, and pepper and blend all the ingredients.

Peel and slice the eggs in half. Serve with the pine nut sauce, either as a dip or to spoon over the eggs.

Mint, Yogurt, and Honey Dip

Use as a dip for melon pieces or other fruit. You can also mix berries or additional pomegranate seeds into the yogurt.

- 1 cup Greek-style yogurt
- ¼ cup mint, minced fine
- 2 tbs. honey

- 2 tbs. pomegranate seeds, optional

Stir all the ingredients together until well mixed.

9

TAPAS IN ATHENS AT A
PHILOSOPHICAL BANQUET

My sabbatical trip to Greece and especially Athens provided a bounty of historical, cultural, and culinary experiences. Along with a large crowd of tourists, I climbed the Acropolis, an ancient, fortified hill, to see the Parthenon and other temples. I wandered around the agora, imagining the many markets and the philosophers who gathered there to teach and debate. I managed to scale the red marble hill called the Areopagus, stopping first to read the text of Paul's speech there in Greek and English. The museums were wonderful, the ancient architecture amazing, but what especially caught my interest was the food and especially the Central Market of Athens. We had many fine meals, eating at neighborhood *tavernas* instead of touristy restaurants. The Central Market was a gastronomic wonder, outdoor and indoor booths filled with beautiful vegetables, fruit, meat being butchered, and fish so fresh they sparkled. Walking through the market made me want to cook; thinking about it still does.

ATHENS: CITY OF ART, PHILOSOPHY,
AND GASTRONOMY

Athens was a resilient city. It was a center of military power; it also experienced great defeats. It thrived through extraordinary "golden" periods, during which its alliances spread throughout Greece and colonies around the northeastern Mediterranean. Military losses were short-lived and only caused Athenians to rebuild their city with more splendor and an even greater emphasis on culture and the arts.

Greek mythology told of two gods competing to become the patron of the region of Attica and the city of Athens. Because of the proximity to the sea, Poseidon was one of the competitors. It was told that he struck one of the rocks of the Acropolis with his trident and a horse sprang forth. Then Athena made an olive tree sprout, full-grown, beside the horse. Both the citizens and the other gods realized that the olive tree was a more valuable gift. Olive trees grew and continue to grow throughout southern Greece, and olive oil was important to the economy of Athens. Owls that lived on the Acropolis during ancient times became the best-known symbols of Athena. They represented wisdom, an attribute of Athena.

At the beginning of the sixth century BCE, Solon the lawgiver assisted in developing a democratic structure for governing the *polis* and its surrounding *chora*. Democracy continued to mature through much of the classical period (approximately 480–323 BCE) only to be interrupted by short periods when the city returned to an oligarchy form of governance. Immediately before its classical period, Athens was conquered by the Persians, who destroyed the city in 480 BCE. The Parthenon, built on the Acropolis and the focal point of the city, was also demolished. The Athenians quickly repelled the Persians, and the city began an extensive rebuilding program.

The quick victory over the Persians was considered a gift from the goddess Athena, by then the patroness of the city. Athena was not only the goddess of wisdom but also of defensive war and a special protector of all Greeks. The new marble Parthenon with its prominent location on top of the Acropolis was dedicated to her. Other temples were constructed on the Acropolis and around the town, including a massive temple for Zeus. A very large outdoor theater sits on the south slope of the Acropolis and is still used for plays and concerts. The agora, the city's public space marked with columns and surrounded by stores and offices, was only a short distance northwest of the Acropolis in the valley. The agora in Athens was characterized in part by the scholars who would gather and debate the great philosophical questions of the day.

The market was also known for its expensive and wonderful selection of food. Fresh fish highlighted a section of the market called *eis tous ikhthyas*, "at the fish." The market at the agora was also known for its professionally baked bread, garden greens, sausages, and thyme, the omnipresent herb that happened to be a favorite of the Athenians.

During its centuries of glory, Athens received food imports not only from around Greece but also from most of the eastern Mediterranean. Goods included a wide variety of fish, eels, herbs, cucumbers, figs, cheeses, radishes, geese, and ducks. Barley was grown in southern Greece, but wheat had to be imported from Egypt and the region around the Black Sea.

Barley cakes were the typical bread at Athenian meals. Honey came from nearby Mount Hymettus and remained famous for centuries.

Not far from the Acropolis and just south of the agora is a large outcrop of red marble. Steps had been carved into its side long ago. The top is relatively flat and commands a view of the agora, the city below, and the Acropolis above. This is the Areopagus. Nine leaders of Athens, called the *archon*, were elected each year, and once their term was finished, they became members of another governing body called the Areopagus, named for its meeting place. The role of the *archon* and the Areopagus changed over the centuries, but they always played an important role in public life. It was this group that functioned as a court to hear serious criminal cases.

After a period of remarkable cultural and academic growth, Athens and its empire were destroyed by its rival Sparta. It was conquered again in the third century BCE from the north by Alexander the Great and the Macedonians, and then by the Romans in the second century BCE. Through most of this time, even after conquest, it remained a free city, first allied with the Macedonians and then with the Romans. The Romans allowed it to continue to keep its institutions and its method of governance. Athens tested this freedom by taking the wrong side in 88–86 BCE in a rebellion against Rome. On the threshold of defeat, Athenian civic leaders met with the Roman general Sulla to instruct him concerning the glorious history of Athens and to dissuade him from sacking their great city. His response was that he was there to punish rebels, not to be given lessons in ancient history.[1] Sulla and the Roman army left the art and architecture in place but destroyed many Athenian residences.

Athens was still known as an intellectual and cultural center of the Roman Empire by the time Paul arrived. Even in difficult times, the city attracted leading philosophers, playwrights, historians, and chefs. Sophocles, Euripides, Socrates, Plato, and Aristotle are just a few of those enticed to the city over the centuries.

Greece had a history of supplying schools for its chefs. A famous school was established near Elis, the town that first organized the Olympic festival and games. It was said to be the earliest of all schools for cooks and supplied many Greek cities with the experts that the wealthy craved for their banquets and other special meals.[2] It also provided a model for other training facilities in the culinary arts. Many centuries later, skilled chefs from Athens were coveted by wealthy Romans and were hired or taken as slaves.

THE ATHENIAN BANQUET

In many ways the Athenian banquets were like other ancient feasts. The history of Greek feasting and banqueting was centuries old by the first century, with early variations described by Homer, Plato, and others. Alexander the Great's conquests and travels, especially Egypt and Persia, provided new foods and extravagances for the banquet. The forms were the same, the types of entertainment remained consistent, and even the omnipresent parasites or party crashers that are described in chapter 5 continued to slip uninvited into the celebrations. There were some differences. Because Greek banquets were male-only events, except for courtesans and mistresses, the male guests often shed their clothes, rearranging them for cover only from the waist down. Courtesans who were present apparently did not even trouble with this formality.

Athenian banquets were also known for the way food was served. Instead of large bowls of lettuce or legumes and cuts of meat with elaborate displays, cooks served small amounts of food on little plates, enough for the guests to have a taste and try another dish. Restaurants that serve small plates, or even larger recipes meant to be shared "family-style," are standard in many countries and increasing in popularity in the United States. It is an excellent way to sample a wide variety of foods and flavors. But the concept is anything but modern, even if the flavorings and food combinations are. Small plates of tapas are common in Spain, usually served with a glass of wine or a pint of beer. Perhaps it was the Moors in northern Africa who first served these little plates. It is still a customary sign of hospitality among the Moors and Arab Bedouins to serve many *meze* plates of food to guests.

Serving a variety of food on small plates was the custom in ancient Athens. The plate might have small amounts of fish, calamari, ham, or sausage, just enough to whet the appetite but not enough to spoil the next course. Guests were teased and pleased with the variety of flavors and textures.

Of course, not everyone enjoyed a meal made of many small-dish delicacies:

> Please listen, cook, my host comes from Rhodes and I'm from Perinthus, and both hate Athenian-style dinners. There's something revoltingly foreign about those Attic dinners. The cook puts down a tray with five little plates on it. One holds some garlic, the next two sea urchins. Yet another contains a sweet cake, or ten little shellfish, and finally a piece of sturgeon. . . . Such a presentation is supposed to offer variation,

but it doesn't fill your belly. I end up smearing my lips, instead of filling them.[3]

Athenian hosts served these little dishes in delicate bowls and cups
from a common table located in the middle of the room, between the
couches for reclining. The central table gave the banquet the sense of collegiality that might have been lost if each diner had a separate table. A servant
or slave stood by to replace the dishes when empty, or to switch the entire
table with a different variety of delicacies. The culinary choices were based
on quality, not quantity. Athenians, as with the banqueters from other cities and cultures, ate pork, lamb, and other meats and poultry, but fish and
shellfish were their favorites.

Greeks adhered to the custom of following the *deipnon* with the symposium. From time to time the usual symposium activities of music, flirt-
ing, and drinking games were set aside for more serious conversation. The
wine was still present, but consumed to promote uninhibited philosophical
thought, not hangovers. Intellectual Athenians were known for their philosophical banquets, symposia where poetry and philosophical writings were
shared and discussions of great, and sometimes not-so-great, ideas were
debated. This section from Plato's *Symposium* illustrates that flute music
and even excessive wine consumption were sometimes set aside for a more
thought-provoking evening:

> So Socrates lay down on the couch. Once he and everyone else had
> finished eating, they performed all the traditional rites—the libations,
> the hymns to Zeus, and so on—and then they turned to drinking. . . .
> "Now gentlemen, what's the easiest way for us to go about our drink-
> ing? I have to tell you that I'm really in a pretty bad state from yes-
> terday's drinking, and I could do with a break. . . . So what do you
> think? How can we best make our drinking easy on ourselves?" At this,
> everyone agreed not to make the party a drunken one, but to drink
> only for pleasure. "Now that we've decided that the amount anyone
> drinks is his own choice, without there being any external compulsion,"
> Eryximachus said. "My next suggestion is that the pipe-girl who's just
> come in is allowed to go; she can play for herself or, if she prefers, for
> the women in their quarters. But today let's spend our time together
> in conversation. . . . I think each of us ought to make the best speech
> in praise of Love he can, moving around the couches from left to right
> and starting with Phaedrus, since he has the first couch and is also the
> prime mover of the topic."[4]

In an effort to continue the Greek tradition of the philosophical symposium, Plutarch developed a list of subjects Romans might discuss during their banquets. They were admittedly "lightweight" compared to the ponderings of Plato and his friends:

- Why do Romans carry their brides over the threshold?
- Why do the Romans forbid human sacrifice?
- Why does sound travel better at night than by day?
- Can new diseases come into being, and if so, how?
- Is wrestling the oldest sport?
- Does sea or land produce the greater number of delicacies?
- Which God do the Jews worship?[5]

PAUL'S SOJOURN IN ATHENS

Paul's time in Athens might have been a surprise both to his followers and to him. His experience in Europe began in Philippi but was cut short by controversy. He and Timothy then walked the one hundred miles to Thessalonica and began their ministry there. His ministry once again was cut short when angry Jews arrived from Philippi and caused problems for him. Paul clearly wanted to remain in Thessalonica but moved on to the town of Beroea in central Greece. Again, conflict caused his stay to be brief, and his next stop was Athens. He likely arrived in Athens sometime in the year 50 CE though it might have been as late as 52 or 53 CE.

It appears Paul never intended to stay long in Athens. Silas and possibly Timothy remained in Beroea with the fledgling Christian community in that town. At some point Timothy joined Paul in Athens but was sent quickly back to Thessalonica "to strengthen and encourage" the young Christian community in the face of the persecutions they had experienced (1 Thessalonians 3:2–3). While waiting in Athens to hear from Timothy, Paul stayed engaged by preaching and debating. If his message resulted in converts and a young Christian community, then so much the better. Paul likely traveled to Corinth before Timothy rejoined him and wrote his first letter to the Thessalonians from that location.

As with most of the communities he visited, Paul began his ministry with the synagogue, presenting his case that Jesus was the very Messiah for which Jews had been waiting. The Book of Acts describes neither a positive nor negative response by the synagogue's members to his teaching.

Acts does describe how he went to the agora every day to debate with the philosophers who were there. It recounts that two schools of thought were represented, Epicurean and Stoic philosophy (Acts 17:16–18). Paul would have been quite familiar with the teachings of both through his studies as a young man in Tarsus. The Academy, an ancient school based on the ideals of Plato, was also a presence in the city.

Paul's Gospel would have first confronted Stoicism. The Stoics believed that the gods existed in all of creation as a divine spark, a *logos* or divine word. This spark constantly brought the world into being until it eventually "blazed out" in a great moment of massive, universal fire. Then the world started over again. The wise person thought and acted according to the divine spark within them. But even though the individual was part of divinity, most Stoics still addressed the divine *logos* that was within them through worship, especially sacrifice and temple worship.[6] Stoic philosophy was quite different from Paul's preaching; still, there were areas where the two overlapped, especially with the reference to Jesus as the *logos*, or *Word* in John's Gospel (see John 1:1–18). Of course, John's Gospel was yet to be written when Paul was actively preaching.

The core belief of Epicureanism was that the gods might exist, but if they did, they were completely separated from the universe of humans and existed only within their own divine realm. Epicureans believed that people had no contact with the gods and, at their death, completely ceased to exist. As a result, they lived for pleasure, believing that it was the greatest good. However, "pleasure" for the Epicureans was different than hedonism because they found it not in rich foods and sensual desire but in living modestly, studying the workings of the world, and limiting one's desires.[7]

Representatives of both these philosophical schools must have believed that Paul and his views were odd. His religious opinions seemed consistent with the monotheism of Judaism, about which they might have had some understanding. But he added an overlay of his beliefs in Jesus and the resurrection of the dead, which was contradictory to their own beliefs. N. T. Wright, in his book *Paul*, suggests that the Athenian philosophers might have believed that Paul was talking about two gods: Jesus and Anastasis (meaning *resurrection* in Greek), and perhaps they were even a divine couple.[8]

After some days of philosophical discussion in the marketplace, he was asked to defend his beliefs at the Areopagus before the city's leaders. This interview was a step beyond just a religious debate. Instead, it was likely some sort of a trial. Paul's ideas were new and perhaps viewed as radical.

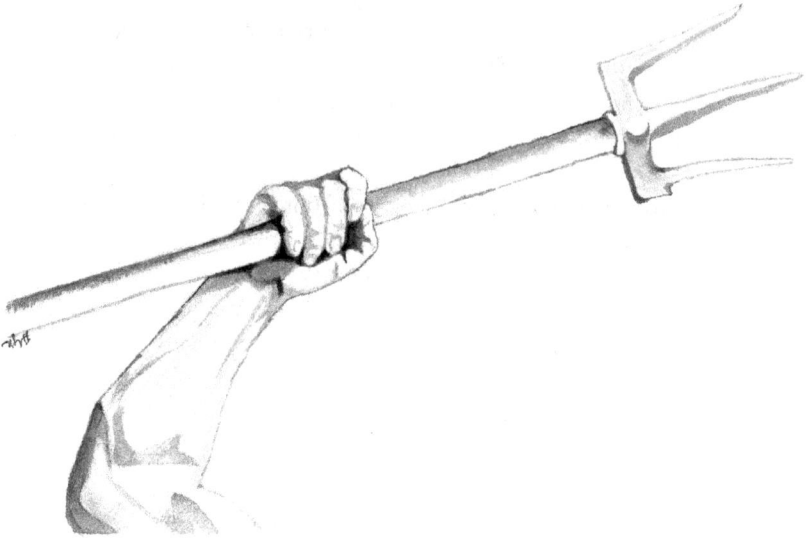

Trident for Tuna Fishing. *Heather Rose*

Were his teachings drastic enough to jeopardize the special status Athens had with the Romans? And was it possible that word of the trouble surrounding Paul had reached Athens from Philippi, Thessalonica, or Beroea? After all, debates were held in the agora; criminal trials happened on the Areopagus.

The text in Acts 17 is well-known. Paul begins his defense with the words, "Athenians, I see how extremely religious you are in every way. For as I went through the city and looked carefully at the objects of your worship, I found among them an altar with the inscription, 'To an unknown god.' What therefore you worship as unknown, this I proclaim to you" (Acts 17:22–23). He ended his defense referring to the resurrection, causing some to scoff at him. However, those on the Areopagus concluded that Paul should return and explain more about his beliefs. After his experiences in Philippi, Thessalonica, and Beroea, he instead decided to leave Athens for Corinth. It should be noted that there were several who became converts based on his talk, including Dionysius the Areopagite, one of the members of the Court of Areopagus and a city leader; a woman named Damaris; and a few others who are not named (Acts 17:34). All in all, Paul's time in Athens was not considered a success.

DINNER FROM THE SEA

Fish and shellfish from the sea and freshwater lakes, rivers, and streams provided an important source of food for the people of the Mediterranean Basin and throughout the Roman Empire. This was true long before the first century. Prehistoric peoples came to realize that a greater number of fish lived in the waters than there were birds and mammals on the land, and almost all the species they caught were edible.

The taste for aquatic protein likely began with the gathering of shellfish at low tide and in tidal pools along the shores of the seas. Extremely primitive housing structures were built along the beach so that early human communities could harvest and prepare food from both land and sea. Fishing became easier and larger fish were caught after the development of spears and harpoons. Drawings of human figures catching fish with harpoons began to appear on cave walls between 23000 and 18000 BCE. One Mesolithic site included an installation for salting and smoking fish, enabling ancient people to store their catch for future consumption. The Franchthi Cave on the coast of Greece contains a large number of tuna bones left between 7900 and 7600 BCE, confirming that tuna was a significant part of the diet of its inhabitants. The archaeological site also proves that the occupants were accomplished sailors and fishermen able to master the open waters of the Mediterranean in search for tuna. Many centuries later, Babylonians used dried fish to make a concentrated fish paste that was added to pottages and stews, incorporating both flavor and protein into their dishes.

History and geography can influence food preference. By the fifth century BCE, fish and shellfish became important foods for the Greeks. The reason was in part a result of geography. Along with Japan and Indonesia, Greece has one of the longest coastlines in the world in relation to its land area. Fishermen used nets, harpoons, tridents, lines with hooks, and a special net and technique called *lamparo* to catch sardines and anchovies. The *lamparo* net was employed at night in conjunction with a light to attract the small fish.[9]

Another technique called *madrague* was employed specifically to catch tuna as they migrated from the Black Sea to the Mediterranean. The fish first had to pass through the Bosporus Strait into the Aegean Sea. Watchtowers were constructed along the strait so the migrating tuna could be spotted, and a labyrinth was assembled using strong nets as a path to a holding area. Fishermen in boats then drove the tuna into the web. Once trapped, large numbers of the fish were caught using tridents. *Madrague* fishing was considered a "bloody business" because of the large number of tunas trapped and killed.[10] The predictability of the migration assisted the fishermen in making very large harvests. The fishermen then cut the tuna into steaks, after which they were salted or marinated in olive oil. Yes, tuna packed in oil is not a modern innovation. Tuna meat and scraps also made a very fine *garum*. Once processed, the tuna was exported for sale around the Mediterranean. Because of the location and the way the fish were caught and prepared, very few people even among the coastal Romans and Greeks had access to fresh tuna.

Fish Markets

Greek and Roman gourmets were selective with their choice of fish: "Fish must be carefully selected at market and keenly bargained for . . . each species will have its own best recipes."[11] The favorite fish of Greek fishermen and diners were sea bream, gray mullet, red mullet, conger eel, turbot, moray eel, and grouper. Tuna was loved along with octopus, squid, and cuttlefish. Sturgeon was one of very few freshwater fish to appear on Greek tables.[12] The agora in Athens dedicated a large section for the sale of fresh and dried fish.

Perhaps the ultimate ancient fish market was located in Rome. The city had robust markets for the sale of food and other goods and services scattered through the city. A market existed around the Forum, and in the year 179 BCE, markets were consolidated into a single building called the Macellum. It has been compared to a modern Oriental covered bazaar with a wide variety of stalls representing many products. However, this building was destroyed during Augustus's reign to make room for the expansion of living spaces as well as government buildings and temples. A new market, the Macellum Liviae, was rebuilt on Esquiline Hill, one of the seven hills of Rome.[13] Other marketplaces met other needs. One example was the market in the *subura*, a suburban district. It was known as a poor, dirty part of the city with thriving "red light" businesses. The market specialized in vegetables from the countryside, chickens, and other poultry. Unlike the Macellum Liviae, this market did not sell fish because of the high price.

A most amazing market was constructed during the reign of the emperor Trajan, around thirty to forty years after the death of Paul. It was a six-floor indoor market that housed 150 shops. The first floor was dedicated to the sale of vegetables and fruit. Above it were large rooms for wines and olive oil. The third and fourth floors were reserved for pepper and other spices. Offices for the grain distributions filled the fifth floor. And finally, customers reached the top floor. The great space was filled with large containers of fish. There were both salt- and freshwater tanks filled with live fish for sale to the wealthy. Discerning gourmets had their choice of a wide variety. The cook could return home with bream, sea bass, or several much-loved eels. Or should he choose, a container of mussels and crabs could become part of a special meal. Small fish such as anchovies or sardines provided a less expensive dinner or appetizers for a larger feast. The seawater for these aquariums was piped in from the nearby port of Ostia, a marvelous engineering feat at that time. The market also sold salted and dried fish, as well as varieties such as tuna that were packed in olive oil. The ruins of the Market of Trajan still exist and illustrate how innovative it was for its time. They also demonstrate how important the access to fresh fish was for the Romans. The agora markets in Athens were not this elaborate but large in their own right, supplying a wide assortment of foods, especially seafood.

Despite their love of seafood, the Greeks and Romans held fishermen in low esteem. Ancient Greeks before and during the time of Homer and Odysseus looked with disdain on fishing and eating fish. Most of Greece was agrarian, and even the heroes such as Odysseus were farmers. Eating fish was described as a last resort food for shipwrecked sailors.[14] While looking back on culinary history, Plato explains, "Fishing, at that time, was an occupation unworthy of a man of good birth, for it takes more skill than strength."[15] Plutarch writes, "It is more noble to buy fish than to catch them."[16]

Fishing was never considered an honorable or even a leisure pastime. Fishing was work. In small, coastal towns, a fisherman and his family also traded and sold the fish. But in large towns and cities, the work of catching and selling fish were separate enterprises. Fishermen sold their catch to wholesalers who then sold the fish at markets. Most fishing operations were small-scale businesses. Several boats with large nets trolled near the coastline, usually along the ridge where the shallow water drops much deeper. The exception was fishing the tuna and bonito runs.

Farm-Raised Seafood

The fruits of the sea were expensive. Even at the markets along the coast and the famous seafood markets in the large cities such as Rome and Athens, the cost of fish and shellfish was exorbitant. Centuries after the death of Paul, the emperor Diocletian set the price of many food items in order to curtail rampant inflation. The cost of fish was double that of pork, triple the price of beef or sheep. Many of the wealthiest Romans reacted to the high cost of their favorite protein by growing their own. It is said that Sergius Orata was the first to make oyster ponds in the Gulf of Baia, at the time of the orator Lucius Crassus, before the Marsian War.[17] At approximately the same time, Licinius Murena developed ponds for a wide variety of fish. These ponds were called *piscinas* or *piscinae* from the Latin word *piscis*, meaning fish. Other wealthy Romans quickly followed in their footsteps by raising their own fish in ponds they constructed. The story was told that Lucullus built a channel through the mountains that cost more than his entire estate in order to bring water to his ponds.

Gaius Hirrius was the first to develop ponds for moray eels. The eels were especially vicious but well-loved as a delicacy for the banqueting table. It was reported that the Roman gourmet Pollio believed the eels tasted much better when they first fed on human flesh. He supposedly punished slaves by feeding them to his morays. More likely, the occasional slave was bitten by an eel while harvesting them and the bite festered, causing the slave to die. Pollio was especially fond of the eel's liver. Other varieties of eel, such as conger and electric, were also considered delicious and are still enjoyed in many countries. As a celebratory gift, Gaius Hirrius gave six thousand eels for Caesar's triumphal banquets. Pliny the Elder was impressed that the fortune in eels was given for free: "He didn't want money or anything else in return."[18]

The Greeks, too, were extremely fond of eels. In fact, as they were with the Romans, eels were a much sought-after delicacy. They were prepared in a variety of ways. The Greeks sometimes simply wrapped pieces of an eel in beet leaves before roasting them. Some were fried in olive oil and modestly served with salt, pepper, and grated hard cheese. They were roasted on spits or boiled, and large ones, such as electric eels, were filleted and then fried. Because they were so expensive, especially by the first century BCE and into the next millennium, those who could afford to eat them often accompanied their dinner of eel with elaborate sauces, including intricate herbed mayonnaise.

Fish and Sacrifice

Unlike barnyard animals such as lambs, goats, pigs, and oxen, fish and other delicacies from the sea were typically not offered on the altar to the gods and, in fact, were considered unsuitable for sacrifice for several reasons. Blood was considered an important element in all sacrifices and, except for a very large fish like a tuna, the necessary blood for the offering would not have been present. Even with tuna, it was important to kill, clean, and prepare the fish for transport to be sold as quickly as possible. Moreover, the sacrificed animal had to be large enough for a community to eat, whether it was a large family, a group that extended to pilgrims temporarily residing at the temple facility, or members of the broader community that lived in the precincts surrounding the place of sacrifice. Fish were just not large enough. Instead, they were savored solely by family and friends at a special dinner or feast.

The Greeks and Romans only sacrificed domestic animals. All types of wild game were exempt. And fish were considered wild game: "Wild game that could be killed willy-nilly, outside the symbolic rigours of formal sacrifice [were] an item for private, secular consumption, as and when desired."[19] Yet it was speculated that the gods would have loved fish and other seafood. Fish were eaten solely for the sake of pleasure, "instead of a wretched and perfunctory sheep for ritual's sake. Forget all that smoking essence of cow and goat, the gods would much rather tuck into a plate of seafood."[20] Eating lamb meat was a religious responsibility; consuming fish was pure contentment. It was a food whose worth was judged solely according to taste, attraction, and, of course, market demand.

There were exceptions to the rules of sacrifice. Athenaeus claimed Agatharchides recorded, in his six-volume European history, that the Boeotians, the residents of the region to the north and west of Athens, sacrificed conger eels, decorating them with wreaths, saying prayers over them, and sprinkling them with *mola*, a grain mixed with salt. On occasion, a large tuna was set aside to be sacrificed to Poseidon, the god of the seas. Because it was such a large fish, one or several fish could feed a goodly number of people. The killing of the tuna certainly was bloody business. But to keep the fish from dying in transit, the sacrifice would have taken place very near where it was caught.

Cooking Fish

Only the wealthy could afford to eat fresh fish on a regular basis. They also had the means to serve it at dinners and banquets prepared with elaborate sauces. People who were not as wealthy could only afford small ones such as anchovies and sardines. Those who could not purchase any type of fresh seafood ate fish that were salted and dried or packed in oil. Salted fish was first rinsed and then soaked before cooking. Average citizens had to be satisfied with *garum*, and even that was expensive. The wealthy who could afford seafood were concerned that they purchased the freshest fish and used the correct style of cooking with the right sauce for each variety. This quotation from the cook's speech in a lost play by Sorades illustrates this interest:

> Shrimps I took first: I cooked them all in a frying pan. A big smooth-hound came next: I've baked the middle pieces, I'm boiling the rest of the stuff, with a mulberry sauce ready. I fetch two very large head steaks of bluefish: into a casserole with that, with a few herbs, cumin, salt, water, and a drop of olive oil. Now then, I bought a very fine sea bass: it's to be cooked in stock with oil and herbs when I have taken off the steaks that are going to be grilled on spits. I bought fine red mullets and wrasses: I put them straight on the grill, adding oregano to an oily sauce. Beside these I bought cuttlefish and squid: a boiled stuffed squid is nice, and so are the tentacles of a cuttlefish, simply roasted. I have made a side salad of all sorts of greens to go with these. Then there was some *hepsetos* (means "fish for frying"), for which I made a well-shaken oily dressing. Then I bought a very sturdy conger, and drowned it in a stock with strong herb flavours. Some gobies and some little rock-fish, naturally: I chopped their heads off, dredged them in a bit of flour, and sent them off to follow the shrimps. Then a lonely bonito, a very fine beast, which I dipped in oil, wrapped in fig-leaves, sprinkled with oregano, and hid like a firebrand under heaped ashes. Beside this I got some little *Phalerum* anchovies: a cup of water over these is plenty; chopping up lots of herbs finely I tip them on with a good jug of oil. What else? Nothing at all. That's the art, and you don't learn it from books and notes.[21]

The Romans especially enjoyed complex sauces for fish. *Apicius* has two chapters dedicated to seafood, one called "The Sea" for shellfish, and the other "The Fisherman" for fish and eels. The sauces are often elaborate and include many ingredients. For example, a sauce for roasted baby tuna includes pepper, lovage, celery seed, mint, rue, dates, honey, vinegar, wine, and oil.[22] His recipes also describe ground fish and shellfish used for force-meat that then was employed for sausages, culinary pâtés, and meatballs. Recipes for many variations of seafood patinas were included as well.

Not everyone desired the complex preparations that the Romans enjoyed. Some Greek gourmets criticized large banquets with complex foods. The fourth-century-BCE poet Archestratus recommends small gatherings with simple but fresh food: "His chief concern . . . was that the true flavor of fresh produce, chosen in the right place and at the right time of year should be allowed to come through and not be covered up with layers of spices and strong seasonings."[23] His method for cooking bonito, a type of tuna, was to place a sprig of oregano in the fish and then wrap it with fig leaves, tied with a string, and then buried under hot ashes. Another very simple recipe for baking sea bream included grated cheese, olive oil, salt, and a bit of cumin.

Fish fillets and other types of seafood were used to make patinas. Earlier chapters explored how cooks utilized different meats, vegetables, and fruits for patinas. A dessert patina is included. In fact, *Apicius* includes thirty-six recipes for patinas, many of which feature fish as the major ingredient. *Apicius* also contains several recipes for seafood stews.

I am inclined to believe that Paul, like most people who lived along the Mediterranean coast, loved fish when he had the opportunity to eat it. His little churches often included several influential and wealthy members who might have provided him with an occasional special meal that included fresh fish from the market. However, my suspicion is that Paul agreed with the poet Archestratus, who lived four centuries before him, that fresh and simply prepared foods, including foods from the sea, were the best.

A PHILOSOPHICAL BANQUET

This is the time to discuss something more significant than football or the latest television series. You can have your guests begin by sharing a description of someone who was significant in their lives. Discuss hobbies, or a book that may have been challenging. Maybe discuss the two philosophies, Stoicism and Epicureanism, described in this chapter. Have fun or become serious. Stay away from politics.

MENU: A PHILOSOPHICAL BANQUET

This meal is designed to be served on small plates, similar to tapas in Spain. If you do not own countless small plates for this feast, then serve several recipes on a large plate.

Appetizers

Mulsum from chapter 5; try a different flavor combination
Parsley and Cucumber Salad with *Apicius* Dressing

Deipnon

Any of the bread recipes in the book
Sautéed Sardines
Tuna and Sauce
Honey-Ginger Glazed Shrimp
Pan-Fried White Fish and Sauce
Calamari in Garlic Butter Sauce
Apicius Meatballs

Symposium

Wine, from the market
Feta Cheese or Halloumi with Pepper and Olive Oil
Dates
Grapes or Other Seasonal Fruit

RECIPES

Parsley and Cucumber Salad

For decades I have been making a French vinaigrette or Caesar salad dressing for our home use. However, these traditional dressings have now been replaced with this salad dressing from *Apicius*. It is very tasty.

- 1 bunch of parsley, large stems removed, and chopped fine
- 2 cucumbers, stems and bottoms removed
- ¼ cup pine nuts, roasted
- 3 green onions, green and white parts chopped
- 2 hard-boiled eggs, shelled and chopped

Apicius Dressing

- 1½ tbs. each fresh mint, fresh coriander (cilantro) leaves, fresh parsley, dried thyme
- 1 small leek, cleaned and the white and light green parts diced
- 2 tbs. small curd cottage cheese
- 1 tsp. each salt and pepper
- ¼ cup red wine vinegar
- ½ cup olive oil

Combine all the dressing ingredients and then stir vigorously with a fork or wire whisk. Check the seasoning. This dressing can be covered and stored in the refrigerator.

Place the salad ingredients in a large bowl. Pour on some of the dressing, to your taste. Toss and serve.

Sautéed Sardines

- Canned sardines packed in oil, 1–2 sardines per person
- 4 hard-boiled eggs, peeled and chopped
- ½ cup parsley, chopped
- ½ cup pickled red onions, from chapter 3

Drain and pat the sardines dry. Sauté until warm. Mix the eggs and parsley and use as a garnish. Top with the pickled red onions.

Tuna and Sauce (Apicius)

Many people prefer tuna medium rare or medium. This is your banquet; prepare it any way you choose. If you lean toward rare or medium rare, use sushi-grade tuna.

- 1 tsp. pepper
- 2 tsp. oregano
- 2 tsp. mint
- 1 shallot, minced
- ¼ cup white wine vinegar
- ½ cup olive oil plus 1 tbs., divided use
- 4 tuna steaks
- 1 tsp. salt

Mix the first six ingredients in a small bowl. Salt the tuna steaks. Heat 1 tablespoon oil in a hot skillet. Sear both sides of the tuna steaks. Turn down the heat; pour the sauce over the tuna and cook until medium. Remove the tuna steaks and allow to sit for 5–10 minutes. Cut each in half for the small-plates banquet. Adjust seasoning, drizzle the sauce over the tuna, and serve.

Honey-Ginger Glazed Shrimp

- ¼ cup honey
- ½ tsp. ginger root, grated and minced
- ½ tsp. fish sauce

- 1 tbs. red wine vinegar
- 1 lb. shrimp, 12–20 count, shelled and deveined

Bring honey, ginger, fish sauce, and red wine vinegar to a boil. Add the shrimp and cook 45 seconds to 1 minute per side. Remove the shrimp. Continue to boil the sauce until it is thick. Cover the shrimp with the sauce and serve.

Pan-Fried White Fish and Sauce (Apicius)

Use your favorite firm white fish for this recipe. For a mild fish, choose either cod or sea bass.

- 1 tsp. each ground cumin, ground coriander, oregano, and rue
- 1 garlic clove, minced
- 1 tsp. vinegar
- 5 pitted dates, cut with kitchen scissors into small pieces

- 1 tbs. honey
- 1 tsp. fish sauce
- 2 tbs. olive oil, divided use
- 1 tbs. *saba* (concentrated grape must)
- 6 fish fillets
- 1 tsp. salt

Combine all ingredients in a bowl except the fish, salt, and one of the tablespoons of oil. Heat a nonstick skillet and add the other tablespoon of oil. Salt the fish fillets and add to the skillet. Briefly cook both sides, then add the rest of the ingredients from the bowl. Bring to a simmer, cover the skillet, and allow the fish to braise until it flakes with a fork. The length of time will depend on the thickness of the fish. Uncover the skillet, remove the fish, and bring the sauce to a boil, allowing it to thicken. Return the fish to the sauce for approximately 1–2 minutes to reheat. Adjust the seasoning and serve with sauce napped over the top of the fillets.

Calamari in Garlic Butter Sauce

I tried this calamari recipe at a small trattoria in Greece. The owner and I are now fast friends, even though she spoke no English and my Greek

is not good. It was too delicious not to make at home. I order frozen calamari online from Vital Choice. It comes cleaned in twelve-ounce packages.

- 12 oz. calamari
- 2 tbs. olive oil

- 2 tbs. butter
- 2–3 garlic cloves, minced

If frozen, thaw the calamari in the refrigerator. If you have access
to fresh squid, have the fishmonger clean them. Cut the solid part of the
calamari into rings. If the tentacles are large, separate them into two parts.
Heat the olive oil and butter. The butter should be melted. Sauté the garlic
in the oil and butter mixture, and then add the calamari. Plate the calamari
and top with the olive oil mixture. You and your guests will want to dip
the olive oil mixture, so have bread available.

Golden rule for cooking squid: Either sauté it 1 to 1½ minutes or, if it's
part of a stew or sauce, no longer than 45 minutes. Anything in between
will turn your squid into rubber. For this recipe, sauté the calamari slightly
longer than one minute.

Apicius Meatballs

After all the fish, those at the feast might want a little red meat. This
recipe has no sauce or special presentation, just a little meat to eat with
your hand.

- 2 lbs. ground lamb or beef
- 2 pieces of whole grain
  bread
- ½ cup red wine
- 2 tsp. myrtle berries
- 1 tsp. peppercorns

- 2 tsp. fish sauce
- 1 tbs. *saba*
- ¼ cup lightly roasted pine
  nuts or slivered almonds,
  roughly chopped

Soak the bread in red wine for thirty minutes. Meanwhile, grind the
myrtle berries and peppercorns with a mortar and pestle or a spice grinder.
While grinding, the outer shell of the myrtle berries will come loose and
can be removed.

Remove the bread from the wine and squeeze to remove most of the
liquid. Then chop the bread into small pieces and mix with all the other
ingredients. Form the meatballs and either fry in oil or bake at 350 degrees.
If baking, turn occasionally. The saltiness comes from the fish sauce. You
may want to add additional salt.

10

FUNERAL FOOD IN PHILIPPI

Modern funerals typically fall into a familiar pattern. There is time for family and friends to gather, usually the evening before the service. It might be for a viewing, or a rosary, or maybe a wake of some sort. The next day, the community gathers for a church service where the life of the person who has died is celebrated liturgically. The casket is then interred at a grave site or a columbarium, or the cremated remains scattered at a place of family significance.

After the interment, family and friends join in a funeral feast. Food is shared. Drink is enjoyed. Those in attendance begin to tell stories and recount memories of the deceased. Instead of tears and mourning, laughter resounds. It is a different type of celebration, certainly one with the offering of good food, but also worship of sorts. Not only is the life of the loved one honored, but the community of family and friends that was nurtured by the

Roman Sarcophagus. *Heather Rose*

one who died is also acknowledged. As the time passes and food is enjoyed, the stories teach the history and culture of the family unit. A grandmother is remembered. The exploits of an adventurous cousin are shared. Funny and poignant stories about the deceased are recalled. In this way the family history is passed down to a new generation, and all of it happens within the context of generosity and hospitality.

Ancient funerals had many of the same characteristics, but with some fascinating differences. Similar to the trade organizations, funeral guilds were organized to prepare feasts for its members. Is it possible that these guilds also provided models for worship in early Christian communities, especially for Gentile churches?

THE CITY OF PHILIPPI

The Book of Acts tells the story of Paul having a vision or a dream in the middle of the night, in which "there stood a man of Macedonia pleading with him and saying, 'Come over to Macedonia and help us'" (Acts 16:9). Paul and his companions were still in the district of Asia Minor, what is now western Turkey. So it was that the Apostle Paul and his followers set sail for the southern coast of Macedonia and arrived in Philippi.

Philippi had a history of both wealth and of falling to conquerors. Gold mines were located near the community, making the town quite affluent. Only five years after being founded by Athenian exiles and named Springs (Krenides), Philip II, the father of Alexander the Great, conquered Philippi for its riches in approximately 356 BCE. He named it after himself and built a road that came to be called the Via Egnatia. The Romans then conquered it in 168 BCE, destroying the town and the area around it. In 42 BCE, it became the site of a landmark battle where Mark Antony and Octavian (later called Augustus) defeated the assassins who killed Julius Caesar. Many of Mark Antony's soldiers were given land to repopulate the city (*polis*) and the surrounding *chora*, and it became a Roman colony in the middle of Macedonia. The town was renamed Antoni Iussu Colonia Victrix Philippensium. Later, Augustus defeated Mark Antony in the same area, and once again war devastated the region. Augustus was determined that the city should be rebuilt, principally for strategic and economic reasons. After the battle in 30 BCE, the troops loyal to Mark Antony were used to repopulate the region, in part because their Italian farms were forfeited to Augustus's own soldiers. Augustus renamed the city Colonia Augusta Iulia Philippensis, or Philippi.[1]

Philippi was in most ways a Roman city. It was designated as an *Ius Italicum*, that is, treated with the same privileges of a Roman city in Italy. Because of the Via Egnatia, a constant movement of troops progressed through the city, bringing even more Romans into the area. Latin was the primary language. In fact, most of the inscriptions in the city found by archaeologists were written in Latin. Philippi was even designed like a Roman city along an east–west axis provided by the Via Egnatia with a Roman-style forum, Roman architecture, and "a magnificent view" of their acropolis.[2] Because of a large contingent of foreign craftsmen, people of commerce, and descendants of ancient Greeks, there is evidence that Greek was also spoken and used as the language to transact business.

With the ongoing support of the emperor, Philippi became and remained a wealthy city. The financial situation certainly was assisted by the gold mines, the terminus of the Via Egnatia, and a port on the Strymonic Gulf of the Aegean Sea. But it was not the major city of trade and commerce for the area. Thessalonica received that honor. Still, migrants from other parts of the Roman Empire, especially Egypt and Asia, moved to Philippi for its business opportunities. But unlike most of the cities where Paul started or helped congregations, Philippi was primarily an agricultural center. Romans arriving there were given parcels of land in the fields and valleys outside the city, so most of the economic development of the area was based on farming.

Grains, vegetables, fruit, and grapes for wine were the principal crops for the area and for much of Macedonia. Very fertile plains started at the foot of the mountains north of Philippi and stretched west toward and into Greece. Fishing was also a major enterprise. Eels were caught in the Macedonian rivers and salted for export. Shrimp were taken from the shore area of the Aegean Sea. A variety of freshwater and saltwater fish were caught. Bass and pike lived in brackish water near the sea, and trout in the streams and lakes near the mountains. Sole was a primary saltwater fish.

Along with other immigrants, Jews must have also formed a small community. Acts 16:13 mentions a "place of prayer" outside the city gate by a river. Paul and his companions went out to that location on the Sabbath day. Was the place of prayer a small synagogue or some other building that the Jews used on the Sabbath? There is archaeological evidence that other, non-Roman religions, especially eastern cults and native Thracians, used this area to gather. Scholars speculate that Paul was searching for a synagogue building or perhaps some other type of space where diaspora Jews and Gentile followers gathered.[3]

That was when Paul met Lydia of Thyatira, a woman who was called a "worshiper of God" (Acts 16:14). The phrase usually meant that the person was a Gentile who was sympathetic to Judaism. Lydia could have been attracted to the monotheism or to the high ethical standards of Judaism. Whatever the reason, she became Paul's first Christian convert on the European continent. The Book of Acts tells us that Lydia and her entire household were baptized (Acts 16:14–15). At this time, members of a household accepted the religion of the person who was the head.[4]

Lydia was wealthy, a successful woman of business. Her wealth enabled her to be independent and head a large household. She was a dealer in purple cloth, a very expensive commodity in the first-century world. Purple dye was available only to the wealthiest people. By Roman law, only the emperor could wear a purple cape. The dye for purple cloth came from a marine snail known now by its scientific name *Bolinus brandaris*. So not only was Lydia wealthy but her customers were powerful and influential people. She provided Paul and his friends with the hospitality of her home which likely also became the meeting place for the new Christian community. The head of the household where the community met often assumed leadership for the church. Was Lydia the head of the Philippian church, especially after Paul was forced to leave?

PAUL AND A VERY DIFFERENT COMMUNITY

The congregation in Philippi cared very deeply for Paul. Even after his departure, they continued to provide monetary support for his ministry with other Christian communities. His letter to the Philippian church is filled with language of love and appreciation. At the same time, he delivered to them additional news regarding his situation and how his imprisonment enabled him to proclaim the gospel message. The same letter included a statement of belief in the form of the beautiful Christ Hymn (Philippians 2:6–11) and enjoined his audience to "work out their salvation with fear and trembling" (Philippians 2:12b).

One of Paul's goals for all his congregations was that they functioned as *shining lights* of example, "so that you may be blameless and innocent, children of God without blemish" amid a culture that exemplified "a crooked and perverse generation" (Philippians 2:14–16). To help fulfill that image, he addressed both internal dissensions that pulled churches away from that vision and outside opposition that caused persecution and suffering that had to be tolerated and overcome.[5] It was in this context that he warned his young congregation regarding the possibility of becoming sidetracked by Jewish traditions, especially circumcision:

> Beware of the dogs, beware of the evil workers, beware of those who mutilate the flesh! For it is we who are the circumcision, who worship in the Spirit of God and boast in Christ Jesus and have no confidence in the flesh—even though I, too, have reason for confidence in the flesh. (Philippians 3:2–4a)

The question of circumcision, and, therefore, the question of whether a Gentile follower of Jesus must first become a Jew or at least adopt certain essential Jewish practices, became a significant issue as the followers of Jesus moved out of Palestine and into the Greco-Roman world. For Paul, it was a distraction. Focusing on issues such as circumcision interfered with what were the more important matters of faith, discipleship, and Spirit.

Food and the feast can build a sense of unity and community and so were considered essential to the worship of early church communities. But they also can define and differentiate communities. As we have seen in previous chapters, the more diverse the community, the more problematic or even divisive the feast can become. If the congregation was primarily Roman or Greek, then the worship feast was one that stressed unity and built community. We only have hints about the makeup of the Philippian Christian community. I suspect that they were primarily Roman farmers and some merchants since the city was a Roman settlement. But we also know that the city had a cosmopolitan nature as well. Lydia's presence speaks to that. As an aside, because many of the members of the congregation likely were farmers, the meals would have been simple and good, with a variety of fresh produce and grains.

Were Jewish Christians part of the congregation? Were there Cilicians, Syrians, and Asians? I can imagine Jewish Christian evangelists from Jerusalem arriving in Philippi and explaining to the congregation that Paul had only taught them part of what they needed to know. This could cause confusion to a group of Roman farmers who had previously believed in a pantheon of gods and goddesses. The arrival of "Christian experts" telling them that circumcision and a new diet were required caused stress within the congregation and strain to the unifying aspects of communal meals.

At one point in the text of Paul's letter to the Philippians, we read a sudden flare of anger. The issues were familiar to him. The church should be a unified community. Perhaps Jewish Christians from outside the church had arrived to recommend circumcision and other Jewish practices be adopted. Perhaps a kosher diet was an element endorsed by visiting Christians. It might even be that Jewish Christians from within the Philippian church, remembering their heritage, then agreed with the visitors or raised the question themselves.

As he did in other letters, Paul used himself as an example. He was Jewish; he was circumcised; he was a Pharisee, and one with great zeal for his religion. Yet for Paul, following Jesus was more important than his past, "For it is we who are the circumcision, who worship in the Spirit of God and boast in Christ Jesus and have no confidence in the flesh" (Philippians 3:3).

Later in the letter, Paul again raised the issue of what was essential in the life of the new community:

> For many live as enemies of the cross of Christ; I have often told you of them, and now I tell you even with tears. Their end is destruction; their god is the belly; and their glory is in their shame; their minds are set on earthly things. (Philippians 3:18–20)

Who are those whose "god is the belly"? This phrase likely refers to food, and especially the demand to eat a kosher diet. It required that they avoid pork and pork sausage; shellfish, such as shrimp; meat whose blood had not been fully drained; and serving meat and milk products at the same meal. The idea of a Jewish diet must have mystified a primarily Roman, Gentile congregation. Pork and pork sausage were well loved and a special part of the diet. Shellfish were abundant just off the shore in the Strymonic Gulf. Did following Jesus require giving up these foods?[6]

On the other hand, some interpreters wonder if those whose "god is the belly" were people whose libertine behavior conflicted with the goal of the Christian community as a shining light. For Paul, an emphasis on either a restrictive diet or an unfettered pursuit of pleasure was a mistake. Their citizenship was in heaven, and their focus must be on "a Savior, the Lord Jesus Christ" (Philippians 3:19–20).

Within some of his communities, the cultural clash clearly originated with Judaism and Jewish Christians; within others, it was the prevailing Greco-Roman religious culture. In Philippi, it was with both. The Book of Acts tells a most fascinating story of Paul and a slave girl who had a spirit of divination and brought significant income to her owners. She followed Paul and his companions for days, crying out that they were "slaves of the Most High God, who proclaim to you a way of salvation" (Acts 16:17). Becoming annoyed, Paul cast out her spirit of divination. Her owners then reacted to the potential loss of income by starting a riot and having Paul and his friend Silas arrested, beaten, and placed in jail. While they were in prison, an earthquake shook the foundations, and before the night was over, the jailer and his household were all baptized. The result of the story is that Paul came into conflict with the magistrates of the city and was forced to leave quickly. It was only his Roman citizenship that kept him from additional jail time.

The cultural conflict with Judaizing Christians certainly threatened the unity and purpose of the young Christian community. But just as real was the cultural clash with the religion of the pagan marketplace. The society of gods and goddesses had no issue with a possessed slave being used to divine the future. Paul was irritated at the slave's attention to him—that is clear from the text. But on a deeper level, the pagan marketplace conflicted with Paul's vision of what it meant to follow Jesus. Ultimately, this conflict may be the real reason Paul was driven from the town.

FUNERAL BANQUET

The actual form of an ancient funeral was similar to that of modern Western funerals, as was the series of events that occurred there, though the details and experiences were quite different. The first step was the actual preparation and laying out of the body. The women of the household took responsibility for preparing the body for burial. In fact, funerals provided women, especially in Greek society, with a rare outlet for social interaction. Greek women ordinarily remained in their homes, in charge of all household responsibilities, including oversight of the servants and slaves. Do note that plebeian women often worked at professions that required them to be in public and that some women owned and ran businesses. Funerals provided many women with the opportunity to associate with others: "It may seem odd to suppose that some women actually looked forward to the next death in the family as an opportunity to meet with their relatives and friends, but such was undoubtedly the case."[7] The preparation involved closing the eyes and mouth of the deceased and placing a strap around the head and chin. The body was washed carefully and rubbed with olive oil. Then it was clothed, wrapped in a sheet, and placed on a couch. The head was propped up with pillows and the couch placed so the feet faced the door. Very wealthy families further dressed their dead with ornate jewelry and even crowns. Finally, relatives were allowed to view the body and sing special songs and dirges.

After the time of preparation and viewing, the deceased was taken to the place of interment. The means of transporting the body must have varied greatly depending on the financial status of the family and the distance to the place of burial. The body might have been placed in a coffin-like box, but more likely it was left in the preparatory sheet. The corpse was carried by the pallbearers or transported in a cart. Mourners followed the deceased to the place of burial.

Then the body was interred, either buried in the ground or cremated. Especially for Greeks, cremation was the preferred method, with the ashes gathered, placed in an urn, and then buried. A grave marker was erected at or near the place of burial. There was very little of what could be called a religious ceremony at the grave site or really at any stage of the funeral. Attendees sang ritualized laments, and one may have said a prayer at the interment, though archaeologists and historians have no such records.

The final step was the funerary banquet. For the Greeks, especially during the classical period (fifth century through 323 BCE), the feast was held at the home of the deceased. This practice was altered by the first century, and the funeral feasts were typically held at a public facility rented for the occasion. Temple banqueting rooms were used, or, as was the custom with the Romans, the funerary feasts were held at or near the tomb of the one who had died. In fact, many funeral and grave facilities had permanent kitchens where feasts were prepared. Regardless of the location, the focus of the funeral changed radically as the friends and family of the deceased moved from the interment to the banquet. The following passage from *Adelphoi*, a play by the Greek writer Hegesippos, quotes a cook referring to his skills at making a funeral banquet a joyful occasion:

> Whenever I turn my talents to the *perideipnon* (banquet), as soon as they come back from the *ekphora* (burial), all in black, I take the lid off the pot and make the mourners smile; such a tickle runs through their tums—it's just like being at a wedding.[8]

The banquet was time to remember and celebrate the good qualities of the deceased, to remember his or her accomplishments. At the same time, delicious food was enjoyed and a sizable amount of wine was consumed.

Occasionally, Greeks and especially Romans made provision for the dead to participate in the feast. Pipes were inserted into the grave so that food and drink offerings could be shared with the departed. These pipes have been dubbed "feeding tubes" by scholars. Most evidence points to the fact that Greeks did not believe that they actually dined with their dead relatives. But not so for the Romans. There are numerous archaeological examples of "feeding tubes" at Roman burial sites, and as stated earlier, a feast was often served at the burial site. In fact, it was customary to attend numerous feasts at the grave: one on the ninth day of mourning as well as the one on the day of the funeral. The festival of Parentalia was a day on the Roman calendar specifically set aside for visiting and eating a meal at family graves. The purpose of these festivals was twofold, to celebrate the memory of the departed and to delight in the feast provided in their honor.

Funeral Association / Burial Society

Associations and guilds played important roles in the lives of many. As such, societies or clubs existed to provide an honorable burial for their members. Since the families of the wealthy could afford a funeral, these associations were typically composed of members of the lower classes: tradespeople, plebeians, and even slaves. These were people who could not otherwise be guaranteed a decent burial. In a sense, membership provided a form of "social security" or "burial insurance."[9] To assist with the services provided for their members, many of these clubs owned a common burial plot, called a *columbarium*. The cost to join the association might be steep, and sometimes new members were required to donate an amphora of good wine along with a cash membership fee, but the ongoing dues were significantly less, and the benefits of being a society member were enjoyed long before the grave.

Funeral associations may have professed to have a funerary or religious objective, but they also were social organizations. Especially in large urban areas, such societies functioned as an extended family or even as a small *polis*, a town within the city. They provided members with colleagues from the same socioeconomic group and even furnished the opportunity of connecting association members with wealthy patrons.

Associations typically assembled once a month. The purpose of some of the meetings was to collect dues, but often it was to hold a banquet. For many of the members, attending this special feast was their only opportunity to imitate the luxury of the wealthy. Funerary feasts were, in the words of one author, "occasion[s] for a festive banquet and the means to pass a day in cordial intimacy."[10]

Most funeral association banquets were defined both by the structure of the organization and by the attention paid to the patrons. Associations characteristically honored two or more patrons, human and divine. One was either a god or goddess, and banquets were held in honor of this divine patron. The god or goddess was usually a lesser member of the divine pantheon, but it could be one of the major ones, such as Diana or Zeus. The feast for the divine patron could be on the day that the association was founded or the "birthday" of the god or goddess.

The association also had a human patron. Funeral associations had rules that described the structure of leadership, the requirements of membership, and the conditions for becoming a patron, including the costs. The patron was wealthy by definition and donated money, food, and sometimes entire banquets for the membership. The occasion of a banquet honoring the patron might be his or her birthday or the birthday of a relative. The association honored the patron with titles of honor and other dedications, lifting their standing in the larger community. The presence of a patron also established a special bond between slaves, freedmen, and those involved in different crafts, creating a way for those who might not have a patron to gain that special relationship.

As with many organizations past and present, the funeral association had different officers, serving according to bylaws and rules. Because of its unusual emphasis, the association needed, beyond a president and secretary, officers specifically related to banquets and funerals. There was one person whose responsibility was to perform rituals. These could be as simple as a prayer and a libation offering of wine. Those in attendance took a sip of wine from a common cup, and then a portion of the wine was poured out as an offering to the host deity. At some occasions, the ritual was more complex, with the person in charge wearing a special robe. Another was designated to sit at the place honor at the banquet. The master of the feast arranged all aspects of the meal, from furnishings to dishes, pillows, couch covers, and the menu. In other words, the master of the feast assumed the same role as the *host* of a standard banquet. Those holding these offices and others were paid with additional servings of food and wine at the feast.

Funeral associations had a variety of space options for meetings and banquets. Temples had meeting and banqueting rooms available for rent. A special meetinghouse, called a *schola*, was an option. Some associations were large and prosperous enough to own their own banqueting facilities. Regardless of the type and location of the building, it was necessary to have a variety of rooms. Especially for large gatherings, a space for food preparation and a standard kitchen were both necessary. Also necessary for the banquet were tables, couches, both small and large banqueting rooms, and, as mentioned above, extras such as pillows and couch covers. Some facilities had courtyards, either for an outdoor meal or to provide an attractive garden view for diners who were feasting inside.

Small groups banqueted in a room with built-in couches against three of the walls, with a U-shaped *triclinium*. A typical *triclinium* configuration seated nine to twelve people. A meetinghouse might have several of these rooms, or perhaps a large room with several *triclinium* arrangements. However, some funeral associations had as many as 350 members or more. Such large associations needed very large rooms, and the *triclinium* arrangement might not be manageable for them. There is evidence that, at least on some occasions and with some groups, benches were necessary to seat the entire membership. I can imagine, in such cases, bench covers and cushions helped to make the setting more comfortable and attractive.

Funeral Food

The feasts were likely as varied as the economic situations of the families. Yet the funeral feast provided the family with an opportunity both to honor the deceased and to extend generous hospitality to family, friends, and other mourners. The characteristic foods of the Mediterranean diet were present.

The only funeral association menu I have found in my research was quite simple: bread, sardines, and wine.[11] But I suspect, even for a simple funerary association banquet, other foods were present. Vegetables, herbs, olives, and nuts could be assumed without being mentioned. A simple dessert of seasonal fruit served with the wine would also be expected. The form of the meal paralleled that of a standard banquet. After the washing of hands and feet, and perhaps the serving of simple appetizers, bread was blessed and shared. With this blessing, the meal, *deipnon*, began. After the food, a simple libation ceremony began the second portion of the banquet, the symposium, with simple desserts and wine that was mixed with water. This was the time for convivial conversation and extolling the virtues of members who had died, as well as the patrons, divine and human, and the other officers of the feast.

Unlike other types of societies, funerary associations met in facilities on the edge of the city or outside of it. This placed them near the burial grounds, where they occupied the same facilities that families used for burial banquets. It should be noted that funeral associations were not just located in Greek and Roman cities. In fact, there is evidence of such associations all around the Mediterranean, including in Syria and Egypt.

The Christian Community and Burial

The New Testament speaks very little about the practical aspects of death and a funeral. Paul and others wrote about a theological perspective of death, but nowhere do they discuss the details of Christian burials. Pagan funeral ceremonies were connected to one of the many in the pantheon of gods and goddesses, so Christians likely gave up membership in associations or simply did not join one if they were not already members. Likewise, Christians may have found the large amounts of wine consumed at many association banquets to be inconsistent with a lifestyle of discipleship. In times of intense persecution, Christian burials and feasts surely became more difficult to hold. Catacomb locations reflect the desire to keep Christian burials secret. In time, a truncated eucharistic (thanksgiving) liturgy replaced the full feast, especially during times of persecution. One can wonder how Christians were buried. Did Christian communities in some way take over the role of the funeral association, collecting dues, arranging for burials, and hosting funeral feasts? Even though we have no evidence of such, were there small Christian burial associations that were separate from the worshiping community itself?

OLIVES AND OLIVE OIL

"Except the vine, there is no plant which bears a fruit of as great importance as the olive."[12] Olive oil is one of the three most important foods in the Mediterranean region, part of the Mediterranean culinary trinity. That was true two thousand years ago and remains so today. In fact, to some degree, the domestication of the olive tree parallels the development of agriculture. Maguelonne Toussaint-Samat, in her classic book *History of Food*, describes how, in many ancient languages, especially Mediterranean and Semitic, the first four letters of the alphabet provide a description of the four poles of ancient civilization, signifying ox, house, camel, and olive oil. These four symbols represent the development of herds, permanent housing, the transport of goods for migration and trade, and finally the development of agriculture.[13]

Olive trees were native to the eastern Mediterranean and, by the fourth millennium BCE, Syrians began using the trees for olives and their oil. One thousand years later, both Palestine and Syria were intensely cultivating the tree. This next spread to Crete, then slowly onto the mainland of Greece and eventually south to Egypt.

In mythology, the Egyptian goddess Isis taught humans how to harvest and use olives. They were considered a gift from the gods. Greek mythology describes how the goddess Athene first gave the trees to the people of Athens, whose fruit was "able to provide a flame giving light by night, to soothe wounds, and to generate a precious food, rich in flavor and full of energy."[14] Divinely planted olive trees were located on the Acropolis and were a significant part of the identity of the city.

The trees were slow to begin producing fruit, some taking as long as seven years, but they lived long, productive lives. Gnarled trees hundreds of years old still produced large amounts of olives. Because of their longevity and productivity, destroying olive orchards even during a war was considered a sacrilege that would then become part of history and mythology. For example, Xerxes conquered Athens in the Persian Wars of 480 BCE. He set fire to the Acropolis, which also burned the divine olive trees. After the Greek victory in Salamis, the Athenians reinhabited their city only to find ruin, ashes, and desolation. It was then that the sacred trees began to grow again from their roots, giving the people hope for the future.

Olives and olive oil were important to other countries and cultures, both in myth and as symbol, representing a variety of far-ranging precepts including "peace, fertility, strength, victory, glory, purification, and sanctity"[15] The olive tree represented that the pantheon of gods and goddesses thought peace more important for humanity than war.

Olive oil played important symbolic and ritual roles for Judaism and Christianity as well. It was an olive leaf that the dove brought back to Noah and his family as evidence that the time of God's angry flood had ended. It was part of the Jewish sacrificial system, with some types of grain offerings made with flour and olive oil. Jewish kings, especially the Davidic kings, were anointed with oil, setting them apart for their role as ruler. At the beginning of his ministry, Jesus was anointed, not with oil but through the spiritual experience at his baptism. The title *Messiah* or *Christ* literally means "anointed one," connecting him symbolically to the kingship of David. Jesus also had another defining experience connected to olives. On the night of his arrest and trial, he and his disciples sought a place for respite and prayer in the Garden of Gethsemane, which was an olive orchard.

Early Christians used olive oil as an element in ritual. The New Testament letter written by James describes how church leaders prayed for and anointed sick members of their community with oil, likely olive oil infused with aromatics: "Are any among you sick? They should call for the elders of the church and have them pray over them, anointing them with oil in the name of the Lord" (James 5:14). The tradition of anointing the sick continued for centuries, and is still practiced among some Christian denominations. This second- or third-century prayer from the ancient Christian text by Hippolytus called *Apostolic Tradition* sums up a number of these themes:

> O God, sanctifier of this oil, as you give health to those who are anointed and receive that with which you anointed kings, priests, and prophets, so may it give strength to all those who taste it, and health to all that are anointed with it.[16]

By the second century, perhaps earlier, olive oil played a role in baptism. Those that were baptized immediately were anointed when coming from the water. The two actions came to be considered part of the same baptismal ritual.

The Olive Tree

Olive trees blanketed much of the Mediterranean region. There were not as many in Egypt or the rest of northern Africa; the soil there was believed to be more appropriate for growing grain. The lands of Palestine, Syria, what is now western Turkey, Greece and the Greek Isles, the Italian Peninsula, southern France, and into southern Spain, were known or would be known for their olive orchards.

The olive is a tenacious tree. Olive trees are evergreen trees with grayish leaves. They can grow up to fifty feet tall, and the average canopy is thirty feet. They live for hundreds of years, sometimes up to five hundred years. They can be cut level to the ground and still grow again from their roots. Olive wood is hard and beautiful, yet the fruit was so valuable that it was difficult to imagine cutting one down. However, the trees were trimmed every year to expose inner branches to light and increase their health and productivity. Trimming took place around the same time that the grape vines were pruned.

The Fruit

Olives are a fruit. Experts call them a *dupe*, a fruit with a single pit or seed, like plums and peaches. The trees require moderate spring weather to flower, and the weather must stay temperate until the petals drop. The fruit itself needs a long, hot growing season. All olive varieties are green until they ripen, and then they turn dark. Depending on the variety, ripe olives range from black to a darkish purple. The green olives in stores and Mediterranean markets were simply harvested before fully ripening. They tend to have a sharper flavor and a much firmer texture.

The growing season culminates in the late fall when olives are the last agricultural product to be harvested. Both Romans and Greeks preferred the oil from green, almost ripe olives. Pliny writes that the riper the olive, the greasier and "less agreeable" the flavor.[17] The oil made from green fruit has a grassy, peppery, fruity taste, while oil made from ripe olives tends to be softer, with a mellow flavor. I suspect Pliny's comments are showing his prejudice, one shared by most Greeks and Romans. He did write, however, that, for an agricultural business, using barely ripened olives made the most sense by providing a compromise between flavor and quantity. The riper olives provided more oil, even if he considered the taste to be inferior.[18] Some producers used a combination of ripe and green olives to create a flavor they enjoyed and believed would sell at a good price. The same is true today. Modern producers in the United States and in some other countries blend several olive varieties as well as olives at different stages of ripeness to produce a favorable flavor.

Pliny and other Romans had strong opinions regarding the best olives and oil in the empire. Of course, they believed it was produced in the Italian Peninsula, "the highest ranked in the world."[19] I am certain that first-century Greeks disagreed. I know they still do! Pliny had praise for oils from the provinces that are now Spain and Croatia, but special praise for Licinian oil produced in the province of Venafro in central Italy as being "exceptionally famous."[20]

Releasing the Oil from the Olive

One of the highlights of my trip to Greece was spending time in orchards and olive mills. I visited two mills, a modern one and another in operation since 1750. The older one finally began using electricity in 1965. Up until then, the method for releasing the olive oil was not much different than it was two thousand years earlier. The stone and press were the same, just powered by donkeys and people instead of electricity. The modern facility was quite a contrast. The technique for extracting the oil was similar, but the equipment was technologically advanced, and I am sure the stainless steel was much easier to clean and keep sanitary. The owners at both facilities were extremely hospitable. After a tour, the manager of the older one took us into a small room where clients were fed while waiting for their olives to be pressed. A delightful light lunch was laid out on a rustic table that might have been as old as the mill: tomatoes with olive oil and fresh oregano, homemade bread, olive tapenade, local pickled vegetables, and a type of grappa called *raki*.

The owner of the modern mill insisted before our tour that we drink Greek coffee (which I love), eat Turkish delights, and get to know one another. Our guide was also extremely knowledgeable and hospitable. He was an executive with Esti Olive Oil, Lelia Foods. Esti olive oils are very difficult to find in the United States and are of very high quality. I was honored and surprised that he took so much time from his work to spend half a day driving us from the city of Kalamata to the olive orchards and mills of the northern Mani Peninsula.

The primary olive of the region for oil is the Koroneiki. It is quite small, about the size of a dime, and oval shaped. This contrasts with the much larger Kalamata olive, which is primarily used for brining and eating. By the first century, there were a large number of olive varieties. Even today, the majority of olives are grown for their oil, though some are specifically raised, harvested, and brined for the table.

I would love to return to Greece, help harvest the olives, and participate in the milling process. I was there two months too early. In most places in the world, the harvest process is almost the same as it was two thousand years ago: Large cloth tarps were spread under the tree. Then workers climbed the trees to shake the branches, while others stood on the ground and hit the tree with long sticks. Olives rained from the tree, which were piled in baskets and carried to the mill. The goal was to collect a maximum amount of fruit without bruising it. The olives began to sour once they were off the tree, so it was imperative to press them as quickly as possible. Only in the last century have some olive producers planted trees closer together, almost resembling hedges, and begun using mechanical tree shakers for the harvest.

Fabricating olive oil is basically a three-part process. The skin of the olive has to be broken and the interior flesh crushed, preferably without breaking the pit or seed. A large circular stone was used for this purpose. The olives were placed in a mill, a stone basin, and the stone was turned by animals or slaves, or in the case of those with meager financial means, by family members. The mashed olives, or pulp, were scooped into thin, straw baskets that were stacked on top of one another, sometimes twenty or more high. The baskets of pulp were then pressed using a screw press. Several men turned a large screw with a handle on top. The intense pressure released the oil, which ran down a trough and into a container. The watery *amurca*, called the *lees*, naturally separated from the oil, leaving a pure product. As today, the first pressing of the olives produced the best oil, now called "extra-virgin." This product was reserved for culinary uses.

Subsequent pressings produced oil for a wide variety of purposes, such as fuel for the small lamps found in most rooms. The lamps were made of clay and looked a lot like ancient versions of Aladdin's lamp, with a wick placed in the spout and a hole on top for adding more oil. Many archaeological sites are literally littered with these lamps. Oil from second and third pressings was also used to make soap, as well as moisturizer that was rubbed on the skin several times a day, especially after baths and other cleansings. Applied to clothing, oil became a waterproofing agent. And it was a primary ingredient in making cosmetics. As already described, oil was a key element for both social and religious rituals.

Olive oil had to be stored in a dark place, preferably in airtight containers. Amphorae of the type used to store wine were also used for oil. After they were filled with oil, the amphorae were sealed with pitch to make them airtight. Once opened, the oil had to be used quickly before it became rancid. Even though good oil was expensive, the rule of thumb was to use it liberally and often. As a note, modern olive oils typically last about eighteen months if stored properly, so the advice is the same today: use liberally and often.

Mediterranean peoples rarely used butter or animal fat, so oils were the normative cooking medium. There were other oils, such as sesame oil, but, except for rare occasions, olive oil was exclusively utilized. Olive oil was used as a marinade for both fish and meat, served as a main ingredient for salad dressings along with vinegar and herbs, and poured over cooked food and fresh vegetables as a flavoring before serving. But primarily, olive oil was used to cook and fry foods. It had a high searing point, especially when compared with other oils available in the ancient world. And it retained some of its flavor. In comparison, the Celts of northern Europe used butter for cooking and did not like the flavor of olive oil, one of the reasons they were considered barbarians by the Romans and Greeks.

The Health Benefits of Olive Oil

The Mediterranean diet, with its overwhelming use of whole grains, legumes, and vegetables, is undeniably healthy. It is just as true in the twenty-first century as it was in the first—that is, if a person had the financial wherewithal to purchase the necessary foods. One of the key elements for health was olive oil. In 1993, Dr. Walter Willett, the chair of the Department of Nutrition at the Harvard School of Public Health, stated at a conference on Mediterranean diets that, "as far as I'm concerned, you can take the whole food pyramid and just pour olive oil over it!"[21]

Olive oil is high in monounsaturated fatty acids, the good fat that helps with HDL cholesterol levels (the "good" cholesterol) and provides a healthy means to store fat-soluble vitamins like A, D, E, and K. Most fats are polyunsaturated and cause lower levels of HDL cholesterol. A diet in which olive oil is the primary fat and large amounts of vegetables are eaten results in healthy blood sugar levels and lower blood pressure. Those people who live on the Mediterranean diet are among the least likely in the world to suffer from coronary heart disease or strokes. Plus, the food tastes good.[22]

A FUNERAL FEAST

It is appropriate to serve this feast outside. Sit on the ground picnic style or at tables. Be sure the gathering is close to the kitchen so it is easy to carry food from the oven to the table. Of course, you can eat the meal in a dining room or living room. Perhaps you will want to serve the appetizers and *deipnon* outside and the symposium inside. Spend the symposium time discussing the life of a significant person who has died. All Saints' Day can be a perfect time for a funeral meal, weather permitting.

MENU FOR A FUNERAL FEAST

Appetizer

> *Mulsum* (recipe from chapter 5)
> Macedonian Olive Salad
> Pistachios, from the market

Deipnon

> Any of the Bread recipes in this book
> Olive Oil for dipping the Bread
> *Minutal* of Apricots
> Ham Steaks with Figs
> Favorite Lentils
> Wine, from the market

Symposium

Pear Patina with Cumin Sauce
Passum, serve slightly chilled

RECIPES

Macedonian Olive Salad

- ½ cup green and black pitted olives
- 4 green onions, finely diced
- 1 cup parsley, chopped

- 2 tbs. olive oil
- 1 tbs. white wine vinegar
- 1 tsp. sumac
- Salt and pepper if needed

Soak the olives in water if they are brined. Dry and finely chop. Add the green onions and parsley to the olives. Add the olive oil and vinegar and stir. Top with ground sumac. Taste and add salt and pepper if needed.

Minutal of Apricots (Apicius)

A *minutal* is a stew, so this is a recipe for pork and apricot stew. You can use less pepper; most Romans would have used more. I recommend cutting the apricots with scissors.

- 1 tbs. olive oil
- 2 tbs. *garum* (fish sauce),
  divided use
- ¾ cup white wine
- 1½ lbs. pork, cut into
  chunks
- 1 tsp. each of cumin, dried
  mint, dill, ground pepper
- ½ tsp. salt
- 16 dried apricots, cut in half

- 1 tbs. flour mixed with
  water to thicken
- ¼ cup honey
- ½ cup *passum* (raisin sweet
  wine), or any good-quality
  sweet white wine
- 2 tbs. red wine vinegar
-
- 4 green onions, cut into
  2-inch pieces

Heat oil, 1 tablespoon *garum*, and the white wine in a pot. Add the pork and cook for 5 minutes, stirring frequently. Then add the cumin, mint, dill, pepper, salt, and apricots. Stir to incorporate the herbs and spices and continue to cook.

Meanwhile, mix the flour and water in a ramekin or small bowl. Stir to blend any lumps that form. In a separate bowl, combine the honey, 1 tablespoon *garum*, *passum*, and vinegar. Add this mixture and stir to coat the pork and apricots. Stir the flour mixture and pour into the stew to thicken. Finally, add the onions. Continue to cook until the apricots are soft and the stew is hot. Adjust seasoning and serve.

Ham Steaks with Figs

- 2–3 ham steaks, cut in half
- 4 dried figs, cut into small pieces with kitchen scissors
- ½ cup *passum* (raisin wine)
- 1 bay leaf
- 1 tbs. honey
- 2 tbs. *saba* (concentrated grape must)

Preheat the oven to 325 degrees. Place the ham steaks on a skillet or nonstick baking sheet with sides. Place the remainder of the ingredients in a pot and simmer until it begins to thicken. With a kitchen brush or a spoon, apply some of the glaze to the ham. Place in the oven to bake. Continue to simmer the sauce. Remove the ham from the oven when it is done. Apply another layer of glaze. Boil the remining glaze until it has the consistency of syrup. Remove the bay leaf and plate the ham. Spoon the sauce over the ham slices.

Favorite Lentils

Yes, the ingredient list is daunting. You can omit herbs if you do not have them. You may also buy coriander and cumin that is already ground. I tend to use a mortar and pestle for all the ingredients, from coriander to lovage, and then moisten them with vinegar.

- ¼ cup olive oil
- ½ yellow onion, chopped
- 2 garlic cloves minced
- 1 cup red lentils
- 5 cups chicken or vegetable stock
- ½ tsp. coriander seeds, ground with mortar and pestle
- ½ tsp. cumin seeds, ground with a mortar and pestle
- ¼ tsp. rue
- ¼ tsp. celery seed
- ½ tsp. lovage or chopped celery leaves
- 2 tbs. red wine vinegar
- ½ tsp. pepper
- Additional olive oil and sumac to garnish

Sweat the onion in olive oil. Add the garlic and cook for another 30 minutes or until the garlic is opaque. Add the lentils and the stock. Then add the herbs and spices, salt, and pepper. Cook for at least 30 minutes or until the dish begins to thicken. Use additional olive oil and sumac to garnish.

Pear Patina (Apicius) with Cumin Sauce (My Recipe)

Apicius used peaches for this recipe. Pears and peaches both work and are delicious.

- 5 pears
- 1 cup white wine
- 2 tbs. honey, plus 1 tbs. additional honey

- 6 eggs
- 1 cup milk

Cumin dessert sauce:

- Poaching liquid from the pears
- ½ tsp. cumin

- ⅓ cup cream
- Skins from the pears

Bring the white wine and honey to a simmer in a pot large enough to hold the pears in one layer. Add the pears, cover the pot with a lid, and poach pears until just turning tender. Remove from the poaching liquid and let cool.

Once the pears are room temperature, carefully remove the skins and save. Thinly slice the pears and remove the core. Grease a pie pan with olive oil. Mix the 6 eggs, milk, and 1 tablespoon of honey. Place pear slices in the pan and pour the egg/milk mixture over top.

Preheat oven to 375 degrees. Bake the patina for 45 minutes or until a knife stuck in the center comes out clean. Remove pan and cool to room temperature

Cumin dessert sauce: Cook the poaching liquid, cumin, cream, and skin from the pears in a small pot. Reduce until it forms a thick sauce. Strain the sauce to remove the skins. Pour the sauce back into the pot to keep warm.

Slice or place a large spoonful of the patina on a dessert plate. Cover with the cumin dessert sauce.

Passum (Raisin Wine)

Use in recipes as an ingredient or drink separately.

- One bottle of a sweet wine, such as an American Chenin Blanc or a German Rhine wine

- ⅓ cup of raisins

Pour wine into a large pot. Heat the wine, but do not bring to a boil. Put raisins in a bowl, and pour over the heated wine. When the wine cools, pour all of the wine and the raisins into a container large enough to hold a bottle of wine. Cover with an airtight lid and let the mixture continue to macerate in a refrigerator for several days. Strain, and the wine is ready to use.

11

A GUILD FEAST IN THESSALONICA WITH DRINKS TO MAKE GLAD THE HEART

Paul arrived in Thessalonica from Philippi and immediately began presenting the good news of the Jesus message and forming a promising Christian community. But he experienced conflict with local authorities and was forced to move to his next destination much sooner than he desired. Yet he wrote that his time in Thessalonica was special, one of kindness and generosity.

THESSALONICA: A CITY OF TRADE AND WEALTH

Thessalonica was a cosmopolitan city. Though not as large as Rome or Alexandria, its population was still over two hundred thousand people. Along with Corinth, Thessalonica was one of the two most important cities for trade in Greece and was the major port in Macedonia. The city was geographically positioned to thrive as a center of commerce because it sat at the crossroads of rivers flowing into central Europe and the important highway, the Via Egnatia. Even more significant was its location at the head of the Thermaic Gulf, a large bay protected by the Chalcidice Peninsula to the east and connecting it to the Aegean Sea and thus to the Mediterranean Sea.

Mosaic of Grape Harvest. *Heather Rose*

Thessalonica was founded in 316 BCE by one of Alexander the Great's successors, Cassander, who happened to be married to Alexander's sister, Thessalonice, for whom the city was named. Thessalonica became Pompey's headquarters during the Roman civil wars. But when Pompey left the city, Thessalonica changed its allegiance and backed Antony and Octavian (Augustus). Earlier chapters have illustrated how cities thrived or suffered according to the generals they supported or opposed. Because it supported the eventual victors, Thessalonica was rewarded with special favors and granted the status of a "free city."

Thessalonica was selected as the capital of the Roman Macedonia Province, which added both to its prestige and prosperity. Trade and wealth eventually enticed people to locate there, bringing in craftsmen and merchants from the other regions of Greece as well as Asia Minor, Palestine, Egypt, Rome, and the rest of Italy. They migrated toward the large centers of commerce such as Thessalonica with dreams of making their fortunes, or at least a better living. Migrants brought with them their own cultures, cuisines, and religions. As an example, a large community of Egyptians in Thessalonica participated in the cults of Isis, Serapis, and Osiris. Some followers of the cult of Isis were "wealthy Romans of high status."[1] The worship of Cabeiri or Kabiroi was popular. The Cabeiri were believed to be dwarf-sized magical creatures that protected crops, and their worship was especially connected to the Greek island of Lemnos.[2]

Still the Greek culture and language continued to dominate even as the city became a center of Roman and international influence. The Greco-Roman pantheon of gods was worshiped, as was the emperor. These gods and goddesses were the objects of public cultic devotion, and coins were minted in their honor. As with cults and guilds, private associations were organized around cultic adoration, typically in the form of feasts, given in honor of a sponsoring god or goddess.

The worship of Dionysus, named Bacchus by the Romans, is an example of religion in Thessalonica. Dionysus was the god of wine: grape cultivation, winemaking, wine consumption, and fertility. Dionysus was worshiped both in the public cult, with official, state-appointed priests, and privately within guilds and other types of private associations. Because of Dionysus's association with wine consumption and fertility, he was also linked to music, theater, and ecstatic dance.

THE GUILD FEAST

In many ways, the guild feast resembles the other special feasts described in this book. Like the religious or the funeral clubs, one of the primary reasons for the existence of the group was to gather for a special meal. The form of this celebration was like that of the banquet: a meal followed by a symposium. The guild feasts allowed those without the social or financial status to host or attend a banquet as described in chapter 5 with men like themselves.

Guilds were typically organized around a common identity, perhaps similar ethical and religious beliefs, shared ethnic backgrounds, or similar occupations. Groups based on professions were the most common. They were different than modern trade unions. The reasons for their existence were not economic or based on political objectives such as improving working conditions. Instead, the purpose was to increase status and honor of the members, as well as to foster social intercourse and a sense of cohesion. Guilds provided "surrogate benefits of an enlarged family or a miniature *polis.*"[3]

Individuals joined a guild by first making application to its leadership. The candidates' names were then submitted to the entire guild for a vote of acceptance. Club bylaws typically defined requirements for membership. One responsibility was financial. The new members paid an entrance fee and monthly dues that were used to purchase wine for the banquets. Additional money was collected for monthly and annual festivals. Members were required to pay fines for misbehavior. For members of some of the poorer guilds, the fees and dues required a large financial commitment, but with guild membership came honor and a relationship with the club sponsor.

The guilds usually had both a human and a divine sponsor. The human sponsor was a wealthy patron who donated food and money to the group and on occasion hosted a formal banquet. Some of the patron banquets included a visit to the baths and massages before the feast. Being a guild patron was an honorable, sought-after status considered a "higher good than simple money."[4] The guild provided the patron with titles, honors, and dedications. It also sponsored feasts on the patron's birthday and the birthdays of his or her family members.

Guild feasts often contained a sacred element, with special celebrations held for their divine patrons. Ceremonies in honor of the deity were part of the symposium with a wine libation, prayers, and songs. The rituals corresponded to the religious piety of the group. For example, some clubs acted out an aspect of the mythology of their divine patron. Members who did particularly well reading their parts received additional servings of the meat. Other groups might hear a reading about their sponsoring god or goddess. Music and dancers were also part of special symposia, though wine and conversation remained the favorite type of entertainment.

"Too many of these clubs were nothing more than groups of disorder- lies and drunks."[5] Some guilds emphasized the social aspect of their group with names related to the consumption of alcohol: "Late Night Drinkers," "Society of Diners," and "Comrades of the Symposium."[6] At various times all guilds were prohibited by imperial edict. Reactions by the guilds varied. After one imperial action, the members of guilds rioted, though usually the response to legal action was not as violent and instead led to renewal of club bylaws. Guild rules typically described model behavior and provided punishment for rowdy conduct.

The feast could be quite simple, in some cases just bread and fish. Of course, the members consumed wine during the symposium. A pig could be sacrificed and roasted for special occasions. The officers, sponsor, and special guests received the largest and most choice parts of the pig with the rest of the meat split among the remaining membership. The fat was offered to the sponsoring god or goddess, so the divine partner had a place at the table. It might seem as though there were advantages to being an officer, but those in charge paid more in dues and fees and had greater responsi- bilities when preparing for a feast. In many cases, the bylaws reflected this greater commitment by assuring that the officers (for example, president, treasurer, or host of the feast) received the best portions of the meat.

Guilds of all types often met in locations that reflected their purpose. Religious clubs would feast in special banqueting rooms connected to a temple. Funeral groups usually gathered in a special banqueting room near the city's burial site. Trade guilds usually met in spaces designed for ban- quets. The location might be a hall specifically constructed for guilds to rent for their feasts. Occasionally a guild became wealthy enough or a sponsor generous enough to buy its own banqueting house. Many of the smaller guilds rented a room in a large house. Some Roman or Greek homes, more like palaces, were built with small rooms facing the street that were leased to businesses, as well as one or more banqueting rooms that opened to courtyard gardens. Surprisingly, many of the grand homes contained spaces that were open to the public. The people of the city could walk into the atrium, gardens, and peristyle to enjoy the peace and admire the art.[7]

Regardless of the location, the banqueting area required a well- equipped kitchen, cistern, and dining space large enough for the member- ship to meet. The ideal space included a built-in *triclinium*, perhaps made of stone, on which cushions and blankets were placed for reclining. As many as thirty-six diners could recline on a large *triclinium*, designed for a small guild. But some guilds had more than 100 members; the College of Carpenters in Ostia recorded 350 names of members.[8] It is unfortunate that archaeological endeavors have not produced evidence describing what furnishings were used for large groups and how the spaces were arranged. We do know that *stibades*, or "straw mats," were essential.[9] Were benches with mats and cushions used along with multiple tables? Were several *triclinia* arranged in one large space or in multiple rooms? Because of the importance of collegiality at the banquet, I suspect the guild preferred to meet as one body, if possible, rather than being divided into separate spaces.

PAUL IN THESSALONICA

Thessalonica was Paul's next destination after quickly leaving Philippi. It was almost one hundred miles west on the Via Egnatia. The road took them through two towns, Amphipolis and Apollonia, that were approximately thirty miles apart, far enough to provide places of rest on the journey. Quite a few years ago, I trained for a three-day, sixty-mile walk. The purpose was to raise money for cancer research. My best day was twenty-one miles. I cannot imagine someone of Paul's health and age walking more than that, even though he lived in a culture of walking and had already journeyed great distances in his travels. I think it realistic to assume that he and Silas walked fifteen to twenty miles a day and stopped at both towns for days of rest.

We do know that his time in Thessalonica was short. Acts mentions that he taught in the synagogue for three consecutive sabbaths (Acts 17:1–2). It seems reasonable to believe that Paul was there long enough after those three weeks to spend time with the young Christian community, organizing and teaching. He likely spent only a total of several months. We do know that Silas and Paul left the city in a hurry, much sooner than they anticipated.[10] Many biblical scholars believe Paul wrote his first letter to the Christian community in Thessalonica while he was in Corinth. Timothy visited the young church at Paul's request and returned with news that it was thriving. He also brought questions from the church for Paul to answer. It is probable that the new community shared one or several meals of thanksgiving with Paul derived from the banquets described earlier, especially the guild or religious feasts, which in turn were based on the model of the banquet in chapter 5.

The first letter to the Thessalonians is the first of Paul's known letters and the first of the books and letters comprising the New Testament. It is interesting because he does not address the usual themes of his later letters. For example, he completely bypasses any mention of circumcision or whether their diets adhere to the kosher rules described in the Hebrew Scriptures. Most obvious, Paul does not discuss justification by faith. Instead, knowing the converts were primarily Greeks, he argues a case to remain steadfast to their renunciation of the gods and goddesses, bidding them to live a moral life consistent with the life and teachings of Jesus. He addresses the issue of suffering by using himself as an example. Another question they asked concerned those who died and whether they would be with God on the other side of the grave. Paul responds that those who died would be raised and present with Christ before those who were still alive (1 Thessalonians 5:1–11). As he does in his other letters, he emphasizes the need for love "for one another and for all" (1 Thessalonians 3:11–13).

Paul and the Synagogue

The Jewish population in Thessalonica was not extremely large but apparently significant enough in size to support a synagogue. One must remember that a first-century synagogue was quite different from a modern one. The synagogue building was used for community meetings and for groups to study the Torah. The surrounding community would have considered the synagogue much like other religious associations.

Paul often began his evangelical efforts at synagogue meetings, where he would use his knowledge of Hebrew Scriptures to make a case that Jesus was the long-awaited Messiah. The response was almost always the same. At first, the people of the synagogue were intrigued. After hearing him several times, the membership divided into two groups: those who believed he was wrong and his teachings were dangerous, and those that found Paul's message compelling. At that point Paul and his small band of followers split from the synagogue to create a Christian community. Some who remained in the synagogue ignored Paul after he left. Others tried to force Paul to leave town, sometimes by violent means. Later in his ministry, groups of faithful Jews attempted to have him arrested and executed. He was helped by the fact that he was a Roman citizen.

Paul's background was supportive of his ministry to Gentiles. He was raised in Tarsus, a city where Greek culture and language dominated. It was known as a scholarly community because of its excellent library. There is speculation that Paul studied rhetoric in a Greek school as well as

Hebrew Scriptures with a rabbi. His knowledge of rhetoric enabled him to debate both Jews and Gentiles. His knowledge of scriptures gave him a foundation for his arguments. Jews outside of Palestine typically used the Septuagint, a Greek version of the scriptures, for their reading and studying at the synagogue. It is also likely that prayers and lectures were in Greek. It makes sense that, when Paul quoted scripture, he used the Greek version, the Septuagint. This gave Greek Gentiles the ability to attend the synagogue and understand lectures and worship. These non-Jews were called *God-fearers* because of their connection to a synagogue. Most did not totally embrace Judaism but believed they benefitted from the radical moral and monotheistic beliefs. It was in this milieu that Paul received his early life education. It made sense to him that Gentiles should be part of a Christian community, just as they had been part of his early synagogue experience.

Later in his life Paul studied in Jerusalem with the great rabbi Gamaliel. He approached his studies with zeal and assumed that the first Christian communities were a perversion of Judaism. He honed his studies of scripture and learned how to debate with Jews using his knowledge and background as a scholar. Even his zealous persecution of early Christians helped him understand the perspective of many Jews and Jewish Christians.

Wine, Vinegar, and Beer

The following is a recipe for making Thasian wine recorded by Florentinus from his treatise *Geoponica*:

> We dry ripe grapes in bunches in the sun for five days; on the sixth at midday, we put them, still warm, into must, with sea-water which has been boiled down to half, then remove them and put them in the vat and press them; then, after a night and a day, we put [the must] in jars. When it has fermented and cleared, we are at a twenty-fifth part of concentrated must. After the spring equinox we transfer into smaller jars.[11]

Wine was a significant part of the ancient Mediterranean diet. Along with olives and grains, wine was one of the three elements of the all-important trinity of Mediterranean foods. It still is. Wine also was considered a special gift of generosity and a drink of great symbolic importance just as it is now.

The average first-century family consumed approximately 350 liters of wine per year. This is an amazing amount, especially when compared to modern consumption. French families are the largest consumers of wine today, and they consume only 60 liters per year. Ancient households were much larger than their contemporary counterparts, with multiple generations and servants or slaves drinking wine. Still, the amount was substantial.[12]

The techniques of grape cultivation and wine production as described by ancient writers such as Pliny the Elder and Cato were well established by the first century CE and were little changed in Italy and other Mediterranean countries until the last century. Large amounts of wine, both red and white, good and mediocre, were produced around the Mediterranean Basin, especially in the north and east.

Ancient farmers harvested their grapes later than their modern counterparts. The result was that some of the water in the grapes evaporated, causing the remaining juice to be more concentrated, resulting in a higher amount of sugar and thus a higher alcohol content. The grapes were collected in baskets that were lined with pitch. The pitch made baskets waterproof so that any juice released by the grapes remained during transport.

Treading the grapes was the first step after the harvest.[13] This process released much of the juice from the fruit. It also exposed the juice to the outer skins, which contained the yeast necessary to begin fermentation. The grape skins and the juice from the treading, called must, were then placed in a wine press where even more juice was extracted. By the first century, presses used wooden beams, cranks, and weights. The press placed significantly more weight on the grapes than feet did and extracted much more juice. It also crushed some of the pips, giving the finished product more flavor.

The must from pressing was drained into large tanks, and then the juice was moved to fermenting vats. These were made of clay and coated with pitch to keep them from leaking and to prevent the must from being contaminated by air. The pitch also gave the wine a slightly resiny flavor, which was enhanced in some wines by storage. The taste of the end product was likely similar to the modern Greek wine *retsina*. The vats were partially buried in the ground for temperature control and sealed.[14] The fermentation process began as soon as the juice came into contact with the grape skins during tramping and pressing:

> There are two varieties of yeast on grape skins; one of those begins the process of turning the sugar in the grape juice into alcohol as soon as the juice comes into contact with the outer skin. Within one or two days, this yeast converts nearly half the sugar in the grapes to alcohol, producing an alcohol level between four and five percent. The initial

yeast dies at this point, killed by the alcohol, and a secondary, slower fermentation begins.[15]

Air was and still is the enemy at every step in the vinting process. Wine that is exposed to air turns sour; in fact, it can develop into vinegar. The wine in amphorae risked being exposed to air because the containers were made of clay. As with the fermenting vats, because clay is porous, small amounts of air constantly leached through the walls and eventually spoiled the wine. The interior was covered with pitch to block air from seeping into the containers and keep the wine from spoiling. The lids were also covered with pitch and sealed onto the opening.

Evidence from archaeology and archaeochemistry confirms that wine was created in a range of colors and flavors. Red wines tended to be of a lighter color than its modern counterparts because the must was left with the skins for a much shorter time. Modern wines produce much of their flavor from the juice sitting with the skins. "No ancient author refers to maceration of red grapes after pressing, except to produce a cheap secondary wine."[16] An exception was Greek *melas*, or black wine. The must mingled with skins for a longer time so its pigment was similar to a modern red. Sometimes the vintners mixed a high-quality mature wine with a newer wine of lower quality. The end product had a much better aroma and flavor. The best wines were heavier and sophisticated by ancient standards and needed no additional flavorings.[17]

Most of the white wines vinted in the first century were very light. The must mixed with the skins and pits for an even shorter time than for reds. The result was that the juice was exposed to less yeast and fermentation and did not produce as high an alcohol content. These wines were usually consumed locally because they did not travel well. Since they were much less substantial, there was less need to mix them with water.[18]

Flavorings were added to wine at three different points: before fermentation, during fermentation, and afterward. Salt, or reduced saltwater, was added before the must was moved to the fermentation vats. Pitch or resin was added during the fermentation process, as a rule, by covering the inside of the vat and lid with either product. On occasion, wines were exposed to smoke during fermentation.

Flavorings added after fermentation and before serving wine were common. *Mulsum* was an aperitif crafted with wine, honey, and sometimes spices. Columella recommended a *mulsum* aged in smoke with the addition of grape must and honey.[19] *Conditum* was a wine flavored with herbs and spices. There was even a travelers' *conditum*, called *conditum viatorium*. It was a form of concentrated spiced wine added to the ordinary wine purchased while traveling. Flavorings such as aloe, saffron, elderberry, myrtle berries, nard, roses, violets, lilac flowers, coriander, celery, anis, almonds, pepper, and cinnamon were common. Grape must that was boiled to the consistency of syrup, called *defrutum* or *saba*, became an additional sweetener.[20]

Passum wine was similar to a modern Italian wine called *amarone*. With both wines, the grapes are placed on drying racks until much of the moisture evaporates and the sugars become quite condensed. Modern amarone has a rich and slightly "raisiny" flavor. The same was true with *passum*.

Serving Wine

The Roman practice was to pour the wine through a strainer, called a *saccus*. Additional flavorings could be added by placing them in the filter. Crushed bitter almonds, anise seed, and snow were commonly used. Only the wealthiest Romans managed to pay to transport snow or ice from the alps to Rome.[21]

Water was then added to the wine. Greeks, Romans, Jews, and others believed wine, when properly used, enabled a person to relax and become less inhibited. However, drunkenness was despised. It was believed that drunkenness caused by unmixed wine resulted in madness and death. Water permitted larger amounts of wine to be consumed without intoxication. Diluted wine also enabled people in the first century to drink water with less fear of becoming ill. People in the ancient world knew that water was often contaminated. The alcohol in the wine provided an antibacterial guard. To ensure that water was safe, sometimes it was boiled before being mixed with wine.

Ancient wine was stronger than modern varietals. Grapes were harvested later in the fall, allowing some of the water in them to evaporate, giving them a larger percentage of sugar to convert to alcohol. Concentrated must was also added during the fermenting process, providing even more sugar. This technique was common with wine that was shipped long distances.

For ordinary meals, water was added to wine in the goblet. For a special meal or banquet, the wine was poured into a *krater*, a large bowl used exclusively for mixing wine and water. The ratio of wine to water was 2:3, or perhaps 1:2. Older men were believed to need stronger wine. Likewise, women, with their "cold" and "wet" nature, were also believed to need stronger wine. Ancient philosophers and medical experts believed that men and women were made up of opposite natures. Men have hot and dry natures relating to earth and fire, and women have cold and wet natures relating to air and water. Men were drawn to roasted meats and women to boiled foods and drink. Women were also more likely to feel sad and melancholic, reacting with tears. Wine was believed to help this condition in women.

Wealthy Romans, like the classical Greeks, imported wine from a variety of regions around the empire. They studied and tasted many different wines and became connoisseurs. Most people drank a wine that was marginally better than vinegar. There is a story about a famous Roman politician named Marcus Antonius:

> He found himself on the wrong side of a political power struggle and hid in the house of an associate of far lower social status. As an act of hospitality his host accidently caused Antonius' death. The associate sent his servant to a neighborhood wine shop to buy a bottle of wine for their guest. When he tasted the usual family wine, the servant decided the quality was not good enough for the noble Antonius. So, he purchased a far better and much more expensive wine. When questioned by authorities, the wine merchant mentioned the servant's "suspicious" behavior. This led the authorities straight to Antonius' hiding place. All for a good glass of wine![22]

The Spirituality of Wine

Wine had great symbolic importance for many of the first-century religions. Even today, a bottle of wine brought to a dinner party is a gift of hospitality and thankfulness. In the first century, wine was a valuable gift to humanity from a god or, in the case of both Judaism and Christianity, the one God. The Greeks worshiped Dionysus and the Romans Father Liber as the god bestowing the gift of the grape to humanity. These gods were thanked at banquets and important meals with a hymn and libation sacrifice. The libation ritual included pouring a small amount of wine on the floor or in a fire and drinking a sip of wine that had not been diluted from a common cup.

Jews used prayers of blessing and thanksgiving over the wine at the weekly Sabbath meal and at Passover when four cups were blessed and consumed. The *Todah* or thanksgiving ritual at the temple was the only sacrifice to include both leavened and unleavened bread (Leviticus 7:11–15). The feast following the sacrifice included the sacrificial lamb, bread, and wine. Psalm 116, a Todah psalm, mentions a cup of wine that is "the cup of salvation" (Psalm 116:12–14, 16).[23]

Christians incorporated both bread and wine as part of their worship feasts in a familiar pattern, giving thanks for bread before the meal and wine before a Christianized symposium. In 1 Corinthians, Paul wrote that he received instructions regarding the sacred feast from the already-existing tradition of the followers of Jesus. The text notes that Jesus added this phrase after blessing the bread: "This is my body that is (broken) for you. Do this in remembrance of me." With the wine, Paul wrote that Jesus said, "This is the new covenant in my blood. Do this as often as you drink it, in remembrance of me. For as often as you eat this bread and drink the cup, you proclaim the Lord's death until he comes" (1 Corinthians 11:23–26).[24] Followers of Jesus have for millennia experienced this practice as spiritually important.

VINEGAR FOR THE KITCHEN

Vinegar literally means "sour wine" and is made by a secondary fermentation. It was extremely important to the people of the Roman world. Vinegar was indispensable for cooking, preserving (pickling), flavoring foods, making medicines, and drinking as an alternative to wine for the poor.

Little is known about the first creation of vinegar, but it likely made itself only months after the vinting of the first wines. It forms when wine or other types of alcoholic beverages are exposed to air. Along with the oxygen, air-breathing (aerobic) bacteria enter the wine and oxidize, that is, combine chemically with the alcohol and oxygen to make acetic acid or vinegar.

Ancient storage methods were prone to leaking oxygen. Amphorae were made from clay and thus porous, allowing small amounts of oxygen to seep into the wine. Eventually they were coated with pitch, which slowed the introduction of oxygen. These large containers were sealed with clay and wax and sometimes with pitch. Still, the lids eventually dried and cracked and allowed air into the containers. The introduction of air and aerobic bacteria occurred most likely when the amphorae were opened and the wine transferred to smaller containers. As today, unless all the wine in a bottle is consumed quickly, the remaining amount will eventually turn sour. Because an amphora held seven gallons, the proper storage and treatment of the wine was essential.

Vinegar was used for many purposes. Hippocrates in the fifth century BCE declared that it had a great medicinal capacity and it was used for that reason for millennia. It was utilized most often in the kitchen as a culinary ingredient and as a preservative when pickling a wide range of vegetables, fruits, and even small fish. Many of the recipes in this book provide examples of the use of vinegar in sauces and marinades. The Romans especially were fond of sweet and sour combinations, and vinegar provided the sour taste that often was balanced by honey or a sweet syrup such as *defrutum*.

It was essential that the right bacteria found its way into the wine. There are certainly unwanted aerobic bacteria present in the air, and the result when one contaminated the wine was less than satisfactory. Consider your half-finished bottle of wine that has "turned." The solution for a consistent product is not much different than it is today. The aerobic bacteria produce what is called a "mother," a "gelatinous scum full of living bacteria which forms on fermenting vinegar."[25] Existing vinegar with both a good taste and a mother was added to wine and was then exposed to the air. Water was added if the alcohol content of the wine was quite high, so the alcohol did not kill the bacteria. A mother of vinegar can be readily purchased online or at many kitchen or health food stores. When making red wine vinegar, I have found that a recipe using one bottle of wine produces enough mother to make several more recipes and still share with friends who wish to make their own. What was essential in the ancient world was that good vinegar with a good vinegar mother was available to produce more. Those who made vinegar industrially simply drained off most of the vinegar from a large barrel to bottle and sell. The mother and rest of the vinegar remained behind and fresh wine was added. The process was repeated continually.

Posca was a common vinegar-based drink believed to have been created by the Romans. It was just vinegar greatly diluted with water. It was also infused with herbs or spices, and sometimes honey was added. *Posca* was primarily consumed by the urban poor and those in the army. The army used it because it was inexpensive, easily stored, and believed to be strength-giving, while wine would make the soldiers drunk. Commanders in the army often drank *posca* in front of their men as a sign of solidarity. Cato, both a senator and a writer concerning agriculture, supposedly liked *posca*, but most of the upper class avoided it, considering it a drink only for the poor, preferring a good-quality wine. As with those in the army, travelers carried a flask of vinegar used as an antibacterial for unhealthy water.

It is believed by many scholars that the vinegar offered to Jesus on the cross was *posca*. Straight vinegar offered to Jesus would have been cruel as if death by crucifixion was not harsh enough (see, for example, John 19:28–29; Mark 15:36).

Very little is known either about the proportion of vinegar to water or the amount of flavorings added to it. Writers saw no need to give the existence of *posca*, a drink for the poor, more than a short nod, and they certainly did not provided recipes.

Beer: The Grandfather of Alcoholic Drinks

Wine from the vine has a fragrance like nectar;
Wine from barley stinks like a goat.
Wine from the vine comes from Bacchus,
Wine from barley comes from bread.

—Julian the Apostate[26]

The short poem by Julian the Apostate succinctly describes the Greco-Roman attitude toward beer compared to wine. This was not always the case. Beer is the oldest alcoholic drink in history. Its production paralleled the earliest years of civilization, both in the Fertile Crescent and in Egypt.

As tribes of people in both regions transitioned from nomadic hunter-gathers to settled farmers, they made two discoveries. Grains that became wet in storage pits sprouted. Moistened grains produced diastase enzymes, which convert starch to sugar or malt. Barley was the most common grain, and it produced the most maltose sugar.

The second discovery was that a watery gruel made with malted barley left sitting for several days underwent an amazing transformation. It became fizzy and slightly intoxicating.[27] The same type of discovery likely occurred with fruit or with honey and water, but only very occasionally. Barley and other grains were a major crop, and storage was simple, so a large amount existed for making beer.

With time and experimentation, the quality of beer increased; "more malt meant more sugar, and a longer fermentation means more of the sugar is turned into alcohol."[28] Boiling the barley mixed with water created even more enzymes and turned more starch into sugar, increasing the alcohol level. At the same time, the drink made with boiling water ensured that the end product was sanitary and safe to drink. The Egyptians developed a brewing technique where rye bread was crumbled into water and left to ferment.

Beer became the preferred drink of Mesopotamia and Egypt. By the year 3400 BCE, beer developed into a sign of civilization in part because the increased consumption of beer paralleled the beginning of written language. Beer became such an important part of the diet that it shaped a significant part of cultural, social, and religious identity. "To make a beer hall" or "to sit in the beer hall" meant "to have a good time." The Sumerian phrase "pouring the beer" referred to a banquet or feast. Egyptians used the phrase "bread and beer" as a greeting similar to "good luck."[29] It eventually was recognized as a gift from the gods. It was centuries before wine began to replace beer, and then only among the wealthy.

I joined an award-winning home brewer and friends to brew a beer following an ancient Egyptian recipe. The recipe was used to make beer for an Egyptian exhibit at the Hood Museum of Art at Dartmouth College in Hanover, New Hampshire.[30] The recipe reflects the fact that Egyptians added additional flavorings, such as date juice, myrtle, cumin, ginger, and honey. As anticipated, the flavor of the beer was different: "there is no residual sweetness in the brew . . . and [it] finishes with indefinable, subtle aromatics that seem unique to our taste buds."[31] The ingredients included dates, honey, gingerroot, and mandrake root. Hops, a component in most modern beer, was not used as a flavoring until the thirteenth century CE. Before then, hops shoots were harvested, cooked, and eaten in a manner similar to asparagus shoots.

Beer in ancient times had surface residue and sediment and so was consumed with straws. Xenophon, Greek philosopher, historian, and military leader, wrote about using straws to drink beer:

> The grains of barley floated on top of the bowls, level with the brim. . . . When thirsty, one took a straw into one's mouth and sucked. It was at full strength, unless one added water, and was very pleasant when one was used to it.[32]

By the first century, beer was little known in the countries Paul traveled to. It was a drink popular in Spain, Gaul (France), and still in Egypt. It was not completely unknown by the Romans. The common Roman soldiers stationed in outlying garrisons drank it on a regular basis. The number of Romans consuming beer was large enough that the drink was described in Pliny the Elder's *Natural History*:

> The nations of the west also have their intoxicant, made from grain soaked in water; there are a number of ways of making it in the various provinces of Gaul and Spain and under different names, although the principle is the same. The Spanish provinces have by this time even taught us that these liquors will bear being kept a long time. Egypt also has devised for itself similar drinks made from grain and in no part of the world is drunkenness ever out of action.[33]

Pliny died in 79 CE while observing the eruption of Mount Vesuvius, and his nephew Pliny the Younger used his uncle's notes to finish the book.

MENU: THE GUILD BANQUET IN EPHESUS

Deipnon

Wine Made with Seawater, or another wine from the market
Red Wine Vinegar
Cornish Hens with Green Sauce
Split Peas with Sausage
Italian Flatbread (*Piadine*)
Mint and Green Peppercorn Dipping Sauce
Chickpeas with Almonds and Pomegranate Seeds

Symposium

Ancient Greek Dessert
Roasted Walnuts and Almonds, from the market

RECIPES

Wine Made with Seawater

There is no seawater in the mountains of Colorado where I live, so I added sea salt to a bottle of wine. The taste should be similar. This may not be your favorite, but it was extremely popular in the first century and is worth a try.

- 1 bottle red wine
- 2 tsp. sea salt
- ½ cup honey

Pour the wine into a pan. Add the salt and honey. Bring the temperature of the burner to medium. Stir until salt and honey dissolve. Do not let the wine boil. You may either drink it warm or let it cool to room temperature.

Red Wine Vinegar

A jar with "mother of vinegar" can be purchased online. Homemade vinegar is delicious. This vinegar can be used for every recipe that calls for red wine vinegar. Be patient. After making your own vinegar you may tell your friends that you are officially part of the Slow Food movement.

- 1 jar of vinegar "mother"
- 1 bottle of dry red wine such as a merlot or a shiraz
- Water

A glass container that holds the equivalent of two bottles of wine plus 1 cup is needed. The container must have a lid. Wash the container and lid and sanitize with boiling water. When container has cooled to room temperature, pour one bottle of wine and the jar of mother into the container. Refill the wine bottle with spring water and add to the jar with the wine. Tightly secure the top. Shake vigorously. Remove the top and replace it with cheese cloth held in place with rubber bands. Allow it to sit for two months. Keep away from sunlight and away from heat. It should be kept at room temperature. Remove the cheese cloth and taste. Strain out the mother and keep it in the original jar to make more vinegar. Pour the finished vinegar into jars and bottles. Use a tight cap on bottles you wish to store for months or even a year. The vinegar will mellow with age. Also make sure the jar of leftover mother has a tight lid. Store the leftover mother in the refrigerator.

Cornish Hens with Green Sauce (Apicius)

The original recipe was called "Green Sauce for Birds." I assume that Cornish hens will be easier to find and will taste better than peacocks.

- 1 hen for every 2 people
- 2 tsp. salt
- 2 tsp. pepper

- 2 tbs. dried thyme, divided use
- 1 garlic clove for each hen

Green Sauce

- Drippings and caramelized bits from roasting pan
- 3 tbs. olive oil, divided use

- 1 tbs. honey
- 1 tbs. fish sauce
- 1 tbs. white wine vinegar

- ¼ cup white wine
- 1 tsp. each ground pepper, ground caraway seeds, and ground cumin
- 1 tbs. thyme
- ½ tbs. mint
- 1 tbs. lovage or chopped celery leaves

- 5–6 pitted dates, cut into small pieces with kitchen scissors, rehydrated with boiling water
- ⅓ cup of finely chopped fresh parsley
- ½ tsp. salt

Preheat the oven to 350 degrees.

Cooking the Hens: Use 1 tablespoon of oil to rub hens inside and out. Rub the hens with salt and pepper. Rub inside with 1 tbs. of the thyme and stuff each hen with 1 peeled garlic clove. Sprinkle outside of the hen with remaining thyme. Oil a roasting pan big enough for 3 hens. Put the hens in the pan along with several ounces of water. Roast for approximately 50 minutes or until the thigh temperature is 160 degrees. Baste every 15 minutes with the pan juices. If the bottom of the roasting pan becomes dry, add another ounce or two of water. Allow to sit for 10 minutes. Using poultry sheers, cut out the backbone and then cut in half along the breastbone. Each half is a serving.

Green Sauce: In a small pot combine the drippings, caramelized bits, 2 tablespoons olive oil, honey, fish sauce, wine vinegar, and wine. Bring to a boil and add the pepper, caraway seeds, and cumin. Stir and then add the thyme, mint, lovage, marjoram, and a sprig of lavender. Turn burner to low and stir in the chopped dates. Finally, add the parsley and salt. If it looks too dry, add a little water just to moisten.

Adjust the seasoning, spoon the sauce over the hens, and serve.

Split Peas with Sausage (Apicius)

This is a simple recipe made special with the addition of meat.

- 2 cups dried peas
- 1 lb. pork stew meat (pork)
- 1 lb. Lucanian sausage from chapter 8, or Italian sausage from the market
- 1 medium yellow onion, minced

- 1 tsp. each ground pepper, oregano, coriander seed, and salt
- 2 tsp. fish sauce (optional)
- 1 tbs. dill
- ¼ cup wine
- 4 cups water

Soak the peas overnight. Drain and rinse. In a large skillet, cook the stew meat. When partially cooked, add the sausage. Continue to cook until almost cooked through. Remove the contents with a slotted spoon and let drain on paper towels. Pour out all the grease but 1 tablespoon. Add the onion and sauté until it becomes translucent. Add the meat back into the skillet. Then add the rest of the ingredients. Cook on medium-low heat until most of the liquid evaporates. Adjust the seasoning and serve.

Italian Flatbread (Piadine)

Piadine is an ancient flatbread that is still very popular in Italy. It works with this menu and is characteristic of flatbread. One of the original ingredients was natron, which is a naturally occurring combination of baking soda and other salts. It was primarily used for medicine and as deodorant. It was also used with vegetables to keep them from discoloring. This recipe cheats a bit by moving it from vegetables to bread.

- 4 cups all-purpose flour
- 1½ tsp. baking powder
- 1 tsp. salt
- 6 tbs. olive oil
- 1½ cups water

Using a food processor and the dough hook, process the dry ingredients for approximately 10 seconds. Add the oil and process until it is combined with the dry ingredients. Add the water and process until it becomes a soft ball, pulling away from the sides. Transfer to a floured surface and knead for a short time, 15–20 seconds. Divide into 8 balls. Rotate the balls with your hands until smooth. Loosely cover the balls with plastic wrap. Rest the dough for 30 minutes.

Place a dough ball onto a floured surface. Pat it to a 5-inch circle and then, using a rolling pin, roll to a 9-inch circle. Keep flouring the surface as needed.

Heat a cast-iron Comal or skillet over medium heat for around 3 minutes. Prick the *piadines* with a fork. Carefully put one *piadine* in the skillet at a time. Cook until spotty, looking like a flour tortilla, 1 to 2 minutes on each side, popping any large bubbles that appear. Remove and wrap with a kitchen towel to keep warm. Continue with the other seven *piadines*. Serve warm.

Mint and Green Peppercorn Dipping Sauce

- ¼ cup red wine vinegar
- ½ cup olive oil
- 2 tbs. fresh mint, chopped fine

- 2 tbs. pickled green peppercorns

Mix all ingredients and allow to sit so the flavors mingle. Stir again before serving.

Chickpeas with Almonds and Pomegranate Seeds

You will find pomegranate seeds at most markets. They can also be ordered online.

Dressing:

- 3 tbs. olive oil
- 2 tbs. red wine vinegar

- 2 tbs. pomegranate molasses
- ¼ tsp. salt and ½ tsp. pepper

Stew:

- 1 tbs. olive oil
- ½ red onion, chopped
- Two 15 oz. cans chickpeas, rinsed
- 2 cups chicken or vegetable stock

- 1 tsp. salt
- ½ cup almond slivers, roasted
- ½ cup pomegranate seeds
- ⅓ cup minced fresh parsley

Combine the four ingredients for the dressing in a small bowl. Whisk thoroughly and set aside.

Over medium heat, pour olive oil into medium-sized pot. Add the red onion and sauté until translucent. Add the chickpeas, stock, and salt. When stock has evaporated and the chickpeas are beginning to break down, remove from the heat. Pour the chickpeas into a serving bowl. Stir in the almonds, pomegranate seeds, and parsley. Restir the dressing and pour it over the stew. Toss the resulting dish as you would a salad. Adjust seasoning and serve.

Ancient Greek Dessert

Since you purchased pomegranate seeds for another recipe, mix ⅓ cup into this dessert,

⅓ cup of each:

- Lightly roasted almond slices, chopped
- Pistachios, chopped
- Dried apricots, chopped
- Raisins, chopped
- Honey

It is easier to cut the dates and apricots into small pieces with kitchen scissors than with a knife. Or you can put all the ingredients except the honey in a processor. After chopping, mix with the honey. Use a small ice cream scoop to serve on small plates. Spread the mixture on bread to eat.

12

TROUBLE DURING
WORSHIP IN CORINTH

All things are lawful to me, but not all things are beneficial.
All things are lawful for me, but I will not be dominated by
anything.
All things are lawful, but not all things build up.

(1 Corinthians 6:12; 10:23)

Conflict happens even in the closest and most loving families. Long-held disagreements can emerge at feasts and special occasions. Most of us have heard stories of the uncle who espouses embarrassing political opinions or the cousin who becomes a belligerent drunk. The meal that should build a sense of unity and familial love instead sows discord.

Divisions certainly existed within the church in Corinth. For example, there were frequent disagreements about sex, marriage, the nature of resurrection, and what was considered proper to eat and drink. Rifts in the community were most prevalent during their worship meals. These issues were predictable to some extent because of the nature of the city itself: a community made of entrepreneurs. Traditional Roman social structure was not as important as acquiring money. An ex-slave who made a fortune from trade was considered the model of success.

The church in Corinth was one that the Apostle Paul founded and nurtured for approximately one and a half years. We know from his letters, those that are part of the New Testament and others that he described that are now unknown, that the relationship between Paul and the church community were sometimes contentious. Paul's first letter addresses the issues that arose in the church after he left Corinth for Ephesus. Their worship practices raised both practical and theological questions.

Finally, instead of an in-depth examination of a type of food, this chapter will end with a Corinthian worship feast that you can reenact with your own fellowship of friends and family.

CORINTH, CITY OF ENTREPRENEURS

The ancient city of Corinth was built on a four-mile isthmus connecting the two major land masses of Greece, Achaia to the northeast and the Peloponnesus to the southwest, and surrounded by the Aegean Sea on the east side and the Adriatic or Ionian Sea on the west.[1] Corinth existed for approximately four thousand years until it was destroyed by invading Romans in 146 BCE. Cicero called the ancient city "the light of all Greece."[2] It was rebuilt by Julius Caesar as a Roman colony in 44 BCE.

Corinth was a city of manufacturing, especially products made of bronze and terra-cotta, and because of its location, the newly built Corinth became a major center of trade and commerce. The road across the isthmus and through Corinth controlled the movement of goods from the two major land masses of Greece. The ports directed much of the traffic of imports and exports to and from Rome and around the Mediterranean Sea.

Corinth's strategic placement resulted in a fast-growing, cosmopolitan population. The original citizens were Roman freedmen. Roman businessmen looking for fast profits soon followed. The city attracted poor immigrants and freed slaves from Italy and Greece, as well as people from Syria, Palestine, and Egypt, all coming to the city to make their fortune. The families usually at the top of the Roman social structure were reluctant to engage in business and trade, believing that this type of vocation was dishonest and beneath them. Filling this void, a few hardworking and lucky migrant citizens became quite wealthy. Still, Corinth had a huge social imbalance. Many people were poor, and over half of the population were slaves. Still, Corinth promised the possibility of wealth and social mobility in a way that few other Roman cities did.[3]

The Greek poet Crinagoras describes Corinth as a city of scoundrels.[4] Before its destruction, it had a universal reputation for sexual promiscuity. This "City of Love" was said to be dedicated to Aphrodite, with a thousand priestesses serving as temple prostitutes. The reality was that it was a port city "having all the problems of a rough, relatively new boomtown adjacent to two seaports."[5]

The congregation in Corinth must have comprised a combination of independent, self-made people and those who were accustomed to the coarse lifestyle of the docks. The acceptance of a crucified Jew as the Messiah was difficult; we know from Paul's description of his message of salvation that it was considered a "folly to Gentiles" and a "scandal to Jews" (1 Corinthians 1:22–25). Yet many Jews from the synagogue and a few God-fearing Greeks did accept the message. Many of the Greeks had already disavowed belief in idols and were drawn to the radical monotheism and high ethical standards of Judaism. Most did not convert but nonetheless attached themselves to a synagogue.

Equally difficult for these early followers was the adoption of a Christian lifestyle and ethic. Church members brought with them their previous religious beliefs, diets, and celebrations. Both Jews and Gentiles were required to restructure their lives in some manner. Unlike under Judaism, members of the new church were not required to be circumcised, and their diets were more flexible. Gentiles had to adhere to stricter views on human sexuality and drunkenness.

When addressing the overarching issue of divisiveness and unity within the young community, Paul writes, "Be in agreement and that there be no divisions among you, but that you be united in the same mind and the same purpose" (1 Corinthians 1:10). For Paul, the unity of the church was of ultimate importance. He made this point with several arguments, one by advising that under no circumstance should a member of the church sue another member in public court (1 Corinthians 6:1–8). The church must present itself internally and to the broader community as a cohesive body. The members brought different gifts to the church, for example, gifts of teaching, leadership, and healing, and as such, they were individually members of what Paul called "the body of Christ" (1 Corinthians 12:27–28). They also belonged to different socioeconomic groups. A few were wealthy. Some were slaves or ex-slaves. Many were poor. Considering these differences, the body was both an expression of unity and diversity. It engaged in a unified purpose, to undertake Jesus's ministry of reconciliation and become a community united by it. Paul taught that all aspects of community life, including what foods were eaten and how the community celebrated its worship feasts, reflected the unity of the body of Christ and its expression through the diversity of its membership.

THE APOSTLE PAUL'S THEOLOGY OF FOOD AND FEASTS

One of the issues faced by Corinthian Christians was whether to eat meat purchased at the market. Most of the meat came from animal sacrifices in pagan temples. Was the Christian who ate this meat somehow involved in the worship of an idol? Paul argues that a meal with sacrificed meat was to be avoided:

> No, I imply that what pagans sacrifice, they sacrifice to demons and not to God. I do not want you to be partners with demons. You cannot drink the cup of the Lord and the cup of demons. You cannot partake of the table of the Lord and the table of demons. . . . "All things are lawful," but not all things are beneficial. (1 Corinthians 10:20–23)

"Meat was tainted with the associations of idolatry even for Paul, the apostle of the clear culinary conscience."[6]

Paul believed differently about meat sold at the market or served at a banquet hosted by an unbeliever, even though this meat had likely been sacrificed to an idol. He argues that idols are not real gods and the followers of Jesus have the freedom to eat whatever they want if they do not knowingly participate in the actual worship of an idol. Paul suggests that, even though followers had the freedom to eat what they chose, they may choose to abstain out of love and to keep from becoming a stumbling block to their sisters and brothers. New Testament scholar N. T. Wright describes Paul's position in this way: he could have dinner with Jewish friends, share a kosher meal with all the rituals and prayers, and then later the same week enjoy the hospitality of Gentile friends and have no guilt about whatever was served to him.[7] Paul used an even stronger example where a Christian might even eat a meal in the temple of an idol and have the freedom to do so, knowing full well that the idol did not exist (1 Corinthians 8:10–13).

What about those who, because of their conscience, chose not to eat meat from the market? Paul reasons that there were those in his congregations with weak scruples. They were the ones who had spent their lifetimes worshiping idols and the gods they represented. They had shared in numerous sacrificial feasts, "imagining themselves to be participating in the life of the god by eating sacrificial meat. . . . They could not now touch meat without feeling themselves being dragged back into the world of idolatry."[8]

Jewish Christians were also challenged by issues of conscience. They had lived their lives without eating pork, meat with blood, or shellfish. Serving meat and milk at the same meal was also forbidden. The idea of eating food sacrificed to pagan gods and goddesses was repugnant to all Jews. Following Paul's dietary example would have violated their culinary DNA.

Paul concludes that there were two opposite positions involved that must be held in tension. One was freedom. Because the idol gods did not really exist, the Christian community had the freedom to eat any of the meat available in the marketplace without any fear that it was first offered in sacrifice. On the other hand, Paul realizes that the "strong" in the community, and especially himself, had a responsibility to those with a "weak" conscience not to use the issue of eating meat to unnecessarily challenge them. Paul claims he was a servant, actually a slave, to everyone, so that their faith might grow instead of being unnecessarily challenged. The result was that decisions should be determined by whether the community was built up in unity: "Do not seek your own advantage, but that of the other" (1 Corinthians 8:1–9; 10:24). "So whether you eat or drink, or whatever you do, do everything for the glory of God. Give no offense to Jews or to Greeks or to the church of God"[9] (1 Corinthians 10:31–32).

Paul provides a second example to prove his point, based on eating in the temple of an idol. A wide variety of banquets and feasts were eaten in spaces rented by pagan temples. They might be guild feasts, birthday banquets, funeral banquets, or simply a gathering of friends. The followers of Jesus had the freedom to attend such banquets if the purpose was feasting with friends rather than the worship of an idol. But what about the person invited to such a banquet whose conscience was weak? Again, Paul concludes that the freedom to eat when and where one chose should not be indulged if it causes someone else to fall (1 Corinthians 8:10–13).

Paul's third example illustrates how the Corinthian worship feast itself promoted division instead of building unity. Even though the meal included food and wine, the purpose was to eat the Lord's Supper. The focus was the unity of the community as the body of Christ. Instead of celebrating the feast as forging unity, Paul claims that each was eating their own supper. One can suppose that the wealthier members ate a more sumptuous meal and even became drunk while other members went hungry: "Or do you show contempt for the church of God and humiliate those who have nothing?" (1 Corinthians 11:22b). After all, as we have seen, even the pagan feasts promoted brotherhood and comradery. The community based on following Jesus should do at least the same.

Paul also provides for his readers and for us an outline of the worship meal. By using the phrase "received . . . handed on," Paul reminds the Corinthians that what he gave to them was from the oral tradition of the early followers of Jesus (1 Corinthians 11:23). The meal began with the blessing of bread: "The Lord Jesus on the night when he was betrayed took a loaf of bread, and when he had given thanks, he broke it and said, 'This is my body that is (broken)[10] for you. Do this in remembrance of me.'" The meal (*deipnon*) followed, and when it was finished a cup of wine was blessed with these words: "'This cup is the new covenant in my blood. Do this, as often as you drink it, in remembrance of me.' For as often as you eat this bread and drink the cup, you proclaim the Lord's death until he comes" (1 Corinthians 11:23–26). It is reasonable to assume that, after the meal, the blessing of the cup began a Christian symposium.[11]

Paul describes the types of symposium activities with his lists of spiritual gifts. We know that the gifts of the Spirit were used within the context of the entire church because they were "for the common good" (1 Corinthians 12:7). They included utterances of wisdom or knowledge, faith, gifts of healing, miracles, prophesy, discernment, various kinds of tongues, and the interpretation of tongues (1 Corinthians 12:8–10). It is probable that key passages of the Septuagint and the letters written by Paul and other apostolic letters were read and discussed. As with other types of banquets and feasts, the community most likely sang a hymn or a psalm.[12]

FOOD FOR THE LORD'S SUPPER

It is unknown exactly what the Corinthian church ate at their worship feasts based on the content of Paul's letter, though we can presume with some confidence. Certainly, bread and wine were not only present but essential. The Gospels tell us that bread was a key element at the Last Supper and was a symbol of a feast with God at the end of time. Wine was also important for the same reason, though some churches used a different drink or just stuck with bread.

Some worship feasts paired cheese with the bread. The cheese was likely a soft cheese or cheese curds.[13] Olives, olive oil, and salt were common additions to many meals, and several ancient texts attest to their presence at the table.[14] Another text demonstrates how some foods were blessed for the Christian feast: A list of fruits appropriate for blessing was then given: "grapes, figs, pomegranates, olives, pears, apples, mulberries, peaches, cherries, almonds, plums; not pumpkins, melons, cucumbers, onions, garlic or any other vegetable."[15] Hippolytus, in *The Apostolic Tradition*, not only gives thanks for the bread and wine but also offers prayers for olive oil, cheese, and olives:

> O God, sanctifier of this oil, as you give health to those who use and receive that with which you anointed kings, priests, and prophets, so may it give strength to all those who taste it and health to all who use it. (Chapter 5)

⌒

Likewise, if anyone offers cheese and olives, he shall say thus: Sanctify this milk which has been coagulated, coagulating us also to your love. Make this fruit of the olive not to depart from your sweetness, which is an example of your richness which you have poured from the tree of life to those who hope in you. (Chapter 6)[16]

Hippolytus described a drink given to the newly baptized of milk mixed with honey along with a cup of wine combined with water:

Over milk and honey mixed together in fulfillment of the promise which was made to the Fathers, in which he said, "a land flowing with milk and honey"; in which also Christ gave his flesh, through which those who believe are nourished like little children, making the bitterness of the heart sweet by the gentleness of his word. . . . (Chapter 21)[17]

Legumes and dishes prepared with grains played a large role at any meal. Vegetables, nuts, fruits, and cheese made the feast special.

The presence of fish created a distinctive meal. In addition, the eating and sharing of fish were important to the Gospel writers, and fish became meaningful symbols for the early Christians. They were the subject of miraculous catches (John 21:4–12; Luke 5:1–11) and the feeding of the four and five thousand (Matthew 14:13–21; 15:32–39; Mark 6:30–44; 8:1–13; Luke 9:10–17; John 6:1–15). The Gospels of John and Luke record that Jesus ate fish with his disciples after his resurrection:

Jesus came and took the bread and gave it to them and did the same with the fish. (John 21:9–14, esp. verse 13)

⌒

They [the disciples] gave him a piece of broiled fish, and he took it and ate it in their presence. (Luke 24:42–43)

The image of a fish became a symbol of Christianity and eventually a representation of the thanksgiving feast. Fish were expensive, so only small amounts or small fish such as anchovies were commonly served. The exception would have been when a wealthy member purchased enough larger fish for the entire community.

We know that Paul collected money from followers of Jesus for the poor in other churches (Romans 15:25–29; 1 Corinthians 16:1–4). Did church members also pay dues to defray the cost of their eucharistic meals in a manner comparable to those who paid dues for Greco-Roman guild and funeral feasts?

YOUR OWN WORSHIP FEAST USING
THE CORINTHIAN MODEL

(I recommend that you read this section before beginning the worship dinner.)

It is certain that worship during the first decades after Jesus's death, and even the first several centuries of Christianity, was radically different than any church service in the twenty-first century. Recent scholarship demonstrates that at least some, if not most, of the first-century Christian worship experiences were modeled on Greco-Roman banquets and other types of community meals, very much like the ones we have studied in this book. The worship meals of Paul's communities likely had the same two-part shape of the banquet, with a *deipnon*, or dinner, followed by a symposium, the difference being that Christians used the symposium for music and discussion instead of as a drinking party. As with Greco-Roman banqueting forms, the *deipnon* was sandwiched between giving thanks for the bread and giving thanks for the wine. The blessing of the wine signaled the shift from the *deipnon* to the symposium. In Christian communities of a more austere nature, a drink other than wine was used. For example, water was the worship beverage in at least one ascetic community. Other ancient communities, especially within the context of a special celebration, used still other drinks. This variety of drinks gives you the option to use an alternative to wine in your own feasts. Still, the normative experience was to bless wine at the beginning of the symposium just as it was for Greco-Roman feasts.

Paul used the phrase "Lord's Supper" in 1 Corinthians (1 Corinthians 11:20). However, it is questionable whether he was coining a new name for the worship event or repeating a phrase from oral tradition. He possibly was using it as a comparison between "your own supper" and "the Lord's Supper" (1 Corinthians 11:21). It became the "Lord's Supper when the diners showed regard for one another; then they were eating with Jesus." The phrase "Lord's Supper" was not otherwise used for the first three centuries of Christian worship.[18]

These feasts are perfectly suitable for six to ten people at your home, though you can easily accommodate more. If on a church property, the celebrating community may wish to use a small room or parish hall instead of the formal worship space. Those participating can either recline on cushions or sit in chairs for the meal. Short tables, such as coffee tables, may be needed if the group elects to use cushions and recline on the floor. The space should be made special with the addition of candles and other appropriate decorations. Remember that ancient worship meals were held in homes, and typically in those owned by wealthier members. After all, they were the ones who had the space to host what would have been a small group of twelve to twenty or an even larger group of thirty or more. It is also possible that a Christian community could have rented banquet space for their meals as did other religious or secular associations, at least until persecutions began in earnest.

Those of us from a liturgical tradition will notice that the order of the feast is reversed from modern or even ancient liturgies from several centuries after the beginnings of Christianity. The blessing of the bread occurred first and included an entire meal. What is frequently called the *Liturgy of the Word* was the symposium, or the second portion of the meal. The symposium would not have focused on scripture readings and a sermon as did later liturgical practices. Consider that no first-century Christian community could have afforded a set of Hebrew Scripture scrolls even if they were available. Most of the Christian letters and Gospels had yet to be written, and those that were would not have been universally available during Paul's lifetime. It is possible that a select number of important prophetic passages from Hebrew Scriptures were copied onto several pages, but we have no historical proof of this practice. Some Hebrew texts could also have been quoted by memory, especially by Jewish Christians. Do remember that the passages of scripture quoted by Christian authors originated from the Septuagint.

In his first letter to the Corinthians, Paul describes the kinds of activities that comprised the Christian symposium: "When you come together, each one has a hymn, a lesson, a revelation, a tongue, or an interpretation. Let all things be done for building up"[19] (1 Corinthians 14:26b–27). In place of a formal sermon, members might share stories they heard about Jesus, a section from one of Paul's letters, or perhaps a biblical passage from memory heard recently at the synagogue. The group then discussed what was shared. Those with the spiritual gift of teaching might lead the discussion. Evidence from the Acts and the Epistles seems to support the belief that sermons typically were not preached during a worship meal. Instead, the proclamation of the Gospel was reserved for a more evangelical setting, where the audience primarily included non-Christians.

As we have seen in previous chapters, a Greco-Roman symposium contained similar elements to the Christian feast: a libation prayer with wine, singing, sharing of some type of philosophical or poetic text, followed by discussion. I seriously doubt that the early Christian communities engaged in the drinking games that were popular at many secular banquets, though it should be noted that Paul's warnings against drunkenness at the Corinthian meals might lead us to assume that at least some of the community members drank too much wine (1 Corinthians 11:21).

HOW TO EAT LIKE A FIRST-CENTURY CHRISTIAN

The people of the Mediterranean Basin ate with the thumb and first two fingers of their right hand. They often used pieces of bread to help. Napkins were not common, but your feasting community may choose to use them at your meals. It was customary, at least among the wealthy, to have spoons available for soup. Most diners drank the broth and then ate the beans and vegetables that comprised the rest of the soup with bread or their right hand. Most Greeks and Romans preferred soup cooked until it was quite thick, making it easier to eat without a spoon.

Most of the menus and recipes in this book are appropriate for this Christian meal. Bread and wine are essential.

A wide range of groups, especially church groups, can enjoy hosting either this ancient feast or the one in chapter 13. We discovered that the meals from our last book, *The Food and Feasts of Jesus*, were used for special studies and banquets by many church groups from around the United States as part of a Lenten series or summer programs. Denominations with ordained ministers might feel more comfortable if a priest or pastor served as the leader during the meal. I have written the blessing of the bread.

The Corinthian Lord's Supper

THE *DEIPNON* (DINNER)

1. Set the tables with the food for the meal. Also place a pitcher, bowl, and towels at the table. Napkins and eating utensils are optional. Light candles as everyone arrives.
2. Those in attendance greet one another with the Kiss of Peace as they join the group. The sharing of the Kiss of Peace was characteristic of early Christian communities. If appropriate, kiss one another on the cheek as do southern Europeans. If not, shake hands or embrace.

3. The guests find a seat at the table and wash hands.
4. Once gathered, the leader and people stand, and the leader holds a whole loaf of bread and says the following words:

> O blessed God, we give thanks for the bounty of this land and for the bread you provide from your creation.
> We give thanks because of your grace given to us in Christ Jesus, who gave himself for our sins to set us free. In him we have redemption through the cross, the forgiveness of sins, according to the riches of his grace that he lavishes on us, the ways he enriches us in our knowledge of every kind, so we are not lacking in any spiritual gift.
> You are faithful, O God and by your love, we are called into the fellowship of your Son, Jesus, who is our Lord.
> May we praise your glory shared with our community gathered for this our work of faith, that the Lord Jesus on the night when he was betrayed took a loaf of bread, and when he had given thanks, he broke it and said, "This is my body which is given for you. Do this in remembrance of me."

Everyone responds by saying, "Amen."

5. The leader breaks the bread in half, an ancient sign of hospitality, and then shares it with all who are present. Each person takes a piece from the loaf. After each person takes and eats of the one loaf, they recline or sit. At this point the meal is served and eaten. A glass of wine can be served during the meal.

THE SYMPOSIUM

1. The dishes are cleared and hands are washed again at the end of the meal.
2. The leader raises a glass of wine and says the following words, "Jesus said, 'This cup is the new covenant in my blood. Do this, as often as you drink, in memory of me." All present say, "Amen."
3. The leader drinks from the glass of wine and shares it with all who are present. Certain foods, such as nuts, fruit, and sweets, are appropriately served as part of the symposium.
4. At this point, everyone's wine glass is filled. Continue to serve the wine during the symposium, keeping Paul's advice concerning moderation in mind.

5. It is appropriate to sing a song or recite a poem. The poem can be a psalm. The song may be shared by an individual or sung by everyone present.

6. It is also appropriate for a question to be raised for discussion. Instead of a question, someone present can tell one of his or her favorite stories about Jesus or share one of the parables. The Parables of the Kingdom (for example, Matthew 13) or sections from the Sermon on the Mount are appropriate (Matthew 5–7). Texts from the crucifixion and resurrection of Jesus can be used during the time before Easter. Again, these stories should be discussed by all who wish to engage in conversation.

7. As an alternative, a passage from one of Paul's letters can be read for discussion. A passage from one of the two letters to the Corinthians is especially appropriate.

   a. 1 Corinthians 8. Discuss how our liberty could be a stumbling block to others.

   b. 1 Corinthians 10:23–11:1. Discuss "lawful" and "beneficial" and Paul's emphasis on "things that build up."

   c. 1 Corinthians 10:14–22. Paul ties the metaphor of the Body of Christ with the bread and cup of worship. Also 1 Corinthians 12:7–14, 27–31 concerning the nature of the bread and cup.

   d. 1 Corinthians 12:1–11, 27–31. Discuss spiritual gifts given "for the common good." 1 Corinthians 13 for the gift of love that is the "more excellent way."

   e. 1 Corinthians 15. Discuss Paul's theology of the resurrection of the dead.

8. Another song may be sung. At the end of the symposium, the leader can dismiss the gathering with these words written by Paul: "The grace of the Lord Jesus be with you. May love be with all of you in Christ Jesus." Everyone says, "Amen."

9. The people once again share the Kiss of Peace before they leave.

MENU FOR A CORINTHIAN LORD'S SUPPER

Deipnon

Any of the Bread recipes in the book
Lamb Bites
Barley and Lentil Soup
Green Beans, Mushrooms, and Herbs
Salad and *Apicius* Dressing (dressing in chapter 9)
Peas and Basil

Symposium

Wine, Dried Fruit, Grapes, from the market
Almonds
Olives

RECIPES

Lamb Bites

I tried a number of lamb recipes for this book. Most are still in my notebook. This one is a favorite of mine. I use a mortar and pestle to grind the garlic and other spices. Grind the garlic with the salt. Then add the peppercorns and coriander seed. Eat leftovers with pita bread.

- 1 leg of lamb, deboned, most fat removed, cut into 1 in. pieces
- ¼ cup olive oil
- 2 garlic cloves
- 1½ tsp. salt
- 1 tsp. pepper

- 1½ tsp. ground coriander seed
- 2 tbs. chopped coriander leaves (cilantro) or parsley
- ¼ cup pine nuts, toasted, optional

Place the lamb pieces in a large bowl. Add the olive oil. Then add the garlic and ground seasonings. With your hands, mix the olive oil, spices, and lamb so that all the pieces are covered. In a large skillet, sauté the lamb until the pieces are brown and crusty on the outside and pink inside. If your skillet is not large enough, cook in several batches. Stir in the chopped coriander leaves or parsley. Finally, stir in the pine nuts. Adjust the seasoning and serve.

Barley and Lentil Soup (Galen)

- ½ cup pearl barley
- ¼ cup olive oil
- 1 leek, washed, and bottom section cut into half rings.
- 1 garlic clove, minced

- ¾ cup red lentils
- 6 cups chicken stock
- 1 tbs. dill weed
- 1 tsp. each of salt and ground pepper

Soak the barley overnight. Pour barley and water mixture into a kitchen sieve to drain water. Let dry. Sauté the leek in olive oil, add the garlic and cook another 30 seconds until the garlic is opaque. Add the barley and cook until it is lightly toasted. Then add the lentils, stock, and the rest of the ingredients. Add additional stock or water if the soup becomes too dry. Cook until soup is thick. As an option, you may add chopped cabbage near the end of cooking.

Green Beans, Mushrooms, and Herbs

- 12 oz. green beans, ends pinched off
- 1 tbs. olive oil
- 6 oz. baby bella mushrooms, tough stems removed and mushrooms sliced
- 1 yellow onion, minced

- ½ cup of water
- 1 tsp. each dried oregano leaves, celery seeds, dried dill weed, and dried basil leaves
- ½ tsp. sumac
- ½ tsp. salt

Blanch the green beans in boiling water and then drain. Pour the olive oil in a heated skillet. Add the beans and sauté for several minutes. Add the mushrooms and onion. Continue to cook until onions turn opaque. Add ½ cup of water to moisten.

Add all the spices and continue to cook until the beans, mushrooms, and onion are hot and look roasted. Adjust the seasoning and serve.

Salad and Apicius Dressing

The recipe for *Apicius* dressing is in the recipes at the end of chapter 9.

- 1 romaine lettuce heart, chopped
- 1 leek, washed, with white and pale green sections chopped fine

- Spring mix lettuces
- ¼ cup parsley, roughly chopped
- 1 tsp. pepper
- *Apicius* dressing (chapter 9)

Mix all the ingredients and dress with *Apicius* dressing.

Peas and Basil (Apicius)

Peas and basil are always a good combination.

- 4 cups dried peas
- 1 leek, white and light green sections, chopped thin
- 1 tsp. each coriander, cumin, dried basil, celery seed, ground pepper

- 2 tsp. each caraway seeds and dill seeds
- ⅓ cup white wine
- 2 tsp. fish sauce
- ¼ cup chopped fresh basil

Soak the peas overnight. Drain, and then boil in fresh water. Skim the top as needed. Then add the leek. Grind the spices that are not already ground.

Drain the peas and return to the pot. Stir in the spices, dried basil, wine, and fish sauce. Bring the liquids to a boil until they are almost evaporated. Add salt to taste, and stir in the fresh basil. Adjust seasonings and serve.

13

A SYRIAN EUCHARISTIC FEAST

Even during the New Testament period, Christian worship was known by several names. One was the use of the word *Eucharist* or "thanksgiving." The word can refer to the prayer over the bread and the cup, but in the early church it was understood as both the prayers of thanksgiving and for the entire feast.[1] The *agape* or "love" feast was also a common name for the worship meals of the early church. Some later writers refer to the agape feast as a meal separate from worship. However, in the first-century Christian communities, the agape feast and the Eucharist were synonymous. The Book of Acts uses the phrase "the breaking of bread" to refer to the worship meal of the Jerusalem community (Acts 2:42). The phrase was not used as prominently as either the Eucharist or the agape feast.[2]

This chapter provides an alternative model for a Christian worship banquet. The feast in chapter 12 is based on Paul's first letter to the church in Corinth; this one relies on material from the *Didache*, or *Teaching*. The Didache is believed by most scholars to have originated among Christians in Syria around the end of the first century CE. It demonstrates the existence of multiple models of the Christian worship feast in the first and second centuries.

Even a quick perusal reveals the differences between the worship meal in Corinth and that in Syria. First, instead of calling the meal the Lord's Supper as Paul does in 1 Corinthians 11:20, the section of the Didache related to the worship feast begins with these words, "About the thanksgiving (eucharist): give thanks thus . . ."[3]

Second, the meal began with a prayer of thanksgiving for the wine before being followed by the prayer of thanksgiving for the bread:

> We give thanks to you, our Father, for the holy vine of your child
> David, which you made known to us through your child Jesus, glory
> to you for evermore.

♫

> We give thanks to you, our Father, for the life and knowledge which
> you made known to us through your child Jesus; glory to you for ever-
> more. As this broken bread was scattered over the mountains, and when
> brought together became one, so let your church be brought together
> from the ends of the earth into your kingdom, for yours are the glory
> and the power through Jesus Christ for evermore.[4]

Third, the "cup-bread" sequence, instead of "bread-cup," may not
have been normative, but it was not unique. There is a strong possibility
that other Christian communities used this order for its worship feasts. For
example, Luke's version of the Last Supper used the cup-bread order with
an additional prayer of thanks for the cup after the meal:

> When the hour came, he took his place at the table, and the apostles
> with him. He said to them, "I have eagerly desired to eat this Passover
> with you before I suffer; for I tell you, I will not eat it until it is fulfilled
> in the kingdom of God." Then he took a cup, and after giving thanks
> he said, "Take this and divide it among yourselves; for I tell you that
> from now on I will not drink of the fruit of the vine until the kingdom
> of God comes." Then he took a loaf of bread, and when he had given
> thanks he broke it and gave it to them, saying, "This is my body, which
> is given for you. Do this in remembrance of me." And he did the same
> with the cup after supper, saying, "This cup that is poured out for you
> is the new covenant in my blood." (Luke 22:14–21)

The Didache was widely known in the early church. It was apparently
prevalent in Egypt where it was translated into Coptic. There are also versions in Latin, Ethiopic, and Gregorian. It was incorporated into a later
treatise known as the *Apostolic Constitutions*.[5]

Third, there was no reference to either the Last Supper, the crucifixion, or the resurrection of Jesus. The word "sacrifice" is not used until the
notes in chapter 14, where the reference is not to the sacrifice of Jesus but
to that of the participant in the meal:

> On the Day of the Lord come together, break bread, and give thanks,
> having first confessed your transgression, that your *sacrifice* may be pure.
> But let none who has a quarrel with his companion join with you until

they have been reconciled, that your *sacrifice* may not be defiled. For this is that which was spoken by the Lord, "In every place, and at every time, offer me a pure *sacrifice*; for I am a great king, says the Lord, and my Name is wonderful among the nations."[6] (Emphasis mine)

YOUR EUCHARISTIC (THANKSGIVING) FEAST FROM THE DIDACHE

The worship included the blessing of wine and bread, prayers, and a meal. But the prayers included no reference to the death and resurrection of Jesus, and there was no language connecting redemption from sin to the cross. The feast seemed to end with concluding prayers after the meal ("after you have had your fill"), and there was no mention of a symposium. The songs, readings, and discussion such as those described in the Corinthian feast could have taken place during the meal or before the prayers at the end of the meal. It is possible that symposia were so common that the author felt no need to mention one here. It is also conceivable that there were no symposium activities.

The Deipnon

1. Set the tables with the food for the meal. Also place a pitcher, bowl, and towels on the table. Napkins and eating utensils are optional. Light candles as everyone arrives.
2. Those in attendance greet one another with the Kiss of Peace as they arrive. The sharing of the Kiss of Peace was characteristic of early Christian communities. If appropriate, kiss one another on the cheek as do southern Europeans. If not, shake hands or embrace.
3. Find a seat at the table and wash hands.
4. The leader shall stand and hold a cup of wine and say the following words:

We give thanks to you, our Father, for the holy vine of your child David, which you made known to us through your child Jesus; glory to you for evermore.

Those gathered echo the prayer by repeating the phrase:

Glory to you for evermore.

5. The leader drinks from the cup and passes the cup so all can drink from it.
6. The leader then takes a loaf of bread and gives thanks by saying,

> We give thanks to you, our Father, for the life and knowledge which you made known to us through your child Jesus; glory to you for evermore.
>
> As this broken bread was scattered over the mountains, and when brought together became one, so let your Church be brought together from the ends of the earth into your kingdom; for ours are the glory and the power through Jesus Christ for evermore.

The people gathered respond,

> Glory to you for evermore.

7. The leader breaks the bread, an ancient sign of hospitality, and then shares it with all who are present.
8. After each person takes and eats of the piece of bread, everyone reclines or sits. At this time the meal is served, and all who are present enjoy the meal. Activities such as singing, reciting poetry, and discussion take place during the meal. The poem can be a psalm. The song may be shared by an individual or sung by everyone present.
9. It is also appropriate to raise a question for discussion. Instead of a question, someone present can tell one of their favorite stories about Jesus or share one of his parables. The Parables of the Kingdom (for example, Matthew 13) or sections from the Sermon on the Mount (Matthew 5–7) are appropriate. Again, these stories or teachings should be discussed by all who wish to become part of the conversation.
10. After everyone has eaten their fill, the leader says,

> We give thanks to you, holy Father, for your holy Name which you have enshrined in our hearts, and for the knowledge and faith and immortality which you made known to us through your child Jesus; glory to you for evermore.
>
> You, almighty Master, created all things for the sake of your Name, and gave food and drink to mankind for their enjoyment, that they might give you thanks; but to us you have granted spiritual food and drink and eternal life through your child Jesus. Above all we give you thanks because you are mighty; glory to you for evermore.

11. The leader and those gathered all say, "Amen."
12. The leader continues by saying,

> Remember, Lord, your Church, to deliver it from all evil and to
> perfect it in your love; bring it together from the four winds, now
> sanctified, into your Kingdom which you have prepared for it; for
> yours are the power and the glory for evermore.
>   May grace come, and may this world pass away.
>   Hosanna to the God of David
>   Marana tha.

13. The leader and those gathered all say, "Amen."
14. The people once again share a Kiss of Peace as they leave.

MENU FOR A SYRIAN EUCHARIST

A Shiraz or another favorite wine
Pita Bread
Middle Eastern Lamb Patties
Zucchini and Cucumber Stew
Lentils and Vinegar
Bulgur and Onions

RECIPES

Pita Bread

Pita bread is one of the favorite recipes for those who bought *The
Food and Feasts of Jesus*. With this recipe I used my KitchenAid mixer with
a dough hook.

- 1 tbs. quick-rising yeast
- 1¾ cups of water, approximately 110 degrees

- 4⅔ cups all-purpose,
  unbleached flour
- 1 tsp. salt
- 3 tbs. olive oil

Place the yeast and warm water in the bowl of your mixer. Wait until yeast
begins to activate, approximately 15 minutes. It will change color and begin to
bubble. Add the flour to the mixture. Then add the rest of the ingredients.

Mix with the dough hook for 5 minutes. Start on the slowest speed and then increase to medium slow. Let the dough rest for 15 minutes and then mix for another 5 minutes. The dough should be slightly sticky and springy to the touch. Add more flour 1 tbs. at a time if the dough is too sticky or water if it is too dry.

Remove and place dough in a large bowl. Cover with a kitchen towel or plastic wrap and allow to rise, approximately 1 hour, until it doubles in size. Punch down the dough, cover, and allow to rise a second time. After the second rise, turn out onto a floured surface and knead for approximately 20 seconds. Divide the dough into 10–12 balls and cover with the kitchen towel or greased plastic wrap. Allow to rise until doubled, an additional hour.

Place a pizza stone, oven bricks, or a thick baking pan in the oven. Preheat to 500 degrees. Roll out each ball of dough on a floured surface until 7 or 8 inches in diameter. Using a floured pizza peel or the back of another baking sheet dusted with flour, slide several pitas onto the baking surface. In several minutes they will puff and then begin to brown. Take out of the oven and stack the pitas on a cloth kitchen towel. Fold the towel over the top of the pitas and cover with another towel so the bread continues to steam as it cools. The recipe makes 10 to 12 pitas. Enjoy.

Middle Eastern Lamb Patties

This is another recipe developed by my friend Wendy MacAllistar.

- ½ cup dried apricots, cut into slivers
- 1 cup boiling water
- 2 lbs. ground lamb
- 1 bunch of green onions, minced
- ¼ cup pine nuts, toasted
- 1 tbs. ground cinnamon
- ½ tsp. nutmeg, grated

- 1 tsp. each salt and pepper, or to taste

The sauce:

- 1 cup Greek yogurt
- 1 garlic clove, minced
- 2 tbs. dill weed
- Sumac to garnish

Prepare a grill. Sliver the apricots with a pair of kitchen scissors. Cover apricots with the boiling water to soften, about 5 minutes. Drain. Combine all ingredients; form into 16 patties. Place 4 each on wooden or metal skewers. Grill until medium or desired. Lamb patties may also be cooked in the oven or in a skillet on the stove top. Adjust the seasoning and serve with the sauce.

Mix the yogurt, garlic, and dill weed. Sprinkle sumac on top.

Zucchini and Cucumber Stew

Apicius recommended peeling cucumbers before cooking or they will cause gas. Good advice.

- 1 clove garlic
- 1 cup Mediterranean-style olives
- One 6 oz. brick of feta cheese cut into squares
- 1 tsp. thyme
- 1 tsp. oregano
- 1–2 tbs. olive oil

The recipe:

- 1 tbs. olive oil

- ½ red onion, chopped
- 2 zucchini squash
- 8–10 myrtle leaves
- 18 myrtle berries, crushed with a mortar and pestle or spice grinder, the black skins removed
- 1 cucumber
- 1 tsp. ground pepper
- 1 tsp. salt
- 1 tbs. sumac

One to two days in advance: Mash the garlic clove with the flat part of a knife. Remove the skin. Place the garlic, olives, feta cheese pieces, thyme, oregano, and olive oil in a jar or a plastic container with a lid. Stir the mixture, cover, and refrigerate.

On the day of your meal: cut the ends off the zucchini and cucumber. Use a vegetable peeler and make lengthwise stripes. Cut in half lengthwise, and then cut the squash into halves. Cut the cucumber in half again, and then cut into little pie shapes.

Using a large skillet, sauté the onion in olive oil. Add the squash. As the squash cooks, add the myrtle leaves and berries. Remove the garlic from the olive and feta mixture. When the squash is almost cooked through, add the cucumber and the olive and feta mixture. Then season with the pepper and salt. Both the cheese and the olives are salty, so be careful not to add too much. Spread the sumac on top and stir it into the vegetable stew.

Adjust the seasoning and serve.

Lentils and Vinegar (Apicius)

- 1 cup red lentils
- 1 tbs. olive oil
- 1 leek, white and light green sections washed and chopped fine
- 1 garlic clove, minced
- 6 cups water or chicken stock

- 2 tbs. red wine vinegar
- 1 tsp. salt
- 1 tsp. ground pepper
- 1 tbs. sumac
- ¼ cup coriander leaves (cilantro) or parsley, chopped fine

Rinse the lentils using a sieve and set aside. Pour olive oil into a pot on medium heat. Add the leek and sauté. Then add the minced garlic and cook briefly. Then add the lentils. Stir and add the vinegar, salt, pepper, and sumac. Turn heat to a simmer and cover. Cook for 20 minutes, then remove the lid. Cook for an additional 10 to 15 minutes or until the lentils are soft and mushy and much of the water has been absorbed. Stir in the coriander leaves immediately before taking the pot off the heat.

Bulgur and Onions

This simple preparation can be a side dish for many of the meat and vegetable recipes in this book.

- 2 cups bulgur, #3 large cut
- 1 tbs. olive oil
- ½ yellow onion, chopped
- 2 garlic cloves, minced

- 3 cups water or chicken stock
- 1 tsp. salt
- 3 tbs. parsley

Use a strainer to rinse and dry the bulgur. Pour 1 tablespoon of olive oil in a warm pot. Add the bulgur, and stir until it is toasty. Add the onion and garlic and continue to stir. Then add the water or stock and salt. Bring to a boil, turn down the heat to a simmer, and cover with a lid. Cook approximately 20 minutes.

While the bulgur is steaming, finely chop the parsley. After 20 minutes, take the lid off the pot and stir in the parsley with a fork. Adjust the seasoning and serve.

14

CONCLUSIONS ABOUT FOOD, FEASTING, AND WORSHIP

There is a fine line between worship and the feast. In our last book, *The Food and Feasts of Jesus*, we described camaraderie and convivial joy that are part of a feast. Meals also define communities by emphasizing culture and identity. This is true whether the banquet is for a gathering of friends, a dinner for a trade organization, a funeral meal, or a eucharistic (thanksgiving) feast for a young Christian community. In every case, the meal defines the nature of the community: its history, culture, and beliefs. The feast is an opportunity for generosity, hospitality, and celebration. These were all elements of the ancient Christian worship-meal and of most feasts—Jewish, pagan, and Christian—of the first century.

It is no wonder that most ancient feasts included a religious aspect. The converse was equally true two thousand years ago; worship almost always included a special meal. This certainly was the case with Jewish feasts for the Sabbath; the great pilgrim celebrations of Passover, Pentecost, and Tabernacles; and for certain other sacrifices such as the thanksgiving (Todah) sacrifice. As we have seen in earlier chapters, Greek and Roman sacrifices and festivals included a feast, whether for an extended family, for a club or society, or for the entire community. These feasts often included elements such as an offering of sacrifice, prayer, singing, poetry, and, most important, fellowship.

This was the milieu into which Christianity was born. It is no wonder that a community meal was a central part of the ancient worship experience. The meal assisted in the building of community that leaders such as the Apostle Paul so cherished. He became upset with the community when it came together and abused the sacred meal:

> For when the time comes to eat, each of you goes ahead with your own supper and one goes hungry and another becomes drunk. What! Do you not have homes to eat and drink in? Or do you show contempt for the church of God and humiliate those who have nothing? (1 Corinthians 11:21–22)

The meal was an opportunity for the church to share its emerging traditions, including a setting where stories about Jesus and letters from Paul and others were discussed.

Just as food and feasts can build community and provide a group with a sense of history and identity, the special meal also can define a community and even differentiate it from others. A weekly Sabbath feast certainly was a defining element of Jewish family life and religion. It still is for many Jews, just as the Sunday dinner was and is for many Christian families. Intoxication and drinking games might be the goal at the symposium of a Roman banquet with male friends, but the guests at a Jewish banquet chose to drink wine and discuss questions about the interpretation of the Torah, the first five books of the Hebrew Scriptures. Greek banquets might include both philosophical discussion and alcoholic indulgence. A first-century guest could easily tell the difference between a Roman banquet and a Jewish one.

Paul and his young communities struggled with how to merge new followers of Christ who came from different religious and cultural backgrounds into a single worshiping and feasting community. The issues became especially complex when the new community was composed of both Jews and Greeks. What could they eat? Was economic diversity problematic for the creation of the worshiping and feasting communities as well? Would members of the Christian community whose experience of a feast always involved intoxication be content with a symposium where telling stories and singing songs was the focus?

FOOD AND THE LIFE OF THE SPIRIT

The spirituality of the feast is one in which God touches humanity through the senses: smell, taste, touch, and sight. It is the reality that God loves us, body and soul. The two are intertwined in the Judeo-Christian tradition and at the feast.

As in the communal meals described in this book, the food and wine open those at the feast to deeply know one another. As they put aside their defenses, the diners become more honest and forgiving. The participants begin to see one another through the lens of love. They also open themselves to God. Is it any wonder that the early followers of Jesus called the worship feast a eucharistic (thanksgiving) and an agape (godly love) meal?

I believe that the Apostle Paul and others, such as the author of the Eucharist in the Didache, understood the spirituality of the Christian feast. Paul's realization was based on his participation in both Jewish religious meals and the feasts described in this book. That was why Paul was disturbed by what he saw as abuses of the worship meal and why it was essential that divisive behavior must stop.

REMEMBERING THE POOR

Rome established a simple welfare system that guaranteed the poor were given flour for bread and porridge. Later, bread was allocated instead of flour. On major festival days, meat was also distributed. Outside the city, farm families and craftspeople facing economic deprivation relied on the generosity of family and neighbors, borrowed money for food and seed for planting, became tenant farmers for wealthy landowners, or sold some of their animals or part of their property. The most desperate sold themselves into slavery.

During times of food shortage, wealthy farmers and traders opened their stores of grain to the populace. They became local heroes, were given honors, and had statues erected as signs of their distinction. Once the time of crisis was over, they received at least a partial payment for the grain gifted to the community.

For most of the empire, the social safety net for the poor was not well planned, but hunger was dealt with on an ad hoc basis. Diseases and deformities due to the lack of protein were common, especially in the *polis*, the cities. The gap between the food available to the wealthiest members of society and the poorest was vast. The wealthy had constant access to vegetables, fruits, protein, and exotic spices and flavorings. The plebeians did not.

One can find a more consistent concern for the needs of the poor among Jewish and Christian communities. Paul makes a point in his letters to describe his collection for the needy in Palestine. In later centuries, Christian churches gathered food and clothing during worship for distribution to the poor. The Jews had a system where the poorer members of society could glean the fields. Jewish towns also kept community food storage facilities where those in crisis accessed a variety of foodstuffs, especially grains and legumes. They even had laws related to those who borrowed food from their neighbors and how those debts could be forgiven.

Food inequality should be a constant concern for all of us. Many religious and civic organizations take seriously their ministry and efforts of assuring that people do not go hungry. Our modern society has the additional issue of urban food deserts, where people living in certain neighborhoods must travel great distances to find a market with fresh vegetables and fruit. Large supermarket chains often shutter redundant stores to reduce overhead cost. Food deserts can be created even in a small town. I live in a small mountain community that is separated by a long and steep hill. At one time, both sides of town had a grocery store owned by the same corporation. The one that made the least money was closed. It was the store in a neighborhood where customers often walked to buy their food. Many people did not have the money or the transportation to travel to the market for fresh foods. It is a seven-mile walk to the other store, and includes a five-hundred-foot incline. A few of our local pastors banded together and pushed the town politicians to provide public transportation buses, which proved to be a great benefit to many.

THE MEDITERRANEAN DIET: ANCIENT AND MODERN

At its best, the diet of those in the ancient Mediterranean Basin resembles the food eaten today in the same region. As illustrated in many of these chapters, the poor often suffered from a lack of protein, and the urban plebeians did not have the same access to fresh fruits and vegetables as farmers did. The very rich often enjoyed an overabundance of protein and wine, which could play havoc with their health. But overall, the first-century Mediterranean diet was a good one for the average person, with a lot of vegetables, fruit, legumes, and whole grains.

There are now two billion people in the world who are overweight, with six hundred million considered obese. Forty-five million US residents attempt to reduce their weight each year and use plans such as the DASH diet, Weight Watchers, Atkins, and the Ketosis diet. These plans are designed so practitioners lose weight quickly. The Mediterranean diet stands out as a different way of eating. It is not a plan for weight loss and especially not rapid weight reduction, though many who follow a Mediterranean dietary plan do lose pounds. It is simply the way the people in the Mediterranean Basin eat, a dietary lifestyle.

The advantages of the Mediterranean way of eating are many. It was and is a nutritionally comprehensive diet consisting of a variety of flavors and foods. It just happens to be an eating plan that is healthy and especially heart healthy, and good for those with pre-diabetes and diabetes. It is no wonder that, for the last several years, *U.S. News and World Report* selected the Mediterranean as the best dietary plan. The decision was made by a panel of top nutritionists, dietary consultants, and doctors specializing in weight loss, heart health, and diabetes.

The daily diet for most of the people who live in the Mediterranean Basin should sound familiar to those who read this book. It consists of vegetables, fruits, grains (primarily whole grains), olive oil (the preferred fat), legumes, protein, nuts, herbs, and spices. Fish and seafood are special, on the menu several times a week. Poultry, eggs, cheese, and yogurt are used moderately, with poultry a once-a-week treat for most people. Meats and sweets are rarely eaten and truly are special-occasion foods. Wine and water are the most frequent drinks. This way of eating has changed very little over the last two millennia.

There is great diversity even within the Mediterranean Basin: Italian, Greek, French, Egyptian, Turkish, Moroccan, Middle Eastern, Spanish, and Portuguese cuisines all consist of different flavors and highlight different foods, using different herbs and spices, and emphasizing distinct ingredients. This variety can also be found among the various regions within the countries themselves. For example, northern Italian food can be quite unlike that found in the south. But the essential elements of the diet remain the same.

As the first-century cook would tell us, the work required to prepare dinner for an average multigenerational family of fifteen people was significant. Even though modern families are much smaller, with two adults typically both working, it does require extra time and energy to prepare an Italian dinner, even a simple one. The use of shortcuts is helpful and sometimes necessary. Purchase chicken stock and a good loaf of whole-grain bread. Buy sausage and cheese instead of making your own. When you do have time to cook, freeze part of the meal to eat on a day when everyone is busy.

As an aside, it is curious that as the people within a region or nation become wealthier, their food becomes less healthy. The flour used for bread becomes more refined, and whole grains and legumes tend to drop from the menu, only to be replaced by more frequent consumption of meat. The opposite is true when a people falls into poverty. Their diet becomes more austere, with proteins other than legumes and eggs too costly to purchase.

There are two other essential elements of the Mediterranean diet that are often missing from modern meals, elements that will bring more fulfillment to your experience of the feast. The first is enjoying meals with other people. Focus your attention on the food and drink, and on your family members and friends. Try eliminating electronics and television. Though it is fun to occasionally eat pizza and a salad from TV trays while watching a movie, make the normative experience the dining room or kitchen table. The second element is physical activity. Walking after a big meal and before a nap is always a good idea.

THE FEAST

Have fun cooking delicious and healthy meals for your family and friends. Use mealtime as an opportunity for fellowship. The feast, whether in a religious setting or around a home dining table, provides a setting for spiritual connection among its partakers. Consider inviting someone who typically eats alone, using the time for companionship and building friendships. Enjoy the feast.

NOTES

CHAPTER 1

1. Marcus Pircius Cato, *On Agriculture*, trans. William Davis Hooper, Loeb Classical Library, ed. Jeffrey Henderson (Cambridge, MA: Harvard University Press, 1934), 3–4.
2. New Revised Standard Version (NRSV).
3. Reta Halteman Finger and Goerge D. McClain, *Creating a Scene in Corinth: A Simulation* (Harrisonburg, VA: Herald Press, 2013), 98–99. See also Moyer V. Hubbard, *Christianity on the Greco-Roman World: A Narrative Introduction* (Grand Rapids, MI: Baker Publishing Group, 2010), 73–74.
4. This book follows a trend among historians where BCE (Before Common Era) and CE (Common Era) are used instead of BC and AD.

CHAPTER 2

1. Christopher Grocock and Sally Grainger, *Apicius: A Critical Edition with an Introduction and the English Translation of the Latin Recipe Text* (Devon: Prospect Books, 2006), 309.
2. Pliny, *Natural History*, trans. H. Rackham, Loeb Classical Library, ed. Jeffrey Henderson (Cambridge, MA: Harvard University Press, 1950), book 19, 493.
3. Patrick Faas, *Around the Roman Table: Food and Feasting in Ancient Rome* (Chicago: University of Chicago Press, 1994), 236.
4. Ibid., 293.
5. Andrew Dalby, *Food in the Ancient World from A to Z* (London: Routledge, 2003), 80.
6. Mark Grant, *Roman Cookery: Ancient Recipes for Modern Kitchens* (London: Serif Publishing, 1999), 27–28.

7. Aspen Pflughoeft, "2,600-Year-Old Blocks of Cheese Found in Pottery at Pyramid in Egypt, Archaeologists Say," *Miami Herald*, September 22, 2022.

8. Dalby, *Food in the Ancient World*, 177.

9. Berthold L. Ullman, "Cleopatra's Pearls," *Classical Journal* 52, no. 5 (February 1957): 193–201.

10. Dalby, *Food in the Ancient World*, 39.

CHAPTER 3

1. Cato, *On Agriculture*, 5. An *iugeriais* is two-thirds of an acre.

2. Ibid., 6–7.

3. Ibid., 3.

4. James S. Jeffers, *The Greco-Roman World of the New Testament Era: Exploring the Background of Early Christianity* (Downers Grove, IL: InterVarsity Press, 1999), 311.

5. Robert Garland, *Daily Life of the Ancient Greeks* (Westport, CT: Hackett Publishing, 1998), 91.

6. Faas, *Around the Roman Table*, 75.

7. Pliny, *Natural History*, book 19, 453.

8. Ibid., 461.

9. Faas, *Around the Roman Table*, 208–9.

10. Pliny, *Natural History*, book 19, 459.

11. Ibid., 455.

12. Ibid., 461.

13. Faas, *Around the Roman Table*, 228.

14. Pliny, *Natural History*, 457–59.

15. Ibid., 501–3.

16. Ibid., 505.

17. Maguelonne Toussaint-Samat, *History of Food*, trans. Anthea Bell (Malden, MA: Blackwell Publishers, 1998), quoting Aristoxenus of Tarentum, 698.

18. Pliny, *Natural History*, book 19, 487.

19. Faas, *Around the Roman Table*, 218, quoting Xenophon, historian and student of Socrates, *Symposium*, 218.

CHAPTER 3 ADDENDUM

1. A denarius was a day's wages for a laborer. The values in this chapter assume each denarius is worth fifty dollars. A more accurate number might be the minimum wage in the United States for an eight-hour day, or fifty-eight dollars per each denarius.

2. Jeffers, *Greco-Roman World*, 184.

3. Ibid., 186–87.
4. Ibid.
5. Even though it might seem as though the *populous integer* parallels the modern middle class, there are important differences. For one, they made up only a small percentage of the population. Second, they had less status in society than those of the modern middle class.
6. Jeffers, *Greco-Roman World*, 188.
7. Ibid., 221.
8. Ibid., 232.

CHAPTER 4

1. Peter Fibiger Bang, *The Roman Bazaar: A Comparative Study of Trade and Markets in a Tributary Empire* (Cambridge Classical Studies, Cambridge: Cambridge University Press, 2009), 105.
2. Paul Erdkamp, *The Grain Market in the Roman Empire: A Social, Political and Economic Study* (Cambridge: Cambridge University Press, 2005), 236.
3. Peter Garnsey, *Famine and Food Supply in the Graeco-Roman World: Responses to Risk and Crisis* (Cambridge: Cambridge University Press, 1988), 6.
4. Ibid.
5. Ibid., 10–11.
6. Ibid., 27.
7. Ibid., 45.
8. Ken Albula, *Beans: A History* (New York: Berg, 2007), 17. Also, Alan Davidson, *The Oxford Companion to Food* (New York: Oxford University Press, 1999), 448.
9. Ibid., 4.
10. Toussaint-Samat, *History of Food*, 44. See also Faas, *Around the Roman Table*, 195.
11. Vetches are called *tares* by the English.
12. Albula, *Beans*, 26.
13. *The Mishnah: A New Translation*, trans. Jacob Neusner (New Haven, CT: Yale University Press, 1988), habbat 18.1.
14. Albula, *Beans*, 26–27.
15. Ibid., 27.
16. Davidson, *Oxford Companion*, 448.
17. William Erskine, Fred J. Muehbaue, Ashotosh Sarker, and Baltram Sharma, *The Lentil: Botany, Production, and Uses* (Wallingford: CABI, 2009), 42.
18. Ibid., 13.
19. Albula, *Beans*, 13.
20. Pliny, *Natural History*, book 16, 519.
21. Erskine et al., *Lentil*, 13.

22. Albula, *Beans*, 17.

23. Pliny, *Natural History*, book 18, 267.

24. Ibid., book 18, 265. Also, Albula, *Beans*, 34–35.

25. Toussaint-Samat, *History of Food*, 45.

26. Albula, *Beans*, 41.

27. Pliny, *Natural History*, book 18, 263.

28. Ibid., 265.

29. Clifford A. Wright, *Mediterranean Vegetables* (Boston: Harvard Common Press, 2001), 108.

30. Ibid., 255.

CHAPTER 5

1. Francis Joannes, "The Social Functions of Banquets in the Earliest Civilizations," in *Food: a Culinary History*, ed. Jean-Louis Flandrin and Massimo Montanari Montanari (New York: Penguin Books, 1999), 33.

2. Ibid. Also, Massimo Vetta, "The Culture of the Symposium," in ibid., 96–97.

3. Douglas Neel and Joel Pugh, *The Food and Feasts of Jesus: Inside the World of First-Century Fare, with Menus and Recipes* (Lanham, MD: Rowman & Littlefield, 2012), 94.

4. Dennis E. Smith, *From Symposium to Eucharist: The Banquet in the Early Christian World* (Minneapolis: Fortress Press, 2003), 23–24.

5. Toussaint-Samat, *History of Food*, 265.

6. E.g., see the discussion of women and banqueting in Neel and Pugh, *Food and Feasts of Jesus*, 95–96.

7. Ilaria Gozzini Giacosa, *A Taste of Ancient Rome* (Chicago: University of Chicago Press, 1992), 23.

8. Faas, *Around the Roman Table*, 95.

9. Eugenia Salza Prina Ricotti, *Meals and Recipes from Ancient Greece* (Los Angeles: J. Paul Getty Museum, 2005), 9.

10. Faas, *Around the Roman Table*, 4.

11. Grocock and Grainger, *Apicius*, 31.

12. Umami now is considered a category of taste in food, along with sweet, sour, salty, and bitter. It corresponds to the flavor of glutamates found in foods such as beef, soy sauce, and mushrooms.

13. I have a difficult time imagining the appeal or the resulting flavor of disintegrating, fermented fish heads and entrails. Perhaps the taste was similar to anchovy paste.

14. These sauces can be purchased at most Asian groceries or online. I bought both through Amazon.

15. Faas, *Around the Roman Table*, 4.

16. See, e.g., Emeril Lagasse's recipe for his Creole seasoning in Julia Childs, *Cooking with Master Chefs*, 27. It includes salt, paprika, garlic powder, dried oregano, cayenne pepper, black pepper, onion powder, and dried thyme. The Creole seasoning then is used in a sauce for étouffée that includes an additional eight ingredients.

17. Faas, *Around the Roman Table*, 182–83.

CHAPTER 6

1. Wayne A. Meeks, *The First Urban Christians: The Social World of the Apostle Paul*, 2nd ed. (New Haven, CT: Yale University Press, 1983), 13.

2. Ibid., 37.

3. Ibid.

4. Ibid., 80.

5. The Torah comprises the first five books of the Hebrew Scriptures.

6. Gunther Bornkamm, *Paul* (New York: Harper & Row, 1969), 7.

7. Jeffers, *Greco-Roman World*, 217.

8. Bornkamm, *Paul*, 10.

9. Before the year 70 CE, Passover was celebrated only in Jerusalem and its suburbs. All the Passover lambs were sacrificed in the temple. It was not a feast celebrated in the diaspora until after the destruction of the temple in the year 70 CE.

10. Neel and Pugh, *Food and Feasts of Jesus*, 76.

11. Toussaint-Samat, *History of Food*, 101–4.

12. Davidson, *Oxford Companion*, 95.

13. Reay Tannahill, *Food in History* (New York: Three Rivers Press, 1988), 23.

14. Ibid., 51.

15. Dalby, *Food in the Ancient World*, 59.

16. Faas, *Around the Roman Table*, 189; Pliny, *Natural History*, book 18, 253.

17. Pliny, *Natural History*, book 18, 255.

18. Quote from a blogger responding to Suanne Lenzer "Tartine's Country Bread: Be Patient, Perfection Is Near," *New York Times*, April 22, 2014.

CHAPTER 7

1. Bornkamm, *Paul*, 29.

2. Sheila E. McGinn, *The Jesus Movement and the World of the Early Church* (Winona, MN: Anselm Academics, Christian Brothers Publications, 2014), 113.

3. Raymond E. Brown, *Introduction to the New Testament* (New York: Doubleday, 1997), 432.

4. Davidson, *Oxford Companion*, 44.

5. Faas, *Around the Roman Table*, 19.

6. Ibid., 18.

7. John Keay, *The Spice Route: A History* (Berkeley: University of California Press, 2006), 51.

8. Ibid., 59.

9. Ibid., 58.

10. Ibid., 60.

11. Orache—a leafy plant that grows wild in alkaline soil. It tastes similar to spinach but with a subtle salty flavor.

12. Faas, *Around the Roman Table*, 20.

13. Athenaeus, *The Deipnosophists, or Banquet of the Learned*, trans. C. D. Yonge (Memphis, TN: General Books [original historic book], 2012), VI-274d.

14. Pliny, *Natural History*, book 12, 21.

15. Ibid., 63.

16. Davidson, *Oxford Companion*, 460.

17. Pliny, *Natural History*, book 12, 21.

18. Dalby, *Food in the Ancient World*, 254.

19. Pliny, *Natural History*, book 12, 63–65.

20. Ibid. Also see Faas, *Around the Roman Table*, 164.

21. Pliny, *Natural History*, book 12, 63.

22. Ibid., 64–65.

23. Taras Grescoe, "This Miracle Plant was Eaten into Extinction 2,000 Years Ago—Or Was It?" *National Geographic*, September 23, 2022, retrieved from https://www.nationalgeographic.com/history/article/miracle-plant-eaten-extinction -2000-years-ago-silphion.

24. Ibid.

CHAPTER 8

1. Scholars estimate the population anywhere from 120,000 to 400,000. See L. Michael White, "Urban Development and Social Change in Imperial Ephesos," in *Ephesos: Metropolis of Asia; An Interdisciplinary Approach to Its Archaeology, Religion, and Culture*, ed. Helmut Koester (Cambridge, MA: Harvard University Press, 1995), 41.

2. Andrew Dalby, *Empire of Pleasures: Luxury and Indulgence in the Roman World* (New York: Routledge, 2000), 162.

3. Ibid., 161, from Cicero, *De lege Manilia*.

4. Jeffers, *Greco-Roman World*, 268.

5. John and Elizabeth Romer, *The Seven Wonders of the World: A History of the Modern Imagination* (New York: Henry Holt and Co., Inc., 1995), 147. I find it difficult to imagine the size and magnificence of the Temple of Artemis after viewing the Parthenon several years ago. As its designation suggests, it must have truly been one of the world's wonders.

6. Ibid.

7. Dalby, *Food in the Ancient World*, 288.

8. Faas, *Around the Roman Table*, 246.

9. Cato, *On Agriculture*, section 139, 121–23. This section of *On Agriculture* has other sacrificial prayers as well.

10. Andrew Dalby, *Siren Feasts: A History of Food and Gastronomy in Greece* (New York: Routledge, 1996), 3–5.

11. Faas, *Around the Roman Table*, 251.

12. Garland, *Daily Life*, 132–34.

13. Toussaint-Samat, *History of Food*, 409.

14. Faas, *Around the Roman Table*, 266.

15. Large Hispanic and Mediterranean markets will sometimes keep a hog's head or two for sale in the meat section. My children, when young, were amazed when we shopped in one of the Hispanic groceries in Dallas to see a whole hog's head in the freezer section.

16. Toussaint-Samat, *History of Food*, 409.

17. Ibid., 410.

18. Pork belly and bacon are basically the same meat from the abdominal area of the pig. Pork belly is unsmoked and not salted. Bacon is long, narrow strips of pork belly and usually smoked and salted.

19. Faas, *Around the Roman Table*, 260–61.

20. Ibid., 253.

21. From Hippocratic text, *Sacred Disease*, in Dalby, *Food in the Ancient World*, 269.

22. Davidson, *Oxford Companion*, 624.

23. Anonymous, *The Homeric Hymns and Homerica*, trans. Hugh G. Evelyn-White (Cambridge: Harvard University Press; London: William Heinemann, 1914).

CHAPTER 9

1. Michael Grant, *A Guide to the Ancient World: A Dictionary of Classical Place Names* (New York: Barnes and Noble Books, 1986), 83.

2. Dalby, *Siren Feasts*, 21.

3. Faas, *Around the Roman Table*, 71–72.

4. Plato, *Symposium*, 8–10.

5. Faas, *Around the Roman Table*, 96–97.

6. N. T. Wright, *Paul: A Biography* (New York: HarperCollins, 2018), 197–99.

7. Ibid., 198.

8. Ibid., 198–99.

9. Martine Duquesne, "To Fish and Not to Fish: An Ethnological Survey of the Fishing Techniques in Collioure, France," *Icon* 6 (2000): 176.

10. Dalby, *Food in the Ancient World*, 334.
11. Ibid., 144.
12. Toussaint-Samat, *History of Food*, 300.
13. Giacosa, *Taste of Ancient Rome*, 17.
14. Toussaint-Samat, *History of Food*, 299.
15. Ibid.
16. Dalby, *Food in the Ancient World*, 146.
17. Faas, *Around the Roman Table*, 324.
18. Ibid., 325.
19. James Davidson, *Courtesans and Fish: The Consuming Passions of Classical Athens* (New York: St. Martin's Press, 1997), 12.
20. Ibid., 15.
21. Dalby, *Food in the Ancient World*, 145.
22. *Apicius*, 295.
23. Andrew Dalby and Sally Grainger, *The Classical Cookbook* (Los Angeles: J. Paul Getty Museum, 1996), 59.

CHAPTER 10

1. Meeks, *First Urban Christians*, 45–46.
2. Ibid., 45.
3. Brown, *Introduction to the New Testament*, 485, note 2.
4. We should wonder if *conversion* had as individualistic a meaning as it does today. We see the same thing happen with Cornelius the centurion, when, after his conversion, his entire household was baptized (Acts 10:48).
5. Brown, *Introduction to the New Testament*, 487.
6. Ibid., 489, esp. note 14.
7. Garland, *Daily Life*, 53.
8. Smith, *From Symposium to Eucharist,* 40, 308, note 141.
9. Ibid., 96.
10. Ibid., 97.
11. Ibid., 100.
12. Waverly Root, "The Olive, a Fruit That Shaped Civilization," *Washington Post*, August 3, 1978. Also, Pliny, *Natural History*, book 15, 291.
13. Toussaint-Samat, *History of Food*, 205.
14. Ibid., 212.
15. Ibid., 211.
16. R. C. D. Jasper and G. J. Cuming, *Prayers of the Eucharist: Early and Reformed* (Collegeville, MN: Liturgical Press, 1987), 36. Also see, Neel and Pugh, *Food and Feasts of Jesus*, 69.
17. Pliny, *Natural History*, book 15, 29.1
18. Ibid.

19. Ibid., 293.
20. Ibid.
21. Nancy Harmon Jenkins, *The Mediterranean Diet Cookbook: A Delicious Alternative for Lifelong Health* (New York: Bantam Books, 1994), 20.
22. Ibid.

CHAPTER 11

1. Jeffers, *Greco-Roman World*, 283.
2. Edith Hamilton, *Mythology* (Boston: Little, Brown and Co., 1969), 479.
3. Smith, *From Symposium to Eucharist*, 96.
4. Ibid.
5. Ibid., 97.
6. Ibid., 98.
7. David L. Balch, *Roman Domestic Art and Early House Churches* (Tübingen: Mohr Siebeck, 2008), 4–5.
8. Smith, *From Symposium to Eucharist*, 103.
9. Ibid., 123.
10. Brown, *Introduction to the New Testament*, 464.
11. Dalby, *Empire of Pleasures*, 149.
12. Neel and Pugh, *Food and Feasts of Jesus*, 127. See also Patrick E. McGovern, *Ancient Wine: The Search for the Origins of Viniculture* (Princeton, NJ: Princeton University Press, 2003), 304.
13. A humorous example of this technique is illustrated in the *I Love Lucy* episode where Lucille Ball tries her hand, actually her feet, at stomping grapes; *I Love Lucy* (season 5, episode 23), 1956.
14. Pliny, *Natural History*, book 18, 315–16.
15. Neel and Pugh, *Food and Feasts of Jesus*, 129.
16. Dalby, *Food in the Ancient World*, 352.
17. Ibid., 353.
18. Ibid.
19. Ibid., 223.
20. Faas, *Around the Roman Table*, 117–18.
21. Dalby, *Food in the Ancient World*, 351.
22. Neel and Pugh, *Food and Feasts of Jesus*, 313.
23. Ibid. The authors suggested that the Todah or thanksgiving feast provided a background for early Christian theology. See chapter 10, "Eating with God—The Todah Feast."
24. This book has neither the time nor the space to debate the "real presence" of Christ. See also Matthew 26:26–29; Mark 14:22–25; Luke 22:14–20 for language regarding the meaning of the bread and wine at the last supper Jesus shares with his

closest followers. The Lukan passage includes a thanksgiving for a cup of wine both before the bread and at the end of the meal.

25. Davidson, *Oxford Companion*, 828.

26. Giacosa, *Taste of Ancient Rome*, 192.

27. Tom Standage, *A History of the World in 6 Glasses* (New York: Walker Publishing Co., 2005), 14–15.

28. Ibid.

29. Ibid., 29, 37.

30. Horst Dombusch, "Pharaoh Ale: Brewing a Replica of an Ancient Beer," American Homebrewers Association, a division of the Brewers Association, 2019, retrieved from www.homebrewersassociation/zymurgy/pharaoh-ale-brewing -a-replica-of-an-ancient-egyption-beer/.

31. Ibid.

32. Dalby, *Food in the Ancient World*, 50.

33. Pliny, *Natural History*, book 14, 285.

CHAPTER 12

1. An isthmus is a narrow strip of land surrounded by water on both sides and connecting two larger land masses.

2. Brown, *Introduction to the New Testament*, 512.

3. Wright, *Paul*, 211.

4. Brown, *Introduction to the New Testament*, 512.

5. Ibid., 513.

6. Andrew McGowan, *Ascetic Eucharists: Food and Drink in Early Christian Ritual Meals* (Oxford: Clarendon Press, 1999), 66.

7. Wright, *Paul*, 254.

8. Ibid., 252.

9. Michael Li-Tak Shen, *Canaan to Corinth: Paul's Doctrine of God and the Issue of Food Offered to Idols in 1 Corinthians 8:1–11:1*, Studies in Biblical Literature, vol. 83, Hemchand Gossai, general editor (New York: Peter Lang, 2010), esp. chap. 5.

10. The Greek word for *broken* appears in some ancient manuscripts and not in others.

11. Paul F. Bradshaw, "Did the Early Eucharist Have a Sevenfold Shape?" *Heythrop Journal* 43, no. 1 (January 2002): 74.

12. Andrew B. McGowan, *Ancient Christian Worship: Early Church Practices in Social, Historical, and Theological Perspective* (Grand Rapids, MI: Baker Academic, 2014), 111–15.

13. McGowan, *Ascetic Eucharists*, 97–98.

14. Ibid., 104, 115.

15. Ibid., 126.

16. Hippolytus, *The Apostolic Tradition*, chapters 5 and 6, in R. C. D. Jasper and G. J. Cuming, *Prayers of the Eucharist: Early and Reformed* (Collegeville, MN: Liturgical Press, 1975), 36.

17. Ibid., chapters 21, 37.

18. McGowan, *Ancient Christian Worship*, 34.

19. Ibid., 74.

CHAPTER 13

1. Ibid., 33. See also Bradshaw, "Did the Early Eucharist," 73.

2. McGowen, *Ancient Christian Worship*, 34.

3. Jasper and Cuming, *Prayers of the Eucharist*, 23.

4. Ibid.

5. Jasper and Cuming, *Prayers of the Eucharist*, 22. Also see, Andrew McGowan, "First Regarding the Cup: Papias and the Diversity of Early Eucharistic Practice," *Journal of Theological Studies* 42, no. 8, pt. 2 (October 1995): 553. Bradshaw, "Did the Early Eucharist," 73–74. Both Bradshaw and McGowan see the possibility that Paul also references the cup-bread order in 1 Corinthians 10:16–17. Some scholars argue that the cup-bread order in Corinthians is merely an inversion for rhetorical reasons, but it can be seen as a different tradition that Paul knew.

6. Jasper and Cuming. *Prayers of the Eucharist*, 20, 24.

BIBLIOGRAPHY

Anonymous. "Orphic Hymn 30 to Bacchus." *The Hymns of Orpheus*. Translated by Thomas Taylor. London: Prometheus Trust, 1792.

Anonymous. *The Homeric Hymns and Homerica*. Translated by Hugh G. Evelyn-White. Cambridge, MA: Harvard University Press, 1914.

Apicius. *Cookery and Dining in Imperial Rome*. Edited and translated by Joseph Dommers Vehling. New York: Dover Publications, 1977.

Aquilina, Mike. *The Mass of the Early Christians*. 2nd ed. Huntington, IL: Our Sunday Visitor Publishing Division, 1965.

Athenaeus. *The Deipnosophists, Or Banquet of the Learned*. Translated by C. D. Yonge. Memphis, TN: General Books, 2012.

Balch, David L. *Roman Domestic Art and Early House Churches*. Tübingen: Mohr Siebeck, 2008.

Bang, Peter Fibiger. *The Roman Bazaar: A Comparative Study of Trade and Markets in a Tributary Empire*. Cambridge Classical Studies. Cambridge: Cambridge University Press, 2009.

Barclay, John M. G. *Jews in the Mediterranean Diaspora*. Berkeley: University of California Press, 1996.

Barydakis, Koula, and Bill Bradley, R.D. *Foods of Crete: Traditional Recipes from the Healthiest People in the World*. Self-published, 2006.

Borg, Marcus J., and John Dominic Crossan. *The First Paul: Reclaiming the Radical Visionary Behind the Church's Conservative Icon*. New York: HarperCollins, 2009.

Bornkamm, Gunther. *Paul*. New York: Harper & Row, 1969.

Botsford, George Willis, and Charles Alexander Robinson. *Botsford and Robinson's Hellenic History*. 5th ed. Revised by Donald Kagan. New York: Macmillan, 1969.

Bradshaw, Paul F. "Did the Early Eucharist have a Sevenfold Shape?" *Heythrop Journal* 43, no. 1 (January 2002): 72–76.

———. *Eucharistic Origins*. New York: Oxford University Press, 2004.

Bremness, Lesley. *The Complete Book of Herbs: A Practical Guide to Growing and Using Herbs*. New York: Penguin Books, 1988.

Brown, Raymond E. *An Introduction to the New Testament*. New York: Doubleday, 1997.

Bugialli, Giuliano. *Foods of Italy*. New York: Stewart, Tabori, & Chang, 1984.

Buttrick, George Arthur, ed. *The Interpreter's Dictionary of the Bible: An Illustrated Encyclopedia*. Vols. 1–4. Nashville, TN: Abingdon Press, 1962.

Carroll, Ricki. *Home Cheese Making Recipes for 75 Homemade Cheeses*. North Adams, MA: Storey Publishing, 2002.

Cato, Marcus Pircius. *On Agriculture*. Translated by William Davis Hooper, Loeb Classical Library. Edited by Jeffrey Henderson. Cambridge, MA: Harvard University Press, 1934.

Celetti, Barbara. *Making Great Cheese at Home: 30 Simple Recipes from Cheddar to Chevre*. New York: Lark Books/Sterling Publishing, 1999.

Cheung, Alex T. *Idol Food in Corinth: Jewish Background and Pauline Legacy*. Sheffield: Sheffield Academic Press, 1999.

Child, Julia. *Cooking with Master Chefs*. New York: Alfred A. Knopf, 1993.

The Complete Mediterranean Cookbook: 500 Vibrant, Kitchen-Tested Recipes for Living and Eating Well Every Day. Boston: America's Test Kitchen, 2016.

Counihan, Carole, and Penney Van Esterik. *Food and Culture: A Reader*. New York: Routledge, 1997.

Cowell, F. R. *Life in Ancient Rome*. New York: Wideview/Perigee, 1961.

Dalby, Andrew. *Empire of Pleasures: Luxury and Indulgence in the Roman World*. New York: Routledge, 2000.

———. *Food in the Ancient World from A to Z*. London: Routledge, 2003.

———. *Siren Feasts: A History of Food and Gastronomy in Greece*. New York: Routledge, 1996.

Dalby, Andrew, and Sally Grainger. *The Classical Cookbook*. Los Angeles; J. Paul Getty Museum, 1996.

Davidson, Alan. *The Oxford Companion to Food*. New York: Oxford University Press, 1999.

Davidson, James. *Courtesans and Fish: The Consuming Passions of Classical Athens*. New York: St. Martin's, 1997.

Davis, Ellen F. *Scripture, Culture, and Agriculture: An Agrarian Reading of the Bible*. New York: Cambridge University Press, 2009.

Dayai-Mendels, Michal. *Drink and Be Merry: Wine and Beer in Ancient Times*. Jerusalem: The Israel Museum, 1999.

Dombusch, Horst. "Pharaoh Ale: Brewing a Replica of an Ancient Beer." American Homebrewers Association, a division of the Brewers Association, 2019. Retrieved from www.homebrewersassociation/zymurgy/pharaoh-ale-brewing-a-replica-of-an-ancient-egyption-beer/.

Duquesne, Martine. "To Fish and Not to Fish: An Ethnological Survey of the Fishing Techniques in Collioure, France." *Icon* 6 (2000): 176–98.

Durant, William. *The Life of Greece: The Story of Civilization*. New York: Simon and Schuster, 1939.

Edmonds, Anna G. *Turkey's Religious Sites*. Istanbul: Damko A.S., 1997.

Erdkamp, Paul, *The Grain Market in the Roman Empire: A Social, Political and Economic Study*. Cambridge: Cambridge University Press, 2005.

Erskine, William, Fred J. Muehbaue, Ashotosh Sarker, and Baltram Sharma. *The Lentil: Botany, Production, and Uses*. Wallingford: CABI, 2009.

Evinskaya, Irina. *The Book of Acts in Its First Century Setting*. Vol. 5: *Diaspora Setting*. Grand Rapids, MI: William B. Eerdmans, 1996.

Faas, Patrick, *Around the Roman Table: Food and Feasting in Ancient Rome*. Chicago: University of Chicago Press, 1994.

Finger, Reta Halteman, and George D. McClain. *Creating a Scene in Corinth: A Simulation*. Harrisonburg, VA: Herald Press, 2013.

Fisher, M. F. K. *The Art of Eating*. New York: Wiley, 1990.

Ford, Bryan, *New World Sourdough: Artisan Techniques for Creative Homemade Fermented Breads*. Beverly, MA: Quarto, 2020.

Frank, Tim. *Household Food Storage in Ancient Israel and Judah*. Oxford: Archaeopress, 2018.

Freedman, Paul. *Food: The History of Taste*. Berkeley: University of California Press, 1982.

———. *Out of the East: Spices and the Medieval Imagination*. New Haven, CT: Yale University Press, 2008.

Furnish, Victor Paul. *The Moral Teaching of Paul: Selected Issues*. Nashville, TN; Abingdon Press, 1985.

———. *New Testament Theology: The Theology of the First Letter to the Corinthians*. New York: Cambridge University Press, 1999.

Garland, Robert. *Daily Life of the Ancient Greeks*. Westport, CT: Hackett Publishing, 1998.

Garnsey, Peter. *Famine and Food Supply in the Graeco-Roman World: Responses to Risk and Crisis*. Cambridge: Cambridge University Press, 1988.

———. *Food and Society in Classical Antiquity: Key Themes in Ancient History*. Cambridge: Cambridge University Press, 1999.

Garnsey, Peter, and Richard Saller. *The Roman Empire: Economy, Society and Culture*. London: Bloomsbury, 2014.

Giacosa, Ilaria Gozzini. *A Taste of Ancient Rome*. Chicago: University of Chicago Press, 1992.

Grainger, Sally. *Cooking Apicius: Roman Recipes for Today*. Devon: Prospect Books, 2006.

Grant, Mark. *Roman Cookery: Ancient Recipes for Modern Kitchens*. London: Serif, 1999.

Grant, Michael. *A Guide to the Ancient World: A Dictionary of Classical Place Names*. New York: Barnes and Noble Books, 1986.

Gray, Patience. *Honey from a Weed: Fasting and Feasting*. London: Prospect Books, 2009.

Grescoe, Taras. "This Miracle Plant Was Eaten into Extinction 2,000 Years Ago—Or Was It?" *National Geographic*, September 23, 2022. Retrieved from https://www.nationalgeographic.com/history/article/miracle-plant-eaten -extinction-2000-years-ago-silphion.

Grimm, Veronica E. *From Feasting to Fasting: The Evolution of Sin*. London: Routledge, 1996.

Grocock, Christopher, and Sally Grainger. *Apicius: A Critical Edition with an Introduction and the English Translation of the Latin Recipe Text*. Devon: Prospect Books, Allaleigh House, 2006.

Grumett, David, and Rachel Muers. *Theology on the Menu: Asceticism, Meat, and Christian Diet*. New York: Routledge, 2010.

Guhl, E., and W. Koner. *Everyday Life of the Greeks and Romans*. New York: Crescent Books, 1989.

Hamilton, Edith. *Mythology*. Boston: Little, Brown and Co., 1969.

Hubbard, Moyer V. *Christianity in the Greco-Roman World: A Narrative Introduction*. Grand Rapids, MI: Baker Publishing Group, 2010.

Jacob, H. E. *Six Thousand Years of Bread: Its Holy and Unholy History*. New York: Skyhorse Publishing, 2007.

James, Michael, *Slow Food: Flavors and Memories of America's Hometowns*. New York: Warner Books, Inc., 1992.

Jasper, R. C. D. and G. J. Cuming. *Prayers of the Eucharist: Early and Reformed*. Collegeville, MN: Liturgical Press, 1987.

Jeffers, James S. *The Greco-Roman World of the New Testament Era: Exploring the Background of Early Christianity*. Downers Grove, IL: InterVarsity Press, 1999.

Jenkins, Nancy Harmon. *The Mediterranean Diet Cookbook: A Delicious Alternative for Lifelong Health*. New York: Bantam Books, 1994.

Jenkins, Steven. *Cheese Primer*. New York: Workman Publishing, 1996.

Johns, Pamela Sheldon. *Italian Food Artisans: Traditions and Recipes*. San Francisco, CA: Chronicle Books, 2000.

Jones, Martin. *Feast: Why Humans Share Food*. New York: Oxford University Press, 2007.

Keay, John. *The Spice Route: A History*. Berkeley: University of California Press, 2006.

Kranzdorf, Hermie. *Herbs and Spices of the World*. Exton, PA: Shiffer Publishing, 1983.

Krasner, Deborah. *The Flavors of Olive Oil: A Tasting Guide and Cookbook*. New York: Simon and Schuster, 2002.

Kreglinger, Gisela H. *The Spirituality of Wine*. Grand Rapids, MI: William B. Eerdmans, 1967.

Kurlansky, Mark. *Salt: A World History*. New York: Penguin, 2002.

Kutas, Rytek. *Great Sausage Recipes and Meat Curing*. 4th ed. Buffalo, NY: The Sausage Maker, 2008.

Lee, Jin Hwan. *The Lord's Supper in Corinth in the Context of Greco-Roman Private Associations.* Lanham, MD: Lexington Books/Fortress Academic, 2018.

Lukacs, Paul. *Inventing Wine: A New History of One of the World's Most Ancient Pleasures.* New York: W. W. Norton, 2012.

Matz, David. *Daily Life of the Ancient Romans.* Indianapolis, IN: Hackett Publishing Co., Inc., 2002.

Maxwell, Sarah. *Greek Meze Cooking: Tapas of the Aegean.* Secaucus, NJ: Chartwell Books, 1992.

McGinn, Sheila E. *The Jesus Movement and the World of the Early Church.* Winona, MN: Anselm Academics, Christian Brothers Publications, 2014.

McGovern, Patrick E. *Ancient Wine: The Search for the Origins of Viniculture.* Princeton, NJ: Princeton University Press, 2003.

McGowen, Andrew B. "First Regarding the Cup: Papias and the Diversity of Early Eucharistic Practice." *Journal of Theological Studies* 42, no. 8, pt. 2 (October 1995): 551–55.

———. *Ascetic Eucharists: Food and Drinks in Early Christian Ritual Meals.* Oxford: Clarendon Press, 1999.

———. *Ancient Christian Worship: Early Church Practices in Social, Historical, and Theological Perspective.* Grand Rapids, MI: Baker Academic, 2014.

Meeks, Wayne A. *The First Urban Christians: The Social World of the Apostle Paul.* 2nd ed. New Haven, CT: Yale University Press, 1983.

Montanari, Massimo. *Food Is Culture.* New York: Columbia University Press, 2004.

Montant, Jane. "Our Anniversary Party." *Gourmet: The Magazine of Good Living* (January 1991).

Morse, Kitty. *A Biblical Feast: Foods from the Holy Land.* Berkeley, CA: Ten Speed Press, 1998.

Neel, Douglas, and Joel Pugh. *The Food and Feasts of Jesus: Inside the World of First-Century Fare, with Menus and Recipes.* Lanham, MD: Rowman & Littlefield, 2012.

Neusner, Jacob, trans. *The Mishnah: A New Translation.* New Haven, CT: Yale University Press, 1988.

Petito, Annie. "Quick and Easy Italian Flatbreads: Meet Piadine." *Cooks Illustrated,* no. 160 (September and October 2019): 10–11.

Pflughoeft, Aspen. "2,600-Year-Old Blocks of Cheese Found in Pottery at Pyramid in Egypt, Archaeologists Say." *Miami Herald,* September 22, 2022.

Pitre, Brant. *Jesus and the Jewish Roots of the Eucharist: Unlocking the Secrets of the Last Supper.* New York: Doubleday, 2011.

Plato. *Symposium.* Oxford World's Classics. Translated by Robin Waterfield. Oxford: Oxford University Press, 1994.

Pliny. *Natural History.* Translated by H. Rackham, Loeb Classical Library. Edited by Jeffrey Henderson. Cambridge, MA: Harvard University Press, 1950.

Pollan, Michael. *Omnivore's Dilemma: A Natural History of Four Meals.* New York: Penguin Books, 2007.

———. *Food Rules: An Eater's Manual.* New York: Penguin, 2009.

Pomeroy, Sarah B. *Goddesses, Whores, Wives, and Slave Women in Classical Antiquity.* New York: Schocken Books, 1975.

Pope, Victoria. "What Is It about Eating That Brings Us Closer? The Joy of Food." *National Geographic* 226, no. 6 (December 2014): 36–53.

Predika, Jerry. *The Sausage-Making Cookbook.* Mechanicsburg, PA: Stackpole Books, 1983.

Rice, David G., and David G. Stambaugh. *Sources for the Study of Greek Religion, Corrected Edition.* Atlanta, GA: Society of Biblical Literature, 2009.

Ricotti, Eugenia Salza Prina. *Meals and Recipes from Ancient Greece.* Los Angeles: J. Paul Getty Museum, 2005.

Robertson, Chad. *Tartine Bread.* San Francisco, CA: Chronicle Books, 2016.

Romer, John, and Elizabeth Romer. *The Seven Wonders of the World: A History of the Modern Imagination.* New York: Henry Holt and Co., Inc., 1995.

Root, Waverly. "The Olive, a Fruit That Shaped Civilization." *Washington Post,* August 3, 1978.

Rosenblum, Harry. *Vinegar Revival: Artisanal Recipes for Brightening Dishes and Drinks with Homemade Vinegars.* New York; Clarkson Publishers, 2017.

Sandt, Huub van de. "'Do Not Give What Is Holy to the Dogs': Food of the Didache in Its Jewish Purity Setting." *Vigiliae Christianae* 56, no. 3 (August 2002): 223–46.

———. "Why Does the Didache Conceive of the Eucharist as a Holy Meal?" *Vigiliae Christianae* 65, no. 1 (2011): 1–20.

Schoff, Wilfred Harvey. *The Periplus of the Erythraean Sea.* London: Forgotten Books, 2018.

Shen, Michael Li-Tak. *Canaan to Corinth: Paul's Doctrine of God and the Issue of Food Offered to Idols in 1 Corinthians 8:1–11:1.* Studies in Biblical Literature, vol. 83. Hemchand Gossai, general editor. New York: Peter Lang, 2010.

Sitwell, William. *A History of Food in 100 Recipes.* New York: Little, Brown, and Company, 2013.

Smith, Dennis E. *From Symposium to Eucharist: The Banquet in the Early Christian World.* Minneapolis: Fortress Press, 2003.

Smith, Dennis E., and Hal E. Taussig. *The Eucharist in the New Testament and Liturgy Today.* Eugene, OR: Wipf and Stock, 2001.

Smith, Jeff. *The Frugal Gourmet Cooks Three Ancient Cuisines: China, Greece, Rome; Delicious Recipes from the Cultures That Most Influenced Western Cooking.* New York: William Morrow, 1989.

Sonnenfeld, Albert. *Food: A Culinary History.* Edited by Jean-Louis Flandrin and Massimo Montanari. Translated by Clarissa Botsford, Arthur Goldhammer, Charles Lambert, Frances M. Lopez-Morillas, and Sylvia Stevens. New York: Penguin Books, 1999.

Soyer, Alexis. *The Pantropheon or, History of Food and Its Preparation: From the Earliest Ages of the World.* Boston: Ticknor, Reed, and Fields, 1863. Facsimile published by Andesite Press, 2015.

Standage, Tom. *A History of the World in 6 Glasses*. New York: Walker Publishing Co., 2005.

———. *An Edible History of Humanity*. New York: Walker Publishing, 2009.

Stone, Rachel Marie. *Eat with Joy: Redeeming God's Gift of Food*. Downers Grove, IL: IVP Books, 1981.

Swenson, Allan A. *Foods Jesus Ate and How to Grow Them*. New York: Skyhorse Publishing, 2008.

Tannahill, Reay. *Food in History*. New York: Three Rivers Press, 1988.

Temin, Peter. *The Roman Market Economy*. Princeton, NJ: Princeton University Press, 2013.

Toussaint-Samat, Maguelonne. *History of Food*. Translated by Anthea Bell. Malden, MA: Blackwell Publishers, 1998.

Trager, James. *The Food Chronology: A Food Lover's Compendium of Events and Anecdotes, From Prehistory to the Present*. New York: Henry Holt and Company, 1995.

Turner, Jack. *Spice: The History of a Temptation*. New York: Vintage Books, 2004.

Ullman, Berthold L. "Cleopatra's Pearls." *Classical Journal* 52, no. 5 (February 1957): 193–201.

Valantasis, Richard, Douglas K. Bleyle, and Dennis C. Haugh. *The Gospels and Christian Life in History and Practice*. Lanham, MD: Rowman & Littlefield, 2009.

Walsh, Carey Ellen. *The Fruit of the Vine: Viticulture in Ancient Israel*. Winona Lake, IN: Eisenbrauns, 2000.

Warrick, Sheridan. *The Way to Make Wine: How to Craft Superb Table Wines at Home*. Berkeley and Los Angeles: University of California Press, 2006.

White, L. Michael. "Urban Development and Social Change in Imperial Ephesos." In *Ephesos: Metropolis of Asia; An Interdisciplinary Approach to Its Archaeology, Religion, and Culture*, edited by Helmut Koester. Cambridge, MA: Harvard University Press, 1995.

Wilson, A. N. *Paul: The Mind of the Apostle*. New York: W. W. Norton, 1997.

Wirzba, Norman. "Eating in Ignorance: Do We Know Where Our Food Comes From?" *Christian Century* 129, no. 11 (May 30, 2012): 24–27.

Wolfert, Paula. *The Cooking of the Eastern Mediterranean: 215 Healthy, Vibrant, and Inspired Recipes*. New York: HarperCollins Publishing, 1994.

———. *Mediterranean Clay Pot Cooking: Traditional and Modern Recipes to Savor and Share*. Hoboken, NJ: John Wiley and Sons, 2009.

Wright, Clifford A. *Mediterranean Vegetables*. Boston: Harvard Common Press, 2001.

Wright, N. T. *Paul: A Biography*. New York: HarperCollins, 2018.

INDEX

Acropolis, 183, 184
Adelphoi (play), 210
Adriatic Sea, 248
Aegean Sea, 191, 205, 225, 248
agape feasts. *See* love feasts
Agatharchides (historian), 195
Agios Theologos. *See* holy theologian
the agora, in Athens, 184–85
agricultural economy, 62–64
agriculture, in developed nations, 35
Akkadians, lentils cooked by, 74
Alcaeus (poet), 87
Alexander the Great (king), 18, 135,
    140–41, 185, 204
allec. *See* fish solids
All Saints' Day, 78
amarone wine, 99, 234
Amazons (warrior women tribe), 161
Amphipolis (town), 229
amphorae. *See* clay containers
anchovy paste, 280n13
ancient farms, 36–38
ancient Greek dessert, 245
ancient pantry, 32–33
anima. *See* life-breath
animal brains, 32
animals: controversies in treatment of,
    176–77; domesticated, 20, 25, 171;
    sacrifice of, 22. *See also* fish

Antioch (city), 135; Christian
    Movement and, 136–40; church in,
    133; feasts in, 152–53; Paul moving
    to, 134
Apicius (recipe collection), 8, 31, 48,
    75, 78, 97–98; chickpeas and eggs
    from, 129; Cornish hens with green
    sauce from, 241–42; legumes in,
    72; lentils and vinegar from, 270;
    Lucanian sausage from, 180–81;
    minutal of apricots by, 221–22;
    pan-fried white fish and sauce from,
    200; pear patina from, 223; peas
    and basil from, 261; pork loin and
    sauce from, 105–6; sauces described
    by, 100; seafood in, 196; split peas
    with sausage from, 242–43; on
    suckling pigs, 173; tuna and sauce
    by, 199
Apicius dressing, 198–99, 261
Apicius meatballs, 201
Apollonia (town), 229
Apollos (evangelist), 164
Apostolic Constitutions (treatise), 264
The Apostolic Tradition (Hippolytus),
    216, 252–53
appetizers, 40–41, 92, 102, 117, 197,
    220
apricots, 18, 221–22

297

ABOUT THE AUTHOR

Douglas E. Neel is a retired Episcopal priest and the co-author of *The Food and Feasts of Jesus* (Rowman & Littlefield, 2012). He owned a catering company specializing in first-century food and currently teaches classes on ancient food and feasts. Neel enjoys making his own cheese and wine and lives in Pagosa Springs, Colorado.

www.ingramcontent.com/pod-product-compliance
Lightning Source LLC
Chambersburg PA
CBHW070402100426
42812CB00005B/1601